LISP, Lore, and Logic

An Algebraic View of LISP Programming,
Foundations, and Applications

W. Richard Stark

LISP, Lore, and Logic

An Algebraic View of LISP Programming, Foundations, and Applications

With 51 Illustrations

Springer-Verlag
New York Berlin Heidelberg
London Paris Tokyo Hong Kong

W. Richard Stark
Department of Mathematics
University of South Florida
Tampa, Florida 33620
USA

Cover: The leaf-pattern making up the cover's background is suggestive of life processes, particularly morphogenesis. At the level of an individual cell, a structure-generating program written in the cell's DNA duplicates the cell. The molecules of the cell play the role of data, which, since they include the DNA, allows the program to create a copy of itself. Morphogenesis is defined in terms of itself, it is recursive. LISP exhibits two features of this process: recursion and the use of its data to express its programs. At its best, LISP programming is capable of graceful self-reproduction and self-modification suggestive of the metabolic processes of life.

Library of Congress Cataloging-in-Publication Data
Stark, W. Richard.
    Lisp, lore, and logic / W. Richard Stark.
      p. cm.
    Includes bibliographical references.
    ISBN 0-387-97072-X
    1. LISP (Computer program language)   I. Title.
QA76.73. L23S72   1989
005. 13′3—dc20   89-19651

Printed on acid-free paper.

Camera-ready copy prepared using LaTeX.
Printed and bound by R.R. Donnelley & Sons, Inc., Harrisonburg, Virginia.
Printed in the United States of America.

9 8 7 6 5 4 3 2 1

ISBN 0-387-97072-X Springer-Verlag New York Berlin Heidelberg
ISBN 3-540-97072-X Springer-Verlag Berlin Heidelberg New York

For my two most patient and enthusiastic supporters, my Mother and my Wife:

Anna Elizabeth May Stark,
and
Judy Kay Ingrao Stark.

Also, my son

Christopher Jon Stark

who always had a joke when one was needed.

Preface

In a jet – flying to Alaska, Europe, or some other equally interesting destination – the most exciting thoughts that come to my mind are of the beauty of the technology that makes it all possible. It is apparent in the evolution of ideas, from beginnings in engineering, physics, and mathematics to a dramatic and practical conclusion in the airplane. To see this particular vision of beauty, one needs to grasp as much as possible of the whole picture – the abstract theory, the practical technology, and the history of its evolution – all at once.

The impact of our abstract dreams is equally visible in the science of computing. Nowhere is this truer than in and around LISP. The theory and technology of nonnumerical computation reaches from esoteric branches of pure mathematics (algebras developed since the early 1930s) and automatic theorem proving (1950s) through LISP (since the late 1950s) to everyday examples of nonnumerical computation and machine intelligence (today). This beautiful stretch of philosophies, ideas, and technologies is the heart of this book. The body is LISP programming and computing.

Our material has developed out of LISP courses taught over the past ten years at the University of Texas at Austin, California State University at San José, the University of South Florida, and AT&T Bell Laboratories. The initial idea was to augment programming with the theoretical foundations of LISP computation – rather than applications in artificial intelligence (the traditional second theme). This idea was inspired by the professional LISP conferences. Could this deep theoretical approach be brought down to the level of an undergraduate course? Would the average LISP-type person really like it?

Students were enthusiastic from the beginning. Each time the material was taught, their interests directed its development. Given the necessary theoretical foundations, they were naturally drawn into the fantastic side of the subject. There is a good deal of that, so the basic design was embellished with exciting examples from LISP's folklore. Folklore lead to appropriately placed historical commentary and photographs of LISP's creators. Students liked this too. Eventually, some real LISP experts took notice and suggested that the massive and wandering manuscript be dramatically simplified and streamlined. This is the result.

As the title LISP, Lore, and Logic suggests, this is a multifaceted presentation. In addition to programming and theory, there are colorful applications (organic chemistry, automatic reasoning, symbolic differentiation, translating natural language, ...), bits of the history (is LISP really a descendent of the lofty lambda calculus?) and a small family album, computational philosophy (unsolvable problems), bizarre consequences of LISP's exceptional power (self-processing, self-reproduction, ...), and more. These topics are tied together by the common theme of computing in LISP. In most cases, they are realized in programming examples and exercises. Individual topics were included for various reasons – for practical value, for beauty and mystery, and often to explain how and why LISP works so well.

The level of presentation here is appropriate for strong students with some experience in computing and at least a sophomore's background in mathematics. As a text, it is appropriate as a primary text for theoretically oriented courses in LISP or as a secondary text for more traditional courses in LISP, artificial intelligence with LISP, computing languages, or the abstract theory of computation. A good deal of material is covered without unnecessary prose. This conciseness may appeal to those who are put off by soft and wordy texts. The dialect is Common LISP.

Just as with the jet, the beauty and power of this subject is best appreciated by those who can understand and appreciate it, as well as use it. This little book is designed to provide all of this to any reader having an aptitude for computing and mathematics, and a taste for the exotic.

W. Richard Stark

working one summer late in the 20th century, in the peace of western New Jersey's farm country.

Acknowledgments

During the years of this text's development, I've received help in one way or another from dozens of friends and a few strangers. Both great and humble, they are

Woodie Bledsoe, Kim Bruce, Alonzo Church, Dan Freidman, Nick Gall, Oscar Garcia, Jim Gaughan, Henson Graves, David Gries, William Hatcher, the researchers of IBM archives, Stephen Kleene, Larry Landwebber, Dallas Lankford, Tony Llewellyn, John McCarthy, the researchers of the MIT Museum, Lynn Montz, John Pedersen, the researchers of the Princeton University archives, Nathaniel Rochester, Phillip Scott, Guy Steele, George Stockman, Cecelia Swift, Carolyn Talcott, Yoshiyasu Takefuji, John Teeter, Ralph Tindell, Robert A. Wallace, Eugene Wang, Daniel Weinreb, Elia Weixelbaum, Kris Wiesenfeld, and my students.

Without your help, this book would still be just an idea.

Contents

0

Introduction

This book is a presentation of LISP which is both practical and theoretical. For the practical, the syntax of the language, the programming styles, and the semantics of computation are carefully developed in four of the first five chapters. For the theoretical, the algebra of interpreters, the lambda calculus as a foundation for LISP, and the algebraic significance of LISP's approach to artificial intelligence, are the topics of the last three chapters. As the title LISP, Lore, and Logic suggests, it goes beyond a simple description of the language and its theory. The additional material consists of historical comments and quotations, photographs of many of those involved in LISP's creation, and interesting examples of LISP's applications.

The level of difficulty is that of an undergraduate calculus course. The material has been designed to appeal to a variety of readers, from the bright freshman to the practicing professional and from computer scientists and mathematicians to chemists, engineers, and philosophers. We assume some experience in computing and at least a sophomore's background in mathematics. The course in which this material was developed was a theoretically oriented LISP programming course – it will serve well as the primary text in such courses. This little book may also be used as a secondary text in courses covering artificial intelligence with LISP, programming languages, and the theory of computation.

The text is organized into eight chapters – each corresponding to a view of LISP. Chapter 1, A First Look at LISP, presents a few words on LISP's origins, followed by a broad and lightly detailed overview of LISP and LISP computing. Chapter 2, Elementary Programming, is a moderately complete presentation of LISP programming in terms of fundamental operations and strategies. In these programs, we are still dealing with only the most basic data structures and functions. Chapter 3, Deeper into Essential Structure, goes back to pick up essential syntactic and semantic details not fully developed in the first two. At this point, we have a good general view of programming. In fact, with a few additional exercises and the first two sections from Chapter 5, there would be a complete baby course in LISP. We now take a short break, giving the reader time to digest Chapters 2 and 3.

In Chapter 4, Computational Philosophy, topics of a more general nature are introduced. The most abstract topic is a sketch of mathematical models of computation. The most practical is a good solid presentation of types of recursion, their computational properties, and efficient strategies for their programming. Chapter 4 concludes with an entertaining section on computational folklore.

Chapter 5, LISP Functions for Powerful Programming, returns to programming to pick up the remaining important ideas. These include debugging tools, applicative operators, macros, structures, function closures, and surgical functions. As applications, there are colorful and nontrivial LISP programs for parallel computing, translating between English and Inuit, altering LISP's listener, processing molecules in organic chemistry, self-processing, and list processing without CONS. We have now completed most of our development of programming.

DIVISION OF TOPICS:

The division of the text between programming, theory, and the algebra of computation is illustrated in this Venn diagram.

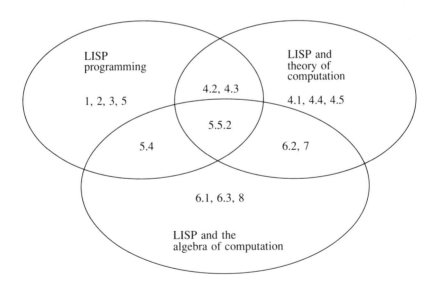

The last three chapters develop the theory and tie it to the language. Chapter 6, Interpreters: From Algebra to LISP, describes the workings of interpreters in general and for LISP in particular. This chapter concludes with a glimpse at compiled functions. Chapter 7, Mathematical Foundations of LISP, is a simplified introduction to the lambda calculus and its relation to LISP. The lambda calculus is interesting as a foundation for LISP and as a bizarrre paradigm for computing in general. Finally, Chapter 8, Automatic Reasoning, Algebraic Intelligence, touches on logic, automatic theorem proving, PROLOG, and the algebraic basis for machine intelligence. This chapter makes the important point that classical machine intelligence is based on fundamental connections between syntax and semantics which exist in algebraic languages. PROLOG is introduced as a sibling of LISP.

There are several paths which the teacher or the independent reader may take through this text. The best are illustrated by paths through the accompanying flow chart. Boxes represent programming chapters, circles represent theoretical chapters.

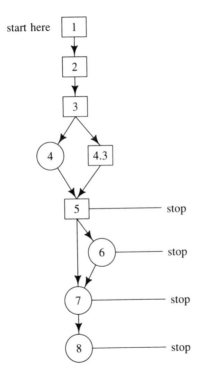

As you get into this text, LISP manuals may be useful. Good manuals listed in the bibliography include Steele[1984] – the bible of Common LISP; Gold Hill Computers[1984] – most of this text's code was developed on their G(olden)C(ommon)LISP for personal computers; Moon[1974]; Pitman[1981]; and Teitelman[1978]; and Weinreb&Moon[1981]. All of the LISP code in this text has been machine verified (directly from the text files) in the Common

LISP of Gold Hill Computers (GCLISP 1.01). Further, implementation sensitive parts of the code have been verified on Symbolics' Common LISP and Texas Instruments' Explorer Common LISP.

> Readers with comments, suggestions, history, photographs, corrections, etc., are encouraged to write to the author. Be sure to include your name and return address.

1

A First Look at LISP

This chapter begins with a sketch of the origins of LISP. The second part of the chapter introduces the most basic and important features of the language. This includes LISP data, LISP terms, and examples of typical LISP-listener responses to the terms.

1.1 The origins of LISP

LISP was created during the years 1956–62 by the mathematician John Mc-Carthy. Working with others and primarily at MIT, McCarthy's goal was to create a language for artificial intelligence. His work was influenced by that of A. Newell, J.C. Shaw, and H. Simon (of Carnegie Institute of Technology) on a nonnumerical language known as IPL2. Newell, Shaw, and Simon presented their work at the first conference on artificial intelligence (Dartmouth, summer 1956). The development of LISP was also influenced by the algebraic features of the terms in the newly developed language FORTRAN.

HISTORY:

In the History of LISP, McCarthy[1981][1] we find the
following story.

...

"My desire for an algebraic list-processing language for artificial
intelligence work on the IBM 704 computer arose in the summer of
1956 during the Dartmouth Summer Research Project on Artificial
Intelligence. ... During this meeting, Newell, Shaw, and Simon

---

[1]All references herein cited as McCarthy[1981] have been taken from McCarthy, John; 1981 *"History of LISP," History of Programming*, Richard Wexelblat (editor), Academic Press, New York. ©1981 by the Association for Computing Machinery, Inc.

Figure 1.1. John McCarthy (courtesy of the MIT Museum)

described IPL2, a list-processing language ... in which they
implemented their Logic Theorist program.

...

[The] FORTRAN idea of writing programs algebraically was [also]
attractive. It was immediately apparent that arbitrary subexpressions
of symbolic expressions could be obtained by composing the
functions that extract intermediate subexpressions, and this seemed
reason enough to go to an algebraic language.

...

There were two motivations for developing a language for the IBM
704. First, IBM was generously establishing a New England
Computation Center at MIT... . Second, IBM was undertaking to
develop a program for proving theorems in plane geometry (based
on an idea of Marvin Minsky's), and I was to serve as a consultant
on that project. At that time, IBM looked like a good bet to pursue
artificial intelligence research vigorously... ."

(Copyright ©1981 by the Association for Computing Machinery,
Inc.)

During the next two years, LISP was developed as a pencil and paper language.

Figure 1.2. IBM 704 (courtesy of the International Business Machines Corp.)

HISTORY:

> "In the Fall of 1958, I [John McCarthy] became Assistant Professor
> of Communication Science ... at MIT, and Marvin Minsky (then
> Assistant Professor of Mathematics) and I started the MIT Artificial
> Intelligence Project. The project was supported by the MIT
> Research Laboratory in Electronics ... No written proposal was ever
> made. When [Professor Jerome] Wiesner [Director of the
> Laboratory] asked Minsky and me what we needed ..., we asked for
> a room, two programmers, a secretary, and a keypunch. ..."
> McCarthy[1981]

LISP was designed for sophisticated nonnumerical computation. The applications include theorem proving, symbolic algebra and calculus, electrical circuit analysis, organic chemistry, game playing, language development, natural linguistics, pattern processing, etc. With its success in such interesting areas, LISP attracted growing interest from nontheoreticians – programmers in artificial intelligence and researchers in other disciplines emphasizing nonnumeric computation. New users began writing larger and larger programs. This shifted LISP's evolutionary forces from mathematical to practical. A large variety of programming tools were added both to LISP itself and to its immediate environment. The original dialects (LISP1 and LISP1.5) were expanded in a variety of directions. These included LISP360, MacLISP, FranzLISP, InterLISP, ZetaLISP, SCHEME, and Common LISP (the long-awaited standard).

1.2   A glimpse into the structure of LISP

Six key features of LISP are introduced in this section. These aspects include
(1) syntax for LISP expressions, (2) the evaluation of LISP expressions, (3) the
special operation QUOTE, (4) user-created functions, (5) conditional expressions
for controlling the course of a computation, and (6) assignments.

TERMINOLOGY:

> LISP is a language whose expressions follow the rules of a formal
> algebraic structure. The rules which determine which strings of
> characters are valid expressions are known as the syntax of LISP.
> The process of computing the intended meaning of an expression is
> *evaluation*. QUOTE is an operation which allows us to deal with an
> expression at the syntactic level (i.e., as a string of symbols) rather
> than with its meaning. Conditional expressions are
> IF...THEN...ELSE... and its generalizations. Finally,
> assignments are generalizations of the familiar
> X:=X+1.

A typical LISP programming session is interactive in that the user interacts
with the LISP listener. The listener is a program loop which reads expressions
from the terminal, checks their syntax, and computes and prints their values.
To the user, the interaction consists of (1) the user entering a LISP-term (at the
terminal), (2) the interpreter evaluating the expression, and (3) displaying the
value (or error message) at the terminal. In our examples, this process is denoted

```
*    LISP-term
     ==> value.
```

The long arrow, ==> used above shows final results. When giving intermediate
steps, a shorter arrow will be used.

   LISP-*term* => *step*−1 => ...=> *step*−*k* => *value*.

These intermediate steps are not shown at the terminal unless a diagnostic function, such as STEP (Section 5.1.2), has been invoked.

To start the LISP listener in the first place, enter a command such as

```
>    LISP
```

at the top level of your system. Once LISP is started, it will run through the
loop

   ..., read *LISP-term*, evaluate, display *value*, read... ,

until the term

```
*    (EXIT)
```

is entered. This term will cause the listener to stop, returning the user to the mode from which LISP was entered.

Example 1: Although we haven't developed LISP's syntax, a first terminal session (with the user's input following the top level prompt > or the LISP prompt *, and the machines response in lower case or following ==>) might look something like this:

```
>   LISP

    Entering Common Lisp

*    (* (- 10 5) 6.1)
     ==> 30.5
*    (IF NIL 4 (1+ 4))
     ==> 5
*    (APPEND '(1 2 3) (LIST 4 5 6 7 8 9))
     ==> (1 2 3 4 5 6 7 8 9)
*    (CAR (LIST 1 2 3))
     ==> 1
*    (EXIT)

>   ...   .
```

1.2.1 Data

For the time being, LISP's data objects may be thought of as consisting of atomic objects (numbers, truth values, the empty list NIL, strings, etc.) and lists of simpler objects. List formation may be applied recursively, so we may have simple lists of atoms

```
(0 1 2 3 4 5 6 7 8 9)
```

and lists containing other lists

```
(0 (1) (2 (3)) (5 (6 (7 8 9)))).
```

Lists differ from sets in that the information that they carry includes the order of their members. Thus, the lists

(1 2 3), (1 3 2), and (1 2 3 2)

are all different, whereas the sets

{1 2 3}, {1 3 2}, and {1 2 3 2}

are all the same. LISP's only restriction on the length of a list is that it fit into available memory.

The empty list may be denoted as either NIL or (), both expressions are computationally equivalent. NIL is also used as a truth value—corresponding to false. T is the constant for true. However, most functions treat all non-NIL values as being equivalent to T.

Later we will use a more fundamental type of data known as dotted pairs. Dotted pairs can be seen at the end of example 9 and in exercise 5.

1.2.2 Functions

LISP places heavy emphasis on functions. In most mathematical and computational languages, function application is denoted

$$f\langle arg_1\rangle, \quad f\langle arg_1, arg_2\rangle, \dots .$$

For example, $\sin\langle 0.145\rangle$ and $\text{expt}\langle 2.0, 0.145\rangle$. In LISP, the equivalent syntax is

$$(F \ arg_1), \quad (F \ arg_1 \ arg_2), \dots,$$

or (SIN 0.145) and (EXPT 2.0 0.145). The infix notation used in arithmetic and logic:

$$(arg_1 + arg_2), \quad (arg_1 \ / \ arg_2), \quad (formula_1 \wedge formula_2)$$

is converted to prefix notation in LISP:

$$(+ \ arg_1 \ arg_2), \ (/ \ arg_1 \ arg_2), \ (\text{AND} \ formula_1 \ formula_2).$$

The basic arithmetic functions of LISP are + (addition), − (subtraction), * (multiplication), / (division), 1+ (increase by 1), and 1− (decrease by 1).

Example 2: The following examples show how LISP will respond to terms using these functions:

```
*   (+ 1 2)
    ==> 3
*   (* (1- 5) (1+ 5))
    ==> 24
*   (/ (* 1 2 3 4) (+ -3 -2 -1 0))
    ==> -4.0
```

(The first * in each input line is LISP's prompt to the listener.) In the second and third cases, * is used in LISP terms as the multiplication function. In the second case, the arguments of * are the terms (1+ 5) and (1- 5), which evaluate to 4 and 6 before multiplication. In the third example, we see that both + and * may be applied to more than two arguments.

We will return to arithmetic and logical functions, but for the present let's go on to list-processing functions. Important functions for list processing include

LIST, APPEND, CAR, CDR, and CONS.

Like + and *, LIST and APPEND can be applied to any number of arguments. LIST returns a list whose elements are its argument values. Given lists as arguments, APPEND returns a list whose elements are the elements of its argument values. CAR and CDR take (nonatomic) lists apart. The value returned by CAR is the first element, that returned by CDR is the rest of the list after the first element is removed. Given an object and a list, CONS returns a larger list formed by adding the given object to the beginning of the given list.

Example 3:   Expressions using these functions are evaluated as follows.
```
*   (LIST 1 2 3 4)
    ==> (1 2 3 4)
*   (APPEND (LIST 1 2 3) (LIST 4))
    ==> (1 2 3 4)
*   (CAR (LIST 1 2 3 4))
    ==> 1
*   (CDR (LIST 1 2 3 4))
    ==> (2 3 4)
*   (CONS 1 (LIST 2 3 4))
    ==> (1 2 3 4)
*   (CONS 1 (CONS 2 (CONS 3 NIL)))
    ==> (1 2 3)
*   (CAR 3)
    ERROR: ATTEMPT TO APPLY CAR TO AN ATOM.
```
In the preceding evaluations; 1, 2, 3, and 4 are LISP constants. This means that they evaluate to themselves:
```
*   3
    ==> 3 .
```
We may also use variables. If X is a variable whose value is (1 2 3 4), then we have the following.
```
*   X
    ==> (1 2 3 4)
*   (CAR X)
    ==> 1
*   (CDR X)
    ==> (2 3 4)
*   (CONS (CAR X) (CDR X))
    ==> (1 2 3 4)
```
User-created functions and methods for binding values to variables are introduced in 1.2.7 and 1.2.8.

Exercises

1. Enter your LISP listener and verify the preceding examples. Experiment with variations of your own.

2. What is a constant? Give examples.

3. In evaluating large terms, innermost terms are evaluated first. For example,

```
*   (APPEND (LIST 1 2 3) (APPEND (LIST 4 5) (LIST 6)))
=>      "    (1 2 3)        "   (4 5)      (6)
=>      "    (1 2 3)   (4 5 6)
==> (1 2 3 4 5 6)  .
```

The (LIST ...) terms are evaluated, then the right-most (APPEND ...), and finally the left-most (APPEND ...). Give a similar analysis of the evaluation of

```
*   (APPEND (CONS 1 (CONS 2 NIL)) (LIST 3 4))  .
```

4. CONS, APPEND, and LIST all produce lists. What is the difference between these functions? Be especially clear in the distinction between CONS and APPEND.

5. Dotted pairs are created by CONS

```
*  (CONS 1 2)
   ==> (1 . 2)
*  (CONS (CONS 1 2) 3)
   ==> ((1 . 2) .3) .
```

Show that when the right-most atom is NIL then the resulting dotted pair is a list.

1.2.3 Expressions in the language

How do LISP terms compare with LISP data? In the preceding examples, ==> is preceded by an expression of the LISP language and followed by a value which is LISP data. In most cases, both the linguistic expressions and the data are lists. Every (finite) list is data. However, only certain lists—known as terms or forms—can be the syntactically correct LISP expressions. To be a form, a list must be either ( ) or it must begin with a LISP function, and the subsequent elements must be LISP subforms (usually). Also, the number of subforms following the function must be appropriate for the function. In evaluating the whole form, the subforms will generally be evaluated first to obtain arguments for the function, then the function will be applied to these arguments.

TERMINOLOGY:

> The words "term" and "form" have nearly the same meaning, so in Chapters 1 and 2, we won't distinguish between them. However, the original use of the word "form" was as a special type of term. Although the distinction has been lost among most mathematicians and computer scientists, it is a useful distinction. For this reason, we will revive it in Chapter 3.

These requirements can be seen in the preceding examples. In the forms which are lists, the first element is a function. The subforms include constants 1, 2, 3, 4, the variable X, and the subforms (LIST 1 2 3 4), (CAR X), and (CDR X). The evaluation of subforms to get values for the function is seen in the second example. If (LIST 1 2 3) and (LIST 4) had not been evaluated, then (APPEND (LIST 1 2 3) (LIST 4)) would have returned (LIST 1 2 3 LIST 4). The response of the listener to violations of these syntactic requirements is shown in the following example.

Example 4: When an incorrect form is submitted to the listener an error occurs.

```
*    (1 2 3 4)
     ERROR: 1 IS AN UNDEFINED FUNCTION.
```

This expression was improper because it did not begin with a function.

```
*    (CAR (1 2 3))
     ERROR: 1 IS AN UNDEFINED FUNCTION.
```

Here, the expression begins with the function CAR, but its argument is not a proper subform. Also, an error will result if the number of subforms is not appropriate for the function.

```
*    (CONS (CAR (LIST 1 2 3)))
     ERROR: NOT ENOUGH ARGUMENTS FOR CONS.
*    (CAR 1 (LIST 2 3 4))
     ERROR: TOO MANY ARGUMENTS FOR CAR.
```

1.2.4 QUOTE

The expression (CAR (1 2 3 4)) seems natural, but it's evaluation resulted in an error because LISP attempted to compute the argument for CAR by evaluating (1 2 3 4). In the form (CAR (LIST 1 2 3 4)), (LIST 1 2 3 4) was successfully evaluated to produce the argument (1 2 3 4) for CAR. However, always using functions such as LIST and CONS to construct arguments is cumbersome.

Another approach is to use the function QUOTE. QUOTE is a one-argument operation that stops the evaluation process before it reaches its argument. Consequently, the argument for QUOTE does not have to be given as a LISP form. QUOTE is special in that its argument is not evaluated. It allows the programmer to introduce arguments directly without having to construct them.

Example 5: Given any data expression, (QUOTE *data-expression*) is a proper LISP form which evaluates to *data-expression*.

```
*    (QUOTE (1 2 3 4))
     ==> (1 2 3 4)
*    (CAR (QUOTE (1 2 3 4)))
     ==> 1
*    (QUOTE (CAR (1 2 3 4)))
     ==> (CAR (1 2 3 4))
*    (CONS 1 (QUOTE (2 3 4)))
     ==> (1 2 3 4)
*    (QUOTE QUOTE)
     ==> QUOTE
```

(QUOTE *data-expression*) may be abbreviated '*data-expression*. Thus, the preceding forms may be expressed as

```
*    '(1 2 3 4)
     ==> (1 2 3 4)
*    (CAR '(1 2 3 4))
     ==> 1
*    '(CAR (1 2 3 4))
     ==> (CAR (1 2 3 4))
*    (CONS 1 '(2 3 4))
     ==> (1 2 3 4)
*    'QUOTE
     ==> QUOTE.
```

QUOTEing is the same in LISP as in a natural language, such as English. Both languages use linguistic expressions for their meaning and require quoting in order to refer to the expression itself (rather than its meaning). In English, the value of

The length of Richard Stark.

is 6 feet 2 inches if he isn't wearing shoes, while the value of

The length of "Richard Stark"

is 13 characters. The English language expression "Richard Stark" is approximately the equivalent of (QUOTE Richard-Stark). Thus, in LISP as in English, quoting is used to give us access to unevaluated expressions. Beside making it easy to present arguments, QUOTE gives LISP computational access to its own forms and functions. (To those already familiar with LISP, we are using both length and quotation here in the sense of English.)

1.2.5   Logical terms

All computer languages allow branching in their programs. When a computation reaches a branch point, the course that it follows is determined by the value of a logical term. Thus, logical terms are used to control the course of a computation.

The logical terms in LISP begin with the constants T for true and NIL for false and are built up using logical functions such as

ATOM, NULL, NUMBERP, ZEROP, <, =, EQUAL, AND,
OR, and NOT.

ATOM, NULL, NUMBERP, and ZEROP test a single argument for being atomic, the empty list NIL, a number, and the number 0. Given two or more numerical arguments, < and = test for the obvious order and for equality. EQUAL tests two arguments of any type for being the same data object. AND, OR, and NOT are not tests, they operate on the truth values of simpler logical terms. AND, OR, and NOT treat non-NIL values as being equivalent to T.

Example 6:   The following evaluations should make sense.

```
*   (ATOM ())
    ==> T
```

The subterm () is treated as an abbreviation for the atomic constant NIL, and so it evaluates to NIL.

```
*   (ATOM '(1 2 3 4))
    ==> NIL
*   (NULL ())
    ==> T
*   (ZEROP 3)
    ==> NIL
*   (< 0 3 10)
    ==> T
*   (AND (ATOM 3) (NOT (ZEROP 3)) (< 0 3))
    ==> T
*   (EQUAL '(1 2 3 4) (CONS 1 (LIST 2 3 4)))
    ==> T
```

Notice that < and AND can be applied to more than two arguments.

Exercises

1. Verify the examples above.

2. Evaluate (= (1- 7) (* 2 3) (/ 24 4) 6). Experiment with similar expressions for > and <=.

3. Evaluate (AND) and (OR). Justify the values returned.

1.2.6   Branching in computations

IF...THEN...ELSE... is used in procedural languages, such as BASIC, FORTRAN, and PASCAL, to control branching in computations. The following syntax is used:

```
IF logical-term
THEN
 statement(s)
ELSE
 statement(s).
```

When a computation reaches this point in a program, it proceeds along the course dictated by exactly one block of statements—depending on the value of the logical term.

In LISP, the course of a computation is usually controlled by COND (for CONDitional) or IF. COND is used in terms of the form

$$(\text{COND } (test_1 \ value_1) \ (test_2 \ value_2)...),$$

where $test_i$ and $value_i$ are forms. When a computation encounters such a form, the forms

$$test_1, \ test_2, \ ...$$

are evaluated until a non-NIL value is encountered. If $test_i$ is the first test form to return such a value, then the form $value_i$ is evaluated. The value returned by (COND...($test_i$ $value_i$)...) in such a case is the value of $value_i$. Thus,

$$(\text{COND } (test_1 \ value_1) \ (test_2 \ value_2) \cdots (test_k \ value_k))$$

is analogous to

```
IF test₁ THEN
 RETURN value₁
ELSE IF test₂ THEN
 RETURN value₂
 ...
ELSE IF testₖ THEN
 RETURN valueₖ .
```

SPECIAL FORMS:

Certain operations which do not evaluate all of their arguments create LISP forms known as *special forms*. The extraordinary way in which forms are presented to COND make it an operation whose forms

$$(\text{COND} \ (test_1 \ value_1) \ \ldots (test_k \ value_k))$$

are special forms.

Forms beginning with IF, AND, OR, QUOTE, SETQ, and DEFUN are also special forms.

These operations cannot be called functions because they don't evaluate all of their arguments in the way that functions evaluate them. This is especially evident in COND. For lack of better terminology, these operations are commonly called *special forms*—probably slang for "special form creating operations" or the like. Of course, COND, IF, ..., and DEFUN, aren't really forms at all.

Suppose none of the tests in (COND ...) has a nonNIL value. In Common LISP, NIL is returned. In some other LISPs, an error will result. Consequently, it is good style to end a (COND ...) in a pair of the form (T $value_k$).

Example 7:

```
*   (COND (NIL 1) (NIL 2) (T 3) (NIL 4))
    ==> 3
```

Let L, M, and V be variables with the values T, NIL, and 2 (respectively).

```
*   (COND ((AND L M) (1+ V)) ((OR L M)  V) (T (1- V)))
    ==> 2
```

Although it wasn't visible to the user, the interpreter evaluated the COND form as follows:

```
evaluate the first test form
    (AND L M) => (AND T NIL) => NIL,
because the first test returned NIL, skip the first value form,
evaluate the second test form
    (OR L M) => (OR T M) => T,
evaluate the second value form
    V => 2,
and return its value.
```

The remaining test forms are not evaluated.

IF generally takes three arguments:

(IF $form_1$ $form_2$ $form_3$).

If the value of $form_1$ is not NIL, then $form_2$ is evaluated and its value is returned by the expression. If not, then $form_3$ is evaluated and its value is returned by the expression. IF is appropriate for branches where there are only two cases.

Exercises

The PRINT function used below is a function which has the effect of printing its argument value before returning a value of its own (see 1.2.8).

1. Evaluate and explain

```
*   (COND (NIL (PRINT 1)) ((PRINT 2) (PRINT 3))
          ((PRINT 4) T) )
    ==> ?
*   (COND ((COND (T NIL) (NIL T)) 1)
          (2 (COND (T NIL) (NIL T))) )
    ==> ?
```

and

```
*   (COND)
    ==> ? .
```

2. Evaluate and explain

```
*   (IF (PRINT 1) (PRINT 2) (PRINT 3))
?
?
==> ? .
```

1.2.7 Lambda functions

LISP uses a mechanism known as lambda abstraction to create new functions. In LISP, *lambda abstraction* is the process of creating a function from a list of variables and a term.

Starting with a LISP term and a list of variables, a new function can be created as a list of the form

(*LAMBDA variable-list term*),

where the variable list contains the variables of the term. LAMBDA may be thought of as an operation that constructs a function from the variables and the term. Given an argument for each variable of the list, the variables are bound to the corresponding argument values and, using these bindings, the term is evaluated. The term's value is the value returned by the function.

Example 8:   From the variable list (X Y) and the term (CONS X (LIST Y)), lambda abstraction creates the function

>   (LAMBDA (X Y) (CONS X (LIST Y))) .

Lambda functions are lists but they are not terms—they are functions.

```
*   (LAMBDA (X Y) (CONS X (LIST Y))) .
ERROR: LAMBDA IS AN UNDEFINED FUNCTION .
```

LAMBDA **itself is not a function—it is a syntactic operator which creates functions given a variable list and a term.** Given arguments, such as 1 and 9, the function can be used in a term

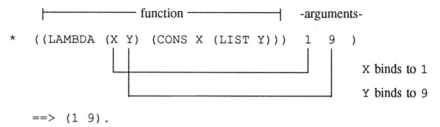

>   ==> (1 9).

The evaluation of this term consists of: (1) give X the value 1 and Y the value 9, (2) evaluate (CONS X (LIST Y)) with these values. (This function is the same as LIST for two arguments.) The importance of the variable list is seen in the following.

```
*   ((LAMBDA (Y X) (CONS X (LIST Y))) 1 9)
    ==> (9 1)
```

If the variable list changes then the function changes.

Exercises

  1. Evaluate the expressions given in the examples.

  2. Use the following functions in terms evaluated by the listener:
```
        (LAMBDA (X Y) (CONS X Y)) ,
        (LAMBDA (X) NIL) ,
        (LAMBDA () 3.14159) .
```
  How does the listener respond when one of these functions (rather than a term beginning with a function) is submitted for evaluation?

  3. A tricky nesting of LAMBDA functions: use the one-argument function

```
(LAMBDA (X) ((LAMBDA (Y) (CONS X Y)) (1+ X)))
```

in a term evaluated by the listener. The argument should be a number. Explain what happened and why.

4. What is lambda abstraction in LISP? Why is lambda abstraction used in LISP?

5. Based on the limited knowledge of "function" available at this point, identify which of the following are functions.

   (a) LAMBDA

   (b) (LAMBDA (V) (QUOTE W))

   (c) (LAMBDA () (ATOM T))

   (d) (LAMBDA (X Y) Z)

   (e) (LAMBDA NIL 3.14159)

   (f) (LAMBDA (LAMBDA) LAMBDA)

   (g) (LAMBDA (V) (V))

   (h) (LAMBDA (V) ((LAMBDA (W) (+ V W)) V))

   (i) ATOM

   (j) IF

1.2.8 Assignments

Usually, we think of an assignment as an operation which names a value or, equivalently, gives a value to a name. In FORTRAN, PASCAL, or BASIC, we often see the assignments

```
  . . .
N := 0
  . . .
N := N+1
  . . .
```

in a program. The first assignment gives the value 0 to the name N. The next assignment retrieves the current value of N from memory, adds 1 to it, and returns the result to the location associated with N. In the usual model for this process, (1) a table associates locations in main memory with names, then (2) each assignment *name*:=*term* has the effect of storing the value of the term in the location associated with the name.

Locations in main memory are remote from the central processing unit. Consequently, moving data to a memory location is very similar to moving data to a terminal or printer, and retrieving a value from such a location is similar to reading a value from a terminal or other input device. This point of view leads to the following more general definition. An *assignment* is an operation which moves information either into or out of the central processing unit. Thus, input and output operations are assignments.

Assignments tend to have effects which influence the future of a computation in ways which are not visible in the future part of the program. For example, if the term N occurs between the first and second assignment statements above, then it may, or may not, have the value 0. If N appears after the second statement, it will probably have a nonzero value. An *effect* is a change in the internal state of the computer which is typically outside of the central processing unit.

Assignments are possible in LISP, but they aren't as important here as they are in most other languages. LISP's assignments include READ and PRINT for input and output, DEFUN for naming user-created functions, and SETQ for naming data values.

First, we will consider only SETQ and DEFUN. The term

    (SETQ name argument)

returns a value (the value of the *argument*), but its computational significance is primarily in its effect. The effect is to bind the value of the argument to the (unevaluated) *name*. Thus, the effects of (SETQ N 0) and (SETQ N (1+ N)) are the same as the assignments N:= 0 and N:= N+1. In

    (DEFUN function-name variable-list term),

DEFUN has the effect of assigning function-name to the user-created function (LAMBDA variable-list term). (In DEFUN, the LAMBDA is implicit.) After such an assignment, we may use function-name in place of the more complicated LAMBDA notation. DEFUN returns function-name as its value. In LISP, most computing is defined in terms of applying functions to arguments. Thus, even when it is the effect—rather than the value—that we are after, a value will be returned.

Example 9: LIST2 is not a function in LISP. Thus, we can use it to demonstrate the effect of DEFUN.

```
*    (LIST2 4 8)
     ERROR: LIST2 IS AN UNDEFINED FUNCTION
*    (DEFUN LIST2 (X Y) (CONS X (LIST Y)))
     ==> LIST2
*    (LIST2 4 8)
     ==> (4 8)
```

DEFUN adds a new function, called LIST2 and equivalent to (LAMBDA (X Y) (CONS X (LIST Y))), to the currently active copy of LISP. Its effect can be seen in the change it caused in the machine's response to (LIST2 4 8).

ANOTHER POINT OF VIEW ON DEFUN:

In Scheme, DEFUN is viewed as a macro or language rewrite-rule assignment. The example just given would be expressed

(DEFUN (LIST2 X Y) (CONS X (LIST Y)))

and would have the effect of adding

"replace terms of the form (LIST2 X Y)
by (CONS X (LIST Y), where X and Y are variables"

to the rules determining computation in the language. Although Common LISP uses only the DEFUN syntax given in the example, the computational effect is the same.

READ and PRINT are functions for simple input and output. For example,

```
*    (READ) XYZ
     ==> XYZ
```

```
*    (CAR (PRINT (CONS 1 2)))
     (1 . 2)
     ==> 1   .
```

READ usually takes 0 arguments and returns as its value the next expression entered at the terminal. PRINT usually takes one argument which it evaluates and prints (the value of) at the terminal. The effect of (READ) is demonstrated by the following:

```
*    (READ) (CONS 0 (LIST 1 2))
     ==> (CONS 0 (LIST 1 2))   .
```

The computational response to (CONS 0 (LIST 1 2)) would have been to return (0 1 2) if (READ) had not preceeded it. Thus, (READ) changed the course of a subsequent computation.

Exercises

1. Give an example of how a simple SETQ assignment can effect the course of subsequent computation.

2. Experiment with binding functions to names using DEFUN and then using SETQ. Try using the functions named in these ways. What is the difference?

3. What is the effect of READ? Can this effect alter the course of subsequent computations?

4. What is the effect of PRINT? What is the value returned by PRINT?

5. Evaluate

   *   (READ) (PRINT 1)

   and

   *   (PRINT (READ)) 1 .

   Does READ evaluate what it READs? Does PRINT evaluate its argument?

1.3   Additional reading

The historical items in this text are from McCarthy[1981] and Stroyan[1984]. Introductory views of LISP from a mathematical point of view are given in Pratt[1979] and Wand[1984]. Good, low-keyed introductions to programming in LISP are given in Friedman and Felleisen[1987], Touretzky[1984], and Weissman[1967]. The original introduction is McCarthy et. al.[1965]. For those interested in Logic Theorist, there is Newell, Shaw, and Simon[1957].

2

Elementary Programming

This chapter shows how the essential features of LISP are used in programming. The first section presents the ideas involved in straightforward (i.e., no loops) computation. Section 2.2 shows how recursive computations are programmed using COND, IF, and DEFUN. In Section 2.3, programs are developed and stored in files which are external with respect to the listener. Search functions are introduced and their importance is explained in Section 2.4. Methods for improving efficiency through the use of extra variables and functions are described in 2.5. Association lists and their application in an English-to-Inuit translator are presented in Section 2.6. Section 2.7 discusses fixed-point computation. Section 2.8 gives additional details on simple input and output functions and the use of streams.

To an extent, the organization of this chapter follows the view of computation of partial recursive function theory (4.1). Specifically, function composition (2.1), recursion (2.2), and search (2.3) are emphasized as fundamental operations.

2.1 Programming straightforward computations

Straightforward programming is programming which cannot jump back to a previous step (thereby creating a loop). It executes each instruction at most once. Straightforward computation relies on the use of constants, variables, function application, function composition, abstraction, and simple branching. Recursive or iterative constructions are not a part of straightforward programs.

ABSTRACTION

There are two types of abstraction. Procedure abstraction is the process of naming complex procedures so that they can be used as

single symbols rather than as segments of code. Data abstraction is
the simplification of complex and commonly used data objects of
similar structure. The simplification is by defining a new data type
to describe the structure involved, and then using simple constants
and variables of this type in dealing with these data objects.

Abstraction moves our thinking, programming, and computing to a
higher and more appropriate level. For example, abstraction allows
us to manipulate a matrix X as a single object

```
READ(X);
X := 2*X + I;
```

rather than as an array of numbers

```
FOR J=1 TO N DO
FOR K=1 TO N DO
 BEGIN
  READ(X[J,K]);
  X[J,K] := 2*X[J,K] + I[J,K];
 END;
```
...etc... .

Example of straightforward programming: CADR, a composition of CAR
and CDR, can be defined to be the function (LAMBDA (X) (CAR (CDR
X))).

```
*   (DEFUN CADR (X) (CAR (CDR X)))
    ==> CADR
*   (CADR ' (1 2 3 4))
    ==> 2
```

CAR, CADR, and CADDR (defined similarly) pick out the first, second, and third
elements of a list. If we wanted to give these functions more appropriate names,
then DEFUN could be used as follows.

```
*   (DEFUN FIRST (X) (CAR X))
    ==> FIRST
*   (DEFUN REST (X) (CDR X))
    ==> REST
*   (DEFUN SECOND (X) (FIRST (REST X)))
    ==> SECOND
*   (SECOND ' (1 2 3 4))
    ==> 2
```

Notice, in SECOND, that defined functions may be used immediately in new
definitions. (Many of these functions are already built into LISP, so the effects
of the assignments are not easily demonstrated.)

Example 1:   We know that CAR and CDR cannot be applied to atoms. Consequently, the preceding functions cause errors when they are given arguments of insufficient depth.

```
*   (FIRST 1)
    ERROR: AN ATTEMPT TO COMPUTE CAR OF AN ATOM
*   (SECOND ' (1) )
    ERROR: AN ATTEMPT TO COMPUTE CAR OF AN ATOM
    ==> NIL
```

(The last term will return an error in some LISPs and NIL in others. If NIL is returned it is because (CAR NIL) ==> NIL. Assume that an error resulted in each case. One way to deal with these problems is to build tests into FIRST and REST which branch to another value—say an ERROR message—when they detect atomic arguments.

```
*   (DEFUN FIRST (X)
     (IF
      (ATOM X)
      'ERROR-IN-FIRST
      (CAR X) ))
    ==> FIRST
*   (DEFUN REST (X)
     (IF
      (ATOM X)
      'ERROR-IN-SECOND
      (CDR X) ))
    ==> REST
*   (FIRST ' (1) )
    ==> 1
*   (SECOND ' (1) )
    ==> ERROR-IN-FIRST
```

Notice that SECOND did not have to be redefined. The original definition of SECOND called on the new definitions of FIRST and REST.

Example 2:   From elementary logic, we know that the logical implication

$$(\alpha \rightarrow \beta)$$

can be defined as

$$((\neg\alpha) \vee \beta),$$

where $\neg$ and $\vee$ are NOT and OR.

```
*   (DEFUN IMPLIES (H C) (OR (NOT H) C))
    ==> IMPLIES
*   (IMPLIES T NIL)
    ==> NIL
```

```
*   (IMPLIES NIL T)
    ==> T
```

Logical equivalence is programmed in terms of IMPLIES and AND.

```
*   (DEFUN IF-AND-ONLY-IF (R S)
      (AND (IMPLIES R S) (IMPLIES S R)) )
    ==> IF-AND-ONLY-IF
*   (IF-AND-ONLY-IF (IMPLIES NIL T) T)
    ==> T
```

Example 3: An integer-valued step function is defined using a conditional with the arithmetic relation "<" in the first test.

```
*   (DEFUN STEP-FUN (X)
      (COND ((< 0 X) 1) (T 0)))
    ==> STEP-FUN
*   (STEP-FUN 0.1)
    ==> 1
*   (STEP-FUN -0.1)
    ==> 0
```

IF could have been used in place of COND here.

Example 4: A LAMBDA function is of the form

```
(LAMBDA variable-list term).
```

The variables in the variable list include the variables of the term, but they are not necessarily restricted to those of the term.

```
*   (DEFUN CONSTANT (X) T)
    ==> CONSTANT
*   (CONSTANT 2.7)
    ==> T
```

CONSTANT returns the value T for each argument. Since constant functions don't depend on their argument, they don't have to have one. In the function (LAMBDA () 3.1416), the variable list is empty and the term is nothing more than a floating-point number.

```
*   (DEFUN PI () 3.1416)
    ==> PI
*   (PI)
    ==> 3.1416
```

Using the fact that * is the multiplication function, we may compute the area of a circle of radius 5. (Don't confuse the * which we have been using as a request for user input with LISP's multiplication function.)

```
*  (DEFUN CIRCLE-AREA (RADIUS) (* (PI) RADIUS RADIUS))
   ==> CIRCLE-AREA
*  (CIRCLE-AREA 5)
   ==> 78.54
```

Example 5: The formula for the surface area of a sphere is

$$spherearea(radius) = 4 * \pi * radius^2 = 4 * circlearea(radius),$$

and the formula for the volume of a sphere is

$$spherevolume(radius) = \frac{4}{3} * \pi * radius^3 = \frac{1}{3} * radius * spherearea(radius).$$

```
*  (DEFUN SPHERE-AREA (RADIUS)
    (* 4 (CIRCLE-AREA RADIUS)) )
   ==> SPHERE-AREA
*  (DEFUN SPHERE-VOLUME (RADIUS)
    (/ (* (SPHERE-AREA RADIUS) RADIUS) 3))
   ==> SPHERE-VOLUME
*  (SPHERE-VOLUME 5)
   ==> 523.6
```

This trick, to establish pi as a 0-argument function rather than a constant, is not good, straightforward programming. A more appropriate approach would be to use SETQ to assign the appropriate value to PI.

```
*  (SETQ PI 3.14159)
   ==> 3.14159
*  PI
   ==> 3.14159
*  (DEFUN CIRCLE-AREA (RADIUS) (* PI RADIUS RADIUS))
   ==> CIRCLE-AREA
```

Now, without changing the subsequent function definitions, we can successfully compute the volume of a sphere of radius 5.

```
*  (SPHERE-VOLUME 5)
   ==> 523.598
```

The slight difference in value shows that the bound variable PI was used rather than the (slightly different) function PI.

The preceding programs involve tests, conditional branching, and calls to other functions, but they do not contain any loops. In programs such as these, there are at least as many program steps as computation steps—so they are limited to algorithms whose computations are no longer than the program. General purpose programming requires the ability to define algorithms which contain loops. In most procedural languages, this is done with a test branch and GOTO, a DO loop, a WHILE block (or its equivalent), or calls to recursive subroutines. In LISP, the primary (or at least the original) mechanism for creating looping computations is recursion.

Exercises

1. Define the function ABSOLUTE-VALUE.

2. Define the function EVENP which, given an integer, returns T if the integer is even, NIL if it is odd. Hint: use INTEGERP.

3. Program a function X-SECOND which, given a list, removes the second member if there is a second member. For example,

```
*    (X-SECOND '(1 2 3 4 5))
     ==> (1 3 4 5)
*    (X-SECOND '(1))
     ==> (1)  .
```

4. Program the approximation

$$e\langle x \rangle = 1 + x + (1/2) * x^2 + (1/6) * x^3 + (1/24) * x^4$$

to the exponential function as a straightforward LISP function.

2.2   Recursive and iterative computations

Recursive processes are processes which are defined in terms of themselves. In mathematics and computing, there are recursive functions, recursive procedures, recursive computations, and recursively defined data objects. In nature, recursive processes are ubiquitous, especially in the life sciences.

2.2.1   A general view of recursion

In LISP, recursive functions usually use names assigned by DEFUN to refer back to themselves. In a DEFUN term, this means that the new function's name is used in the term defining the function, or there may be a ring of functions each defined in terms of the next.

Example 6:   The factorial function of mathematics is defined recursively by the equations

$$
\begin{aligned}
factorial\,\langle n \rangle &= 1, & \text{if } n = 0\\
&= n * factorial\,\langle n - 1 \rangle, & \text{if } 0 < n.
\end{aligned}
$$

In LISP, the mathematics would be translated directly into

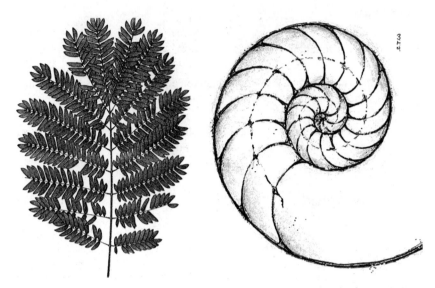

Figure 2.1. Natural recursion in genetically programmed morphogenesis: fern and chambered nautilus.

```
*   (DEFUN FACTORIAL (N)
    (COND
     ((ZEROP N) 1)
     ((< 0 N) (* N (FACTORIAL (1- N))))) ))
    ==> FACTORIAL .
```

(Notice that several lines may be used in entering a LISP term. This is possible because the listener makes no attempt at evaluation until the parentheses have been balanced.) In the computation involved in

```
*   (FACTORIAL 3)
    ==> 6 ,
```

the function calls itself four times. Some of the intermediate steps in the computation are shown in the following.

```
*   (FACTORIAL 3)
    => (* 3 (FACTORIAL 2))
    => (* 3 (* 2 (FACTORIAL 1)))
    => (* 3 (* 2 (* 1 (FACTORIAL 0))))
    => (* 3 (* 2 (* 1 1)))
    => (* 3 (* 2 1))
    => (* 3 2)
    ==> 6
```

This view of the computation of (FACTORIAL 3) shows the terms which must be evaluated to obtain the final value. The LISP system will generally store these terms in stack memory with the left-most expressions near the bottom of the stack, and the right-most at the top of the stack.

STACK MEMORY:

Stack memory is a form of memory which is similar to the lists we have been working with. In stack memory, new items are stored only at the top of the stack—as if they were CONSed onto a list. In stack memory, an item can be read or deleted only from the top of the stack.

Optional: another view of this computation can be had by evaluating (STEP (FACTORIAL 3))—see 5.1.2 for a discussion of STEP.

Given functions f and h, f is *defined in terms of* h if either (1) f is a (LAMBDA variable-list term), where h is used in the term, or (2) there is an intermediate function g such that f is defined in terms of g and g is defined in terms of h. f is *recursively defined* (i.e., f is *recursive*) if f is defined in terms of itself.

There are four ways in which a function f can have a recursive definition. First, f is defined using an f-to-f loop:

```
(DEFUN f variable-list term-involving-f).
```

Second, f is defined in terms of h, and h is defined using an h-to-h loop:

```
(DEFUN f variable-list1 term1-involving-h)
(DEFUN h variable-list2 term2-involving-h).
```

Third, for $g_1, ..., g_k$, f is defined in terms of $g_1, ...,$ and g_k is defined in terms of f:

```
(DEFUN f variable-list₀ term₀-involving-g₁)
(DEFUN g₁ variable-list₁ term₁-involving-g₂)
. . .
(DEFUN gₖ variable-listₖ termₖ-involving-f).
```

Actually, the first way of defining f is the special case $k = 0$ of the third. The fourth way, described in 4.2, involves LABELS.

2.2.2 Programming recursive computations

The distinction between the useful recursive self-reference and useless circular self-reference is subtle, but critical. Most of us find it difficult to think in circles—at least in meaningful circles—but that is exactly what is required in recursive programming. The only way to develop the skill is to study examples and to create recursive programs of your own. This section contains several examples of elementary recursive programs.

Example 7: To a mathematician, the term *list* can be defined recursively as follows:

L is a *list*, if L is an atom and L=NIL, or (CDR L) is a list.

This definition translates into LISP as

```
*   (DEFUN LISTP (L)
      (IF
        (ATOM L)                              ;test for exit
        (NULL L)                              ;exit clause
        (LISTP (CDR L))                   ;recursive clause
      ))
      ==> LISTP
*   (LISTP '((THE ARCTIC) IS (THE LAND (OF THE
          (MIDNIGHT) SUN ))))
      ==> T .
```

LISTP is applied to three successive CDR's of the original list ending with

```
...=> (LISTP '((THE LAND...)))  =>  (LISTP ( ))
    => (NULL ())  => T.
```

In the preceding example, the "*;*" convention has been used to add comments to the function's definition. Whenever a semicolon appears on a line submitted to the listener, the semicolon and everything to the right of it is ignored by the listener.

Example 8: The length of a list is 0 if it is atomic (i.e., length$\langle()\rangle$ = 0), otherwise its length is 1 more than the length of its CDR.

```
*   (DEFUN LENGTH (L)
      (IF
        (NULL L)                              ;test clause
        0                                          ;exit clause
        (1+ (LENGTH (CDR L)))        ;recursive clause
      ))
      ==> LENGTH
*   (LENGTH
      '(IN SUMMER THE ARCTIC IS THE MOST BEAUTIFUL PLACE
        ON EARTH) )
      ==> 11 .
```

In this computation, LENGTH called itself ten times (the last time with the empty list as its argument).

Example 9:   Given an object and a list, the object is a member of the list if it is equal to an element of the list. This idea can be implemented by testing for equality between the given object and the first element of the list, then recurring with the object and the CDR of the list.

```
*    (DEFUN MEMBERP (OBJECT LIST)
     (COND
       ((ATOM LIST)   NIL)                        ;exit clause
       ((EQUAL OBJECT (CAR LIST))   T)            ;exit clause
       (T   (MEMBERP OBJECT (CDR LIST)))) ;recursive clause
     ))
     ==> MEMBERP
*    (MEMBERP 'INUIT '(IT IS THE HOME OF THE INUIT))
     ==> T
*    (MEMBERP
     'REINDEER
     '(AND OF OTHERS (POLAR-BEARS REINDEER WOLVES BIRDS))
     )
     ==> NIL
```

This last term returns a value of NIL because REINDEER is never equal to the first element of a CDR of the list.

Example 10:   The up and down sequence

9 28 14 7 22 11 34 17 52 26 13 40 20 10 5 16 8 4 2 1

is the Collatz sequence starting at 9. Given an arbitrary starting number (9 in this case) as c_0, the successors, c_{n+1} to the current number c_n, are computed by the following rule:

if $c_n = 1$, then there is no successor   (exit)
if c_n is even, then $c_{n+1} = c_n/2$ (case 1)
otherwise, $c_{n+1} = 3 * c_n + 1$ (case 2).

This two-case recursive procedure generates a sequence which is not monotonic (i.e., changing in more than one direction). For a typical starting number, the sequence meanders up and down, but eventually reaches 1 and stops. However, mathematicians have not proved—despite a considerable effort—that this must always be the case. To begin research on your own, define COLLATZ as follows.

```
*    (DEFUN COLLATZ (N)
     (PRINT N)                             ;each N is printed
     (COND
       ((EQUAL N 1)   1)                            ;exit
       ((EVENP N)   (COLLATZ (ROUND (/ N 2)))))    ;case 1
```

```
(T   (COLLATZ (1+ (* 3 N))))  ))                        ;case 2
==> COLLATZ
```

COLLATZ is an integer function, yet the division in case 1 returns a floating-point value. Consequently, ROUND (the function which rounds off a floating-point number to the nearest integer) is applied to (/ N 2) to produce an integer for COLLATZ. If your LISP does not have ROUND, use TRUNCATE.

FORESHADOWING PROGN SYNTAX:

COLLATZ is a LAMBDA function
(LAMBDA (N) (PRINT N) (COND...))
with more than one term following the variable list. This is discussed in detail in 3.2.3, but for now, we can say that, when several terms appear after the variable list, they are evaluated in order, and the value of the last one is returned as the value of the function. In such a case, the list of terms is called the *body of the function*. The values of terms which precede the last term are not returned, so they are present for their effect, and the body is said to be an "implicit PROGN".

ALGEBRAIC SYNTAX VERSUS NATURAL LANGUAGE SYNTAX:

Traditional English-language practice would have ended the previous sentence with the period inside of the quotation

... to be an "implicit PROGN."

rather than outside

... to be an "implicit PROGN".

as we have. The period belongs to the sentence's global syntax rather than the quoted expression's syntax. From an algebraic point of view, the traditional syntax is grotesquely tangled and, therefore, incorrect. In a text dealing with an algebraic language and emphasizing syntactic issues the traditional approach would be inconsiderate of the readers' peace of mind, so we will deliberately use the nontraditional and nontangled syntax.

The (PRINT N) in the body of Collatz causes each argument to be printed during the computation. Thus, the user can see the computation in progress.

```
*   (COLLATZ 27)
    27 82 41 124 62 31 94 47 ...
    3077 9232 4616... 2 1
    ==> 1
```

There are about 111 steps in this computation, with the largest integer visited being 9232. ((PRINT N) will actually display the steps vertically rather than horizontally, as shown here. To get a horizontal display, use PRIN1 and TERPRI.)

For more information on this function, see Lagarias[1985] and Wagon[1985]. We will go deeper into the interesting theoretical aspects of this and similar functions in 4.3.3.

Example 11: A version of the append function might be defined (by a mathematician) for lists $l1$ and $l2$ as follows:

$$\begin{aligned} \text{append} \langle l1, l2 \rangle \\ = l2 & \qquad \text{if } l1 \text{ is nil,} \\ = \text{cons} \langle \text{car} \langle l1 \rangle, \text{append} \langle \text{cdr} \langle l1 \rangle, l2 \rangle \rangle & \qquad \text{otherwise.} \end{aligned}$$

In LISP, this is

```
*   (DEFUN APPEND (L1 L2)
     (IF
      (ATOM L1)                        ;if L1 is NIL, exit
      L2                               ;with the value L2,
      (CONS (CAR L1) (APPEND(CDR L1) L2)))));else recur.
    ==> APPEND
*   (APPEND '("ARCTIC" COMES FROM)
     '(THE GREEK WORD FOR BEAR))
    ==> ("ARCTIC" COMES FROM THE GREEK WORD FOR BEAR)
```

PLAY:

Not because bears live in the arctic, but because the Great Bear constellation contains the North Star and the North Star points the way to the arctic. The Greek for bear is

'arkos' $= \alpha\rho\kappa\omega\sigma$.

However, we don't need to define APPEND, because as we have already seen, a version is built into the language. That version can take any number of arguments.

Example 12: Given a main s-expression, an old s-expression, and a new s-expression; SUBST replaces all occurrences of the old in the main by the new. The substitutions may be at any level, so SUBST must look deeper than just the members of the main argument. We would like to have SUBST work as follows:

```
*   (SUBST 10 'X '(+ X (* 2 X)))
    ==> (+ 10 (* 2 10)) .
```

To get this behavior, we program SUBST as follows:

```
*   (DEFUN SUBST (NEW OLD MAIN)
    (COND
      ((EQUAL OLD MAIN)  NEW)    ;if main=old return new
      ((ATOM MAIN)  MAIN);if main is atomic return MAIN,
      (T                         ;otherwise
       (CONS                     ;join the results of
        (SUBST NEW OLD (CAR MAIN)) ;replace NEW for OLD
        (SUBST NEW OLD (CDR MAIN));in each half of MAIN.
    ))))
    ==> SUBST .
```

Just for fun, we'll apply SUBST to itself. Using FUNCTION (see Section 3.4) to recover the definition of SUBST for use as OLD in SUBST, we will replace all occurrences of MAIN by M.

```
*   (SUBST 'M 'MAIN (FUNCTION SUBST))
    ==> (LAMBDA (NEW OLD M)
    (COND
      ((EQUAL OLD M) NEW)
      ((ATOM M) M)
      (T (CONS (SUBST NEW OLD (CAR M))
         (SUBST NEW OLD (CDR M)) ))))
```

Notice that the substitution of M for MAIN is at all levels in the definition. The original definition of SUBST can be condensed by using SUBST to replace each variable by its first initial.

```
*   (SUBST 'N 'NEW
      (SUBST 'O 'OLD (SUBST 'M 'MAIN (FUNCTION SUBST))) )
    ==> (LAMBDA (N O M) (COND ((EQUAL O M) N)
                             ((ATOM M) M)...))
```

Example—the simplest recursive function: According to the definition of "recursive function", the function O, defined as follows, is recursive:

```
*   (DEFUN O () (O))
    ==> O
*   (O)
    ... <infinite computation> ...  .
```

In this definition, the variable list is empty (), and the term (O) applies the 0-ary function O to an empty list of arguments. In the evaluation of (O), every occurrence of (O) is replaced by an occurrence of (O); thus, we have

$$(O) => (O) => (O) => \cdots => (O) => \cdots.$$

Most readers will probably guess that this pointless computation is the result of having neither an argument to simplify nor an exit clause in the definition of O.

2.2.3 Rules for recursive programming

The accidental occurrence of infinite computations and errors caused by missing exit clauses, malfunctioning control structures, or applications of CAR/CDR to atoms can be avoided by following some simple *rules for recursive programming*.

(1) Use control functions such as COND or IF.

(2) Have all recursive clauses in COND or IF preceded by exit clauses.

(3) When a function is applied recursively, it should be applied to arguments that are in some sense simpler than those to which it is currently applied.

(4) Clauses in which CAR or CDR are used must be preceded by pairs whose test clause is satisfied when the arguments are sufficiently simple (e.g., atomic).

In (3) and (4), the notion of "simple" can be anything as long as, with each pass through the CONDitional, the arguments get one step closer to satisfying an exit clause.

Exercises

Most of the functions discussed in this section are built into LISP. So, in order to experiment with them as we have them defined, our definitions must be entered into the listener's environment.

1. A recursive definition is one that involves self-reference. Does this mean that $x = x^2 + \frac{1}{4}$, is a recursive definition of x?

2. Which of the rules for recursive definitions are violated in the definition of O?

3. What notion of "simpler" is used in FACTORIAL's definition?

4. Define LENGTH as we did above, then submit the term (LENGTH ' POLE) for evaluation. Explain the result. Change a clause in LENGTH's definition to prevent such problems.

5. Formulate a recursive definition for the exponent function (for nonnegative integers). Use the definition to program the LISP function POWER.

6. The sequence

        1 1 2 3 5 8 13 21 34 ...

is known as the *Fibonacci sequence*. It starts with $1, 1$, then each new number is the sum of the two numbers immediately before it. Program a function FIBONACCI which, given a positive integer k, will return the kth element of the sequence. For example,

```
*    (FIBONACCI 10)
     ==> 55 .
```

Show that this sequence can also be computed by

$$FIBINACCI \langle N \rangle = \frac{1}{\sqrt{5}} \left(\left(\frac{1 + \sqrt{5}}{2} \right)^{N+1} - \left(\frac{1 - \sqrt{5}}{2} \right)^{N-1} \right).$$

(An interesting discussion of this sequence is given in Knuth[1973], pages 78–85.)

7. Program a function MIN which, given a list of numbers, returns the smallest number in the list.

8. Define the function PRIME such that, for every positive integer n, PRIME$\langle n \rangle$ = (n) if n is prime, = NIL otherwise.

9. Define the function SORT such that given a list l of integers between -100 and +100, SORT$\langle l \rangle$ is a list consisting of the same numbers but given in nondecreasing order.

10. Define REDUCE so that given a list l, REDUCE$\langle l \rangle$ is a list formed from l by removing every element of l which occurs again later in l. For example,

```
*    (REDUCE
     '(E S K I M O - M E A N S - R A W - M E A T
       - E A T E R) )
     ==> (K I O N S W M - A T E R)   .
```

11. CONSEL takes two arguments—an object and a list—and returns the result of CONSing the object onto every element of the list. For example,

```
*    (CONSEL 'ARCTIC '((DREAM) (ADVENTURE)
                        (EXPLORATION) ))
     ==> ((ARCTIC DREAM) (ARCTIC ADVENTURE)
                         (ARCTIC EXPLORATION) ) .
```

12. Given a list l, PERMUTE$\langle l \rangle$ returns a list of all permutations (i.e., distinct rearrangements) of l.

13. Write a well-behaved recursive function using AND or OR in place of COND and IF.

14. Evaluate (STEP (FACTORIAL 3)) to get a picture of the computation. Explain how the indentation of the resulting list of terms corresponds to the term's position in stack memory.

15. Given a list $(e_1...e_k)$ representing a set, POWER-SET returns the set of all subsets of the given set.

2.2.4 Iteration

For simple iteration, LISP provides DO. A DO form has the following syntax:

```
(DO
    ((var-1 init-val-1 incr-1) ...
     (var-j init-val-j incr-j))
    (termination-test
      termination-form-1 ... termination-form-k )),
```

where j and k are nonnegative integers.

In its computation, a DO term such as this performs the following steps:

(0) bind each variable, *var-i*, to the corresponding initial value, *init-val-i*, (for $i=1,...,j$);

(1) evaluate the termination-test, if T is the value returned, then execute *termination-form*-1,..., *termination-form-k*, then stop; else continue;

(2) bind each *var-i* to the corresponding increment value, *inc-i*, (for $i = 1,...,j$);

(3) go to step 1.

The value returned by (DO ...) is that of *termination-form-k*.

Example 13:   The following function counts (silently) from M=0 to M=N (N is a given nonnegative integer):

```
*    (DEFUN COUNT-UP-TO (N)
     (DO
      ((M 0 (1+ M)))
      ((= M N)
       M )))
    ==> COUNT-UP-TO
*    (COUNT-UP-TO 10000)
     ==> 10000   .
```

A view of the computation performed by COUNT-UP-TO is provided by using STEP (see 5.1.2).

```
*   (STEP (COUNT-UP-TO 10))
    (COUNT-UP-TO 10)
     10
      10 = 10
     (DO ((M 0 (1+ M))) ((= M N) M))
      0                           ;M gets its initial value
       0 = 0
      (= M N)
       M
        M = 0
       N
        N = 10
       (= M N) = NIL
      (1+ M)                      ;M gets its next value
       M
        M = 0
       (1+ M) = 1
      (= M N)
       M
        M = 1
       N
        N = 10
       (= M N) = NIL
      . . .                                        ;  . . .


      (1+ M)                      ;M gets its last value
       M
        M = 9
       (1+ M) = 103
      (= M N)
       M
        M = 10
         N
        N = 10
       (= M N) = T          ;termination-test is satisfied
      M
       M = 10          ;value of termination-form returned
     (DO ((M 0 (1+ M))) ((= M N) M)) = 10
    (COUNT-UP-TO 10) = 10
    ==> 10
```

ITERATION VS. RECURSION:

The depth of (i.e., the amount of) stack memory used is indicated
by the degree of indentation. Notice that in this computation the

depth of stack memory is determined by the syntax of the function, not the size of the argument. Program a purely recursive version of COUNT-UP-TO without DO then STEP through it. The degree of indentation and consequently the depth of stack memory used will depend on the value of M. For sufficiently large M, the recursive version will experience a STACK OVERFLOW ERROR and abort while the DO version will reach completion.

DO binds its variables, $var-1,...,var-j$, in parallel (i.e., as if all of the bindings were done at the same time). Thus, for m<n, the binding of $var-m$ to either $init-val-m$ or $incr-m$ will not effect the value to which $var-n$ is bound. If $var-m$ is used in either $init-val-n$ or $incr-n$, then we may wish to use the most recent value of $var-m$—such an evaluation and binding scheme would be said to be serial (i.e., as if the bindings were done one after the other). Serial binding is done by using DO* in place of DO.

Example 14: The following definition of FACTORIAL uses two variables which must be bound serially—thus DO* is used.

```
*   (DEFUN FACTORIAL (N)
    (DO*
    ((I N (1- I)) (J 1 (* I J)))
    ((<= I 1)
    J )))
   ==> FACTORIAL
*   (FACTORIAL 6)
   ==> 120
```

The computation of FACTORIAL⟨6⟩ follows.

```
*   (STEP (FACTORIAL 6))
    (FACTORIAL 6)
     6
     6 = 6
    (DO* ((I N (1- I)) (J 1 (* I J))) ((<= I 1) J))
    N
     N = 6
    1
     1 = 1
    (<= I 1)
    I
     I = 6                   ;I is given its initial value
    1
     1 = 1
    (<= I 1) = NIL
    (1- I)                   ;I is given its next value
```

```
I
  I = 6
  (1- I) = 5
(* I J)
  I
    I = 5
  J
    J = 1
  (* I J) = 5
(<= I 1)
  I
    I = 5
  1
    1 = 1
  (<= I 1) = NIL
(1- I)                          ;I is given its next value
  I
    I = 5
  (1- I) = 4
(* I J)
  I
    I = 4
  J
    J = 5
  (* I J) = 20
(<= I 1)
  I
    I = 4
  1
    1 = 1
  (<= I 1) = NIL
    . . .
(1- I)                          ;I is given its next value
  I
    I = 2
  (1- I) = 1
(* I J)
  I
    I = 1
  J
    J = 120
  (* I J) = 120
(<= I 1)
  I
    I = 1
```

```
1
  1 = 1
  (<= I 1) = T   ;the termination-test is satisfied
  J   ;the value of the termination-form is returned
  J = 120
  (DO* ((I N (1- I)) (J 1 (* I J))) ((<= I 1) J))
       = 120
  (FACTORIAL 6) = 120
==> 120
```

Compare this computation with the one given for FACTORIAL in 2.2.1.

Exercises

1. Program LENGTH using DO in place of recursion.

2. Program REDUCE using DO in place of recursion.

3. Evaluate (STEP (COUNT-UP-TO 10)) for both the iterative and the recursive versions of COUNT-UP-TO. Explain the difference in the use of stack memory in each case. Explain the difference in the results of evaluating

   *   (COUNT-UP-TO 10000)

for the two definitions.

4. Is it possible for recursion to be more efficient than iteration? Hint: see Saint-James[1984].

2.3   External files

The creation and use of files external to LISP is an implementation-dependent issue. As such, it is a bit out of place in a chapter which is concerned with the use of implementation-invariant features for elementary programming. However, it is a practical necessity at this point because files allow the programmer to preserve his or her code from one LISP session to another.

To preserve function definitions from one LISP session to another, they are written into a file just as they would be entered at the terminal. The user can create or edit definitions in such a file from within the LISP system by using the LISP function ED. The file is permanently stored outside of any particular LISP session. These files are read into the listener by the LISP function LOAD.

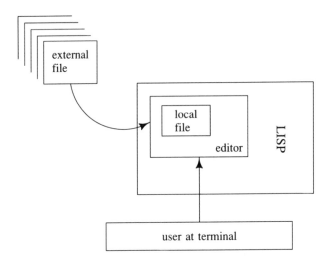

Figure 2.2. A LISP editor used to modify external files.

When a file is LOADed, the LISP terms that it contains have exactly the same effect as if they had been typed in at the terminal.

A term of the form

$$(\text{ED } file-name)$$

has the effect of setting up an editor (with the named file at hand) within the LISP session. When the editor is up and running, keyboard input is switched from the listener to the editor, and the screen shows the file being edited rather than the user interacting with the listener. While the editor is active, the file may be modified. The mechanism for saving the file and returning to LISP is an implementation-dependent key chord (a combination of keys pressed simultaneously). The terms in the file have no effect on the listener's environment until they are LOADed. This is done by the form

$$(\text{LOAD } file-name).$$

The argument *file-name* for these functions is a string defining a path to the file.

Example 15: Suppose that we are in a LISP session when we notice that the SPHERE-VOLUME defined a few days earlier has been forgotten.

```
*   (SPHERE-VOLUME 5)
    ERROR UNDEFINED FUNCTION: SPHERE-VOLUME
```

We decide to create a file, called "ROUND-FUNS," of circle and sphere functions. The effect of

```
*    (ED "ROUND-FUNS")
```

is to bring up the editor (with a file called ROUND-FUNS). We type function definitions into the new file ...

```
editor with file: ROUND-FUNS.
-----------------------------------------------------
  (DEFUN CIRCLE-AREA (RADIUS)
   (* PI RADIUS RADIUS) )
  (DEFUN SPHERE-AREA (RADIUS)
   (* 4 (CIRCLE-AREA RADIUS) RADIUS) )
  (DEFUN SPHERE-VOLUME (RADIUS)
   (/ (* RADIUS (SPHERE-AREA RADIUS)) 3.0) )
```

Since we are in the editor, there is no prompt (i.e., *) and the editor does not respond as the listener would have. After the appropriate key-chord, we are back in the LISP session where we can try again:

```
*    (SPHERE-VOLUME 5)
     ERROR UNDEFINED FUNCTION: SPHERE-VOLUME   .
```

Obviously, the interpreter wasn't aware of the definition that we recorded in the file, so we need to load the file:

```
*    (LOAD "ROUND-FUNS")
          CIRCLE-AREA
          SPHERE-AREA
          SPHERE-VOLUME
*    (SPHERE-VOLUME 5)
     ERROR: UNDEFINED SYMBOL PI   .
```

(Not all LISPs will list function names being defined as we have shown here.) The file must be reedited to contain a definition of PI. We return to the editor:

```
*    (ED)   .
```

Since ROUND-FUNS is the file at hand, it is the default file when no other file name is given to ED. Now that we are back in the editor, type an assignment for PI into the file.

```
editor with file: ROUND-FUNS.
-----------------------------------------------------
    . . .
  (DEFUN SPHERE-VOLUME (RADIUS)
   (/ (* RADIUS (SPHERE-AREA RADIUS)) 3.0) )
  (SETQ PI 3.14159)
```

A good idea is to identify globally bound variables such as PI by a special syntax such as *PI* or -PI-; when the programming gets complicated, this makes them easy to identify. However, the use of special characters is not necessary.

Return to the LISP session and LOAD the new file.

```
*   (LOAD "ROUND-FUNS")
        CIRCLE-AREA
        SPHERE-AREA
        SPHERE-VOLUME
        3.14159
*   (SPHERE-VOLUME 5)
    ==> 523.598
```

OK, it's working. We'll return to the editor and SAVE the file, exit back to LISP, kill the current session, and go home for dinner:

```
*   (EXIT)   .
```

The advantage of all this is that in killing the LISP session we didn't lose the definitions saved in the file. Days later we can bring up the listener, reLOAD the definitions stored in ROUND-FUNS, and use SPHERE-VOLUME immediately.

We have just seen external files used as sets of language-extending assignments. These files are created in an iterative fashion:

..., write code, test it in LISP, rewrite code, ...

and used for their effect. For the creation and use of such files, ED and LOAD are our primary tools. In addition to these procedure files, there are data files. They tend to be created from the output of a single computation and may be used as the input of another. Data files usually have no permanent effect on the computational environment. Such files are treated as streams (2.8) of data.

Exercises

1. Create a file containing definitions for PI, CIRCLE-CIRCUMFERENCE, CIRCLE-AREA, SPHERE-AREA, and SPHERE-VOLUME. Write, test, and edit the file until the functions work perfectly.

2. Show how to link external files so that the loading of one file will automatically trigger the loading of another.

3. The values returned during the loading of a file can be observed by using the :PRINT option as follows:

```
   *   (LOAD path-to-file :PRINT T)   .
```

Try this when loading the file created in exercise 1.

2.4 Searching

Searching is as valid and essential a tool for general computation as is recursion or function composition.

2.4.1 Is searching a sign of ignorance?

Algorithms and programs for searching through data sets or parts of individual objects (e.g., searching the nodes of a tree) are ubiquitous. However, it is easy to get the impression that searching is from the wrong side of the intellectual tracks. It may seem that searching is something that must be resorted to when one doesn't really understand the operations and relations involved in describing the desired object(s). For example, a solution to the second-order equation

$$x^2 + 5x + 21 = 0$$

may be found by searching (possibly using an algorithm, such as Newton's method, which tells us where to look next) or by analytical means (using the quadratic formula). We would expect anyone who knows the rudiments of algebra to use an analytic method, because it is faster and more accurate. The fact that even the best mathematicians may have to use search algorithms to find the roots of equations of order five or more could be nothing more than an indication of the current limits of mathematical knowledge. Maybe it is analogous to the use of statistics, in place of the more powerful methods of mathematical analysis, in areas of science lacking appropriate fundamental models.

The deterministic point of view presented in the previous paragraph is consistent with nineteenth-century science, but not with twentieth-century physics, computer science, or mathematics. In mathematics, rigorous proofs have established that simple algebraic equations of order five or more cannot, in general, be solved analytically. This leaves only search algorithms. Similarly, rigorous mathematical arguments in the study of models of computation (4.1) have shown that many functions which are computable with search operations can never be computed without them.

Thus, searching is as valid and essential a part of both mathematics and computer science as is Boolean algebra. This is not to say that search-based algorithms can never be replaced by equivalent algorithms (i.e., algorithms that return the same value) which make no use of search. The claim is only that many important algorithms have no search-free equivalents.

2.4.2 Kinds of search

In this subsection, we look at well-known search algorithms, such as Newton's method for finding roots, searching through natural numbers, Boolean search (as in using a truth table for determining the whether or not a Boolean formula is satisfiable), and the depth-first search of a tree.

Example 16: Given a differentiable real-valued function $F\langle x\rangle$ and its derivative $DF\langle x\rangle$, say,

$$F\langle x\rangle = 17 \cdot x^4 - 5 \cdot x^3 + 3 \cdot x + 10,$$
$$DF\langle x\rangle = 68 \cdot x^3 - 15 \cdot x^2 + 3,$$

we define these functions in LISP.

```
*    (DEFUN F (X)
      (+ (* 17 X X X X) (* -5 X X X) (* 3 X) -10) )
     ==> F
*    (DEFUN DF (X) (+ (* 68 X X X) (* -15 X X) 3))
     ==> DF
```

Newton's method may be used to find a solution of $0 = F\langle x\rangle$ Recall from calculus that we start with an arbitrary number a_0 and generate a series $a_0, a_1, a_2, \ldots$ of numbers which doesn't end until (and unless) we reach a number a_k for which $0 = F\langle a_k\rangle$ holds (to some predetermined degree of accuracy). Given an a_k for which the equation fails, the next number a_{k+1} is computed from a_k by

$$a_{k+1} = a_k - \frac{F\langle a_k\rangle}{DF\langle a_k\rangle}.$$

This formula contains a kind of intelligence to be used in directing our search. It is coded in NEWTON+:

```
*    (DEFUN NEWTON+ (X) (- X (/ (F X) (DF X))) )
     ==> NEWTON+   .
```

Using NEWTON+, our search is defined as follows.

```
*    (DEFUN NEWTON-SEARCH (X)
      (IF                                              ;If
       (ZEROP (F X))              ;we have found our root
       X                          ;then return it else
       (NEWTON-SEARCH (NEWTON+ X)) ))   ;keep searching.
     ==> NEWTON-SEARCH

*    (SETQ ROOT (NEWTON-SEARCH 100.0))
     ==> 0.894791
*    (F ROOT)
     ==> 0.0
```

Notice that the definitions of NEWTON+ and NEWTON-SEARCH do not depend on the particular F or DF.

In case there are several roots, this algorithm will return only one of them. If there are no real roots, then the search will go on for ever.

Example 17: Assertion—"every even integer greater than 2 is the sum of two primes." Suppose that this property is defined by a function P-SUM:

```
*    (DEFUN P-SUM (N)  ...)
     ==> P-SUM .
```

For every natural number n, (P-SUM n) returns either T (in case n is the sum of two primes) or NIL. Since the search can be restricted to primes less than one half of $n+1$, P-SUM will always return a value.

Being skeptical of the assertion above, we begin our investigation by searching for a solution to the Boolean equation NIL = P-SUM<n>.

```
*    (DEFUN NUMBER-SEARCH (N)
       (IF                                                        ;If
         (NOT (P-SUM N))      ;if we have found the exception
         N                                    ;then return it,
         (NUMBER-SEARCH (+ 2 N)) ))      ;else keep looking.
       ==> NUMBER-SEARCH
```

If NIL = P-SUM⟨n⟩ has a solution in the even integers greater than 2, then the least solution is the value returned by (NUMBER-SEARCH 4), and we have proved the assertion to be false. If no solution exists, then (NUMBER-SEARCH 4) never returns a value.

This example deals with a mathematical claim known as Goldbach's conjecture. *Goldbach's conjecture* is the simple and unsolved assertion made in the first sentence of this example.

Example 18: Let L be a Boolean-valued function of Boolean variables V1, V2, V3, V4. To determine if T=L⟨V1, V2, V3, V4⟩ has a solution, our search will progress through the usual lexicographical (i.e., as in the dictionary) Boolean ordering of values for V1, V2, V3, V4, as follows:

V1=NIL	V2=NIL	V3=NIL	V4=NIL	;first binding
=NIL	=NIL	=NIL	=T	;second binding
=NIL	=NIL	=T	=NIL	;third binding
...	...	...	...	
=T	=T	=T	=T	;last binding.

The function BOOLEAN-SEARCH will use B-NEXT (a "next" function analogous to 1+, but for lists of Boolean values).

```
*   (DEFUN B-NEXT (BV-LIST)      ;given a list of Boolean
                                 ;values, NEXT-B returns the
                      ;next (in the usual Boolean order) list.
      (REVERSE (SUB-B-NEXT (REVERSE BV-LIST))) )
    ==> B-NEXT
*   (DEFUN SUB-B-NEXT (REV-BVL)
      (COND
        ((ATOM REV-BVL)  NIL)      ;exit, process completed
        ((NULL (CAR REV-BVL))(CONS T (CDR REV-BVL)));exit
        (T  (CONS NIL (SUB-B-NEXT (CDR REV-BVL)))))
              ;replace T by NIL and return with the CDR
      ))
    ==> SUB-B-NEXT
```

We'll test B-NEXT just to be sure.

```
*    (B-NEXT '(T NIL NIL T T T))
     ==> (T NIL T NIL NIL NIL)
```

Now, we can define the search function.

```
*    (DEFUN BOOLEAN-SEARCH (B-FUN BV-LIST)
       (COND
         ((APPLY B-FUN BV-LIST)  BV-LIST)
                                          ;exit with solution
         ((NOT (MEMBER NIL BV-LIST))  NIL)
                                  ;exit at end of search
         (T
          (BOOLEAN-SEARCH B-FUN        ;continue search on
            (B-NEXT BV-LIST) ))        ;next set of values
       ))
     ==> BOOLEAN-SEARCH
```

(The function APPLY used in BOOLEAN-SEARCH is defined in Section 3.4. For the time being, we need only know that its arguments consist of a function and a list of arguments for the function. The value returned by APPLY is the value of that function when applied to those arguments.)

The Boolean formula for which we are searching for a solution is L. The following definition for L is used in testing BOOLEAN-SEARCH:

```
*    (DEFUN L (V1 V2 V3 V4)
       (AND V1 V2 (OR V3 (NOT V4)) (NOT V3)) )
     ==> L
*    (BOOLEAN-SEARCH 'L '(NIL NIL NIL NIL))
     ==> (T T NIL NIL)
*    (L NIL NIL NIL NIL)
     ==> NIL
```

```
*   (L T T NIL NIL)
    ==> T    .
```

THE BOOLEAN SATISFACTION PROBLEM:

The problem of finding a set of values for the variables of a
Boolean term which cause the term to return T is known as the
Boolean satisfaction problem (because these values are said to
satisfy the term). This problem is a representative of that infamous
family known as NP-complete problems. Although it has not been
proven, it is generally believed that the time required to solve an
NP-complete problem is an exponential function of the size of the
(description of the) problem.

Example 19: Given a binary tree, we wish to find a node satisfying a certain
test. We will search the tree—moving from one unsatisfactory node to one of its
children, then back up—until a node passing the test is found or until we have
tested every node. Our algorithm will be what is known as a depth-first search.

The binary tree is generated from a given TREE node by functions L-CHILD
⟨node⟩ and R-CHILD⟨node⟩, where nodes without children are identified by
TERMINAL⟨node⟩. The last node is defined by LAST⟨node⟩. We will use
L-CHILD, R-CHILD, and TERMINAL to define our movement through the
tree, and NODE-TEST and LAST to limit our search. For example,

```
*   (DEFUN DF-SEARCH (N)
      (PRINT N)                         ;print search position
      (COND
       ((NODE-TEST N)  N)      ;solution found, end search
       ((TERMINAL N)                    ;terminal node
        (NOT (LAST N)) )
              ;backtrack and continue if not last node
       ((EQ T (SETQ TEMP (DF-SEARCH (L-CHILD N))))
                        ;if T after searching L subtree
        (DF-SEARCH (R-CHILD N)) ) ;then search R subtree
       (TEMP  TEMP)
              ;if TEMP is nonNIL, then TEMP is the node
       (T  NIL)  ;no node satisfies TEST-NODE,end search
      ))
    ==> DF-SEARCH  .
```

The search is the computation initiated by (DF-SEARCH TREE). It continues as long as the value returned by DF-SEARCH is T. The following illustration
shows the order in which one tree's nodes are visited by DF-SEARCH.

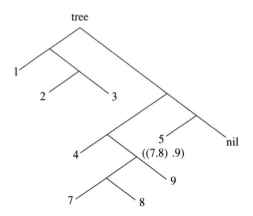

Figure 2.3. An s-expression viewed as a tree domain for searching.

```
*    (SETQ TREE '((1 . (2 . 3)) (4 . ((7 . 8) . 9)) 5))
     ==> ((1 2 . 3) (4 (7 . 8) . 9) 5)
*    (DEFUN NODE-TEST (N) (EQUAL N '((7 . 8) . 9)))
     ==> NODE-TEST
*    (DEFUN LAST (N) (NULL N))
     ==> LAST
*    (DEFUN TERMINAL (N) (ATOM N))
     ==> TERMINAL
*    (DEFUN L-CHILD (N) (CAR N))
     ==> L-CHILD
*    (DEFUN R-CHILD (N) (CDR N))
     ==> R-CHILD
*    (DF-SEARCH TREE)
     ((1 2 . 3) (4 (7 . 8) . 9) 5)

     (1 2 . 3)
     1
     (2 . 3)
     2
     3
     ((4 (7 . 8) . 9) 5)
     (4 (7 . 8) . 9)
     4
     ((7 . 8) . 9)
     ==> ((7 . 8) . 9)
```

COMMENTS ON SEARCHING:

Search algorithms are especially important in the classical approach

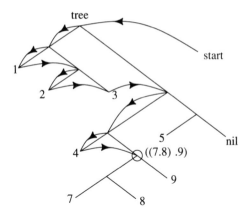

Figure 2.4. A depth-first search of the tree.

to artificial intelligence. A clear and concise presentation of several basic search procedures is given in Chapter 4 of Winston[1984].

An especially thorough and informative discussion of searching is given in Knuth[1973], Volume 3.

The very time-consuming searches so common in artificial intelligence are known as combinatorial searches, NP searches, or NP-complete searches. The time required for NP-complete searches is (believed to be) exponential in the size of the problem's description. The Boolean search described above is a search of this type. See Cook[1971].

Exercises

1. Apply the Newton's method search defined in this section to $f\langle x\rangle = x^2 - 2$. Does it find the square root of 2? Explain.

2. *Binary search.* Suppose that we are given a continuous real-valued function $f\langle x\rangle$ and arguments `left` and `right` such that $f\langle left\rangle * f\langle right\rangle$ is negative. Step 1, let $mid = (left + right)/2$. Step 2, if $f\langle mid\rangle = 0$, then return *mid* (as the root of f) and stop. Step 3, set $left' = (left\ or\ mid)$ and $right' = (right\ or\ mid)$ so that $f\langle left'\rangle * f\langle right'\rangle$ is negative. Step 4, go to step 1. Program SQUARE-ROOT using a binary search.

3. Use BOOLEAN-SEARCH to find a solution to

```
L=(LAMBDA  (V1 V2 V3 V4)
          (AND V1 (OR V2 (NOT V3) V4))).
```

4. An example of this section suggests that it is possible to search the infinite set of natural numbers $0, 1, 2, 3, \ldots$ for a solution to $T=TEST\langle n \rangle$ if TEST is a function which always returns either T or NIL given a natural number n. If there is a natural number n for which our test is true, then our searching strategy will eventually find it. How can we search all the s-expressions in this sense?

5. A list of the form

$$((symbol_1 . value_1) \ldots (symbol_k . value_k) \ldots)$$

is an association list. These lists may be used with the function ASSOC to define arbitrary finite functions. Given a symbol and an association list, ASSOC returns the left-most pair whose CAR is equal to the symbol, or—if no such pair exists—NIL is returned. Program ASSOC⟨symbol, alist⟩. This important function is discussed further in 2.6.2.

6. Try NEWTON-SEARCH starting just below the root bound in the example.

```
*    (NEWTON-SEARCH -1.0)
     ==> ???
*    (NEWTON-SEARCH 0.0)
     ==> ???
```

Explain the results.

7. In a preceding example, we have "If no such solution exists, then (NUMBER- SEARCH 4) never returns a value." Explain why this situation does not disprove the assertion of the example.

8. Experiment with BOOLEAN-SEARCH. Save the function in a file for later use.

2.5   Extra variables and functions, for efficiency

If $f\langle x \rangle = x + x^2 + x^3$, then computing the value of $f\langle t^2 - 1 \rangle$ by

$$f\langle t^2 - 1 \rangle = (t^2 - 1) + (t^2 - 1)^2 + (t^2 - 1)^3$$

is inefficient compared to computing

$$g\langle t \rangle = t^2 - 1$$

and then

$$f\langle x \rangle \text{ for } x = g\langle t \rangle.$$

The extra function has saved two squarings and two subtractions.

Example 20: In this example, we compare the efficiency of two versions, MAX1 and MAX2, of the maximum function. The following definition for MAX1 is inefficient:

```
*   (DEFUN MAX1 (NUMBERS)
     (COND
      ((ATOM NUMBERS)  NIL)                ;exit, no numbers
      ((ATOM (CDR NUMBERS))  (CAR NUMBERS))
                          ;one number left, return it
      ((< (MAX1 (CDR NUMBERS)) (CAR NUMBERS))
       (CAR NUMBERS))
       ;the first number left is the largest, return it
      (T  (MAX1 (CDR NUMBERS))) ))
                          ;the first is not the biggest
    ==> MAX1
*   (MAX1 '(3 1 41 5 9))
    ==> 41   .
```

In a single pass, (CDR NUMBERS) is computed up to three times, and (MAX1 (CDR NUMBERS)) up to two times. When the value of a single term (with no effect and with identical bindings for its variables) must be computed more than once, then we have inefficient programming. Using extra functions allows us to avoid redundant computations at the expense of an extra call to each function.

```
*   (DEFUN MAX2 (NUMBERS)
     (IF
      (ATOM NUMBERS)                       ;exit, no numbers
      NIL
      (CO-MAX2 (CAR NUMBERS) (MAX2 (CDR NUMBERS)))
        ;call CO-MAX2 with the first and MAX of the rest
     ))
    ==> MAX2
*   (DEFUN CO-MAX2 (M N)
     (COND
      ((NULL N)  M)
          ;if N (the MAX of the rest) is NIL, return M
      ((< M N)  N);if N is larger than M, then return N
      (T  M)                       ;otherwise; return M
     ))
    ==> CO-MAX2
*   (MAX2 '(3 1 41 5 9))
    ==> 41
```

Given a list of k numbers with the largest last, both CDR and MAX2 are applied $k + 1$ times. However, had the same list been given to MAX1, MAX1 would have been called $2k - 2$ times and CDR $3k - 1$ times. A better approach avoids the

calls to CO-MAX2 by using a LET variable (2.9) or an &OPTIONAL variable
(3.2.3).

In general, this problem occurs when a program must compute the value of
a term $t = t\langle x_1, \ldots, x_k \rangle$ at several places in a larger term. If the functions
between successive t computations have no effect, then the computations will
return the same value and the time invested in the subsequent computation has
certainly been wasted. However, when functions having an effect are evaluated
between the first and last t computation, t's value(s) could change. In this case,
the issue of efficiency is replaced by the question of correctness. An example
is COLLECT.

Example 21:   We wish to program a function COLLECT of 0 arguments, such
that the value returned by

```
*    (COLLECT)
```

is the list of all subsequent inputs preceding the next NIL. In other words, if
the COLLECT form is followed by inputs

```
KNUD RASMUSSEN WAS AN ETHNOGRAPHER NIL HE STUDIED
THE INUIT NIL ,
```

then the value

```
    ==> (KNUD RASMUSSEN WAS AN ETHNOGRAPHER)
```

should be returned between the inputs NIL and HE. OK. In our first attempt to
program this function, we define

```
*    (DEFUN COLLECT1 ( )
      (IF
       (NULL (READ))
       NIL
       (CONS (READ) (COLLECT1)) ))
     ==> COLLECT1 .
```

A test on the preceding input returns the incorrect value

```
    ==> (RASMUSSEN AN NIL STUDIED INUIT) .
```

The problem is in the term (READ) used in both the test (NULL (READ))
and as a part of the value (CONS (READ) (COLLECT1)) to be returned.
Each (READ) had an effect which changed the values of subsequent (READ)s.
Specifically, in the test, (READ) consumed the inputs KNUD, WAS, ETHNO-
GRAPHER, HE, THE, and NIL, leaving the intermediate inputs for the (READ)
in the value term. This definition for COLLECT1 is incorrect.

In cases such as these, we must avoid evaluating a given term more than
once. One approach is to introduce a subfunction with a variable for the value

of the repeated term. In general, define $f\langle x_1, \ldots, x_k \rangle$ using $co-f\langle x_1, \ldots, x_k, y \rangle$ by

$$f\langle x_1, \ldots, x_k \rangle = co-f\langle x_1, \ldots, x_k, t\langle x_1, \ldots, x_k \rangle \rangle$$

where $co-f$ is defined just as we had originally defined f but with y replacing each occurrence of $t\langle x_1, \ldots, x_k \rangle$. Again, LET or &OPTIONAL can be used to avoid the call to $co-f$.

Example 22: According to this strategy, COLLECT2 is defined as

```
*    (DEFUN COLLECT2 ( ) (CO-COLLECT2 (READ)))
     ==> COLLECT2
*    (DEFUN CO-COLLECT2 (Y)
       (IF
         (NULL Y)
         NIL
         (CONS Y (COLLECT2)) ))
     ==> CO-COLLECT2
*    (COLLECT2)
     KNUD RASMUSSEN WAS AN ETHNOGRAPHER NIL HE STUDIED
     THE INUIT
     ==> (KNUD RASMUSSEN WAS AN ETHNOGRAPHER)    .
```

An improvement on this definition's efficiency is the point of exercise 3.

Exercises

1. Adjust DF-SEARCH to make it into B(readth)F(irst)-SEARCH. The bredth-first search of a tree is defined by

    (a) let NODE-LIST:=(ROOT);

    (b) if the first member of NODE-LIST passes TEST, then return that node and stop, else set
    NODE-LIST := (APPEND (CDR NODE-LIST)
    (ALL-CHILDREN (CAR NODE-LIST)))
    and continue;

    (c) if NODE-LIST is not empty, then go to (b), else stop.

    (See Winston[1984], page 95, for a discussion of various search techniques.)

2. (Optional) A different approach to COLLECT, using an &OPTIONAL variable, is

    ```
    *    (DEFUN COLLECT3 (&OPTIONAL (Y (READ)))
           (IF (NULL Y) NIL (CONS Y (COLLECT3))) )
         ==> COLLECT3  .
    ```

Test this version.

3. Use the fact that (COLLECT2) => (CO-COLLECT2 (READ)) to simplify the definition of CO-COLLECT2.

4. Define a function COLLECT* which uses the first input, no matter what it is, as a delimiter for both beginning and ending the list. For example,

```
*   (COLLECT*)
```

followed by

```
THE WORD "ESKIMO" IS A TERM REFERRING TO THE INUIT
```

would use THE as the delimiter and return the value

```
==> WORD "ESKIMO" IS A TERM REFERRING TO .
```

2.6 Other list functions

Eight new list functions—MEMBER, NTH, REVERSE, LAST, ASSOC, RASSOC, ACONS, and PAIRLIS—are covered in this section. The two most important are MEMBER and ASSOC.

2.6.1 MEMBER and more

LISP has a built-in MEMBER function. If the list is $(e_1 \ldots e_k)$, then

```
(MEMBER object list)
```

returns $(e_j \ldots e_k)$ in case e_j is the first occurrence of the value of the object, NIL otherwise. Notice that this value contains all of the information, of the truth values T and NIL.

As it stands, MEMBER implicitly uses EQ (a restricted equality test described in 3.2.2) to compare the value of the object with potential matches in the list. EQ can reliably test symbols for equality. Thus, if the object we are searching for is not a symbol (or another atom reliably recognized by the EQ of your dialect), then we must specify that the test be EQUAL. In particular, to perform a routine search for a nonatomic object, use

```
(MEMBER object list :TEST EQUAL).
```

To have another relation as a test, use the following syntax:

```
(MEMBER object list :TEST binary-relation).
```

Example 23: The following example illustrates the need for and the use of alternate test relations.

```
*    (MEMBER
     'NANSEN
     '(PROFESSOR NANSEN WANTED TO BE CARRIED TO THE
       NORTH POLE) )
     ==> (NANSEN WANTED TO BE CARRIED TO THE NORTH POLE)
*    (MEMBER
     '(SPECIAL)
     '(AT A (SPECIAL)
        PLACE HIS SHIP WOULD FREEZE INTO THE ICE) )
     ==> NIL
*    (MEMBER
     'ICE
     '(THEN (THE DRIFTING ICE CAP) WOULD CARRY HIM
       (TO THE POLE))
      :TEST 'MEMBER )
     ==> ((THE DRIFTING ICE CAP) WOULD CARRY HIM
           (TO THE POLE))
```

PLAY:

> Professor Fridtjof Nansen was one of the great arctic explorers. His ship, the Fram, was designed with a round hull so that the freezing ice of the polar ice cap would lift rather than crush her. The ship was frozen in at a precisely calculated point north of Siberia in 1893. At first, all went as expected, but before reaching the pole, the ice and the Fram began drifting away. Nansen and a friend left the ship on cross-country skis and began crossing hundreds of miles of floating ice to reach the pole. The miraculous conclusion is described in the *Encyclopedia Britannica* under "Nansen" (Volume 15,©1971, William Benton Company).

Access to elements of a list—other than the first few—is possible by using the following functions. A list consisting of the last element of a given list is returned as the value of

(LAST *list*),

the $(k + 1)^{\text{th}}$ element of a list is the value of

(NTH *k list*),

and (in many dialects) the reverse of the given list is

(REVERSE *list*).

Notice that the CAR of a list is the 0th element according to NTH.

2.6.2 Functions for association lists

An *association list* is a list of dotted pairs of symbols and their values. Such lists are of the form

$$((symbol_1 \; . \; value_1) \; ... \; (symbol_j \; . \; value_j)).$$

The value associated with a symbol is usually recovered by ASSOC, while new associations are added by CONS, ACONS, or PAIRLIS.

APPLICATIONS:

> Association lists are used by interpreters to store local bindings. They can also be used to define finite functions of such an arbitrary nature that no reasonable pattern exists between the independent and dependent variable values (e.g., a function which translates from one language to another).

The syntax for ASSOC is

(ASSOC *symbol alist*),

where *alist* is an association list. If *alist* contains a pair of the form (*symbol.value*), then the value returned is the first such pair. If it contains no such pair, then NIL is returned. A reverse of this function is

(RASSOC *value alist*),

which returns the left-most association (*symbol.value*) in which the values match. By returning the full pair, rather than just the associated value or symbol, an ambiguity between the associated value NIL and the NIL indicating that there is no association is avoided.

ACONS has the syntax

(ACONS *symbol value alist*),

where *symbol* and its association with *value* are to be added to *alist*. The value returned is the same as that of (CONS (CONS *symbol value*) *alist*). In particular, any previous association with symbol remains in the alist. Several associations can be added by

(PAIRLIS (*symbol_1 ...*) (*value_1 ...*) *alist*).

This is equivalent to a series of applications of ACONS.

Example 24: The use of association list functions are illustrated trivially as follows.

```
*    (SETQ ALIST (PAIRLIS '(A B C D) '(1 2 3 4 5) NIL))
     ==> ((A . 1) (B . 2) (C . 3) (D . 4))
*    (ASSOC 'C ALIST)
     ==> (C . 3)
*    (RASSOC 3 ALIST)
     ==> (C . 3)
*    (ASSOC 3 ALIST)
     ==> NIL
*    (SETQ ALIST (ACONS 'E 3 ALIST))
     ==> ((E . 3) (A . 1) (B . 2) (C . 3) (D . 4))
*    (RASSOC 3 ALIST)
     ==> (E . 3)
```

Nontrivial examples of the use of these functions are given in the following subsection.

2.6.3   Example: translation between Inuit and English

Before getting into the colorful example of talking with the Eskimos, we'll look at an example of the use of association lists in record keeping.

Example 25:   Suppose your research involves maintaining the daily temperature records of Thule, Greenland. ASSOC can be used to recover the data for a given day (in a certain year):

```
*    (ASSOC 200 '((118 . -3) (119 . -0)...(200 . 79)...
        (365 . -10)))
     ==> (200 . 79)   .
```

The records cover most days since 28 April 1945, so we'll use a top-level list associating years with sublists which associate days with temperatures.

```
*    (SETQ THULE-RECORDS
     '((1945 . ((118 . -3) (119 . -0)...(200 . 79)...
        (365 . -10) ))
       (1946 . ((1 . -11) (2 . -12)...(365 . -29)))
       ...
       (1988 . ((1 . -33)...)) ))
     ==> ((1945 . ((118 . -3)...))...(1988 . (...)))
```

Given a year and a day, THULE-TEMP, looks up the association list for the year and then the temperature for the day.

```
*    (DEFUN THULE-TEMP ()
       (PRINC "Enter day and year (or nil nil to exit).")
                          ;instructions to the user.
       (LET*
```

```
((DAY (READ)) (YEAR (READ)))
                              ;the day and year are read
 (Y-VALUE (ASSOC YEAR THULE-RECORDS))
                                ;year records found
 (D-VALUE (IF Y-VALUE (ASSOC DAY (CDR Y-VALUE))
                      NIL))                    ;day
 (T-VALUE (IF D-VALUE (CDR D-VALUE)
                      NIL)) )         ;the temp
(COND
 ((AND (NULL DAY)(NULL YEAR))  NIL)        ;exit
 (T-VALUE      ;if a temp was found it is returned
  (PRINC "TEMPERATURE = ") (PRIN1 T-VALUE)
  (TERPRI) (THULE-TEMP) )
 (T                          ;no data was found
  (PRINC "NO DATA FOR REQUESTED DATE") (TERPRI)
  (THULE-TEMP) ))))
==> THULE-TEMP
```

Notice that LET* is serial in its variable bindings. We can now search our data base.

```
*   (THULE-TEMP)
    Enter day and year (or nil nil to exit). 200 1945
    TEMPERATURE = 79
    Enter day and year (or nil nil to exit). 1 1988
    TEMPERATURE = -33
    Enter day and year (or nil nil to exit). nil nil
    ==> nil
```

Example 26: While you are in Thule collecting data, you'll need to be able to talk with the natives (Inuit) and to understand them when they talk to you. So, we'll build a translating function.

```
*   (SETQ *DICTIONARY* '((INUIT . MANKIND/MAN)
                        (KABLOONA . WHITE-MAN)
                        (UBLAKO .  TOMORROW)
                        (KIKAQ . GNAWED-BONE)
                        (QUJANGNAMIK .
                               THANKS-TO-THE-GUESTS)
                        (TAIMALILERDLE . LET-IT-BE-SO)
                        (ILORRAINIK-TIKITUNGA .
                               I-AM-A-FRIEND)
                        (ALU .  VERY-MUCH) ...
                        (UNA-I-KTO . IT-IS-COLD) ))
    ==> ((INUIT . MANKIND/MAN)...)
*   (DEFUN INUIT-TO-ENGLISH (INUIT-WORD-LIST)
     (IF
```

Figure 2.5. Inuit

```
     (NULL INUIT-WORD-LIST)
     NIL
     (CONS
      ((LAMBDA (X) (IF (NULL X) (CAR INUIT-WORD-LIST)
         (CDR X) ))
       (ASSOC (CAR INUIT-WORD-LIST) *DICTIONARY*) )
      (INUIT-TO-ENGLISH (CDR INUIT-WORD-LIST)) )))
   ==> INUIT-TO-ENGLISH
```

Now, when the shaman smiles and says *Hey kabloona, ublako una-i-kto alu*, you can run to your PC for a translation.

```
*   (INUIT-TO-ENGLISH '(HEY KABLOONA UBLAKO
                        UNA-I-KTO ALU))
   ==> (HEY WHITE-MAN TOMORROW IT-IS-COLD VERY-MUCH)
```

So, he's giving you a weather report. But, now you must be able to respond. We'll create an ENGLISH-TO-INUIT translator by merely replacing ASSOC in INUIT-TO-ENGLISH by RASSOC and a CDR by CAR.

```
*   (DEFUN ENGLISH-TO-INUIT (ENGLISH-WORD-LIST)
    (IF
     (NULL ENGLISH-WORD-LIST)
     NIL
     (CONS
      ((LAMBDA (X) (IF (NULL X)
         (CAR ENGLISH-WORD-LIST) (CAR X)))
       (RASSOC (CAR ENGLISH-WORD-LIST) *DICTIONARY*) )
      (ENGLISH-TO-INUIT (CDR ENGLISH-WORD-LIST)) )))
   ==> ENGLISH-TO-INUIT
```

```
*   (ENGLISH-TO-INUIT '(LET-IT-BE-SO OLD MAN))
   ==> (TAIMALILERDLE OLD INUIT)
```

Exercises

1. Use the built-in MEMBER to define ASSOC.

2. Alists are usually updated by adding new associations to the front. Thus, an association list may contain several pairs for a given symbol. (This is inefficient from the point of view of space, but it allows earlier alists to be remembered when the time comes to back out of a computation.) Occasionally, it can be appropriate to rebind symbols rather than just add new bindings to the front. Use ASSOC and SUBST to define a function REBIND(*symbol, new-value, alist*) which changes a symbol's binding.

3. The complexity of ASSOC-based function definitions: Suppose that $y = F\langle x \rangle$ is implemented using ASSOC and an association list for all $(x . y)$ pairs in the graph of $F\langle\ \rangle$. Express the average time to compute $F\langle x \rangle$ in terms of the number D of elements in F's domain.

2.7 The fixed-point style of computation

Computations which repeatedly apply a function or process to its own output until the input equals the output are called *fixed-point* computations. In the abstract, such a computation is defined in terms of a function $f\langle x \rangle$ by a procedure such as

1. read(x)

2. until $x = f\langle x \rangle$ do $x := f\langle x \rangle$

3. print(x).

This procedure generates the values

$$x, f\langle x \rangle, f\langle f\langle x \rangle\rangle, f\langle f\langle f\langle x \rangle\rangle\rangle, f\langle f\langle f\langle f\langle x \rangle\rangle\rangle\rangle, \ldots.$$

In some cases, this process will lead to a y for which $y = f\langle y \rangle$.

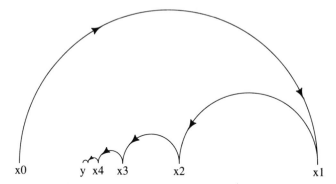

Figure 2.6. The dynamics of a fixed-point computation.

The term "fixed-point" comes from the fact that the value returned is a solution to the equation $y = f\langle y \rangle$ (expressing the property of y of being fixed or unchanged under the action of f).

Example 27:   In LISP, the procedure above is defined

```
*   (DEFUN F-FIXEDPOINT (X)
    (SUB-F-FIXEDPOINT X (F X)) )
    ==> F-FIXEDPOINT
```

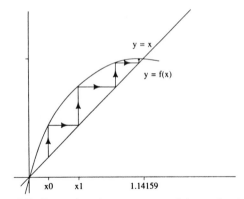

Figure 2.7. Computing the square-root of 2 as a fixed-point.

```
*   (DEFUN SUB-F-FIXEDPOINT (X Y)
    (PRINT X)   ;this allows us to see the computation.
    (IF
    (EQUAL X Y)        ;the fixed-point has been found.
    X
    (SUB-F-FIXEDPOINT Y (F Y)) ))       ;keep searching.
    ==> SUB-F-FIXEDPOINT
```

A function $F\langle x\rangle$ with a fixed-point at the square root of 2 is constructed as follows. At the square root of 2, we want $f\langle x\rangle$ to satisfy two conditions: it must have a local extremum $f'\langle x\rangle = c \cdot (x^2 - 2)$, and it must have a fixed-point $f\langle x\rangle = x$. Upon integration, the first equation leads to $f\langle x\rangle = c \cdot \left(\frac{1}{3}x^3 - 2x\right)$, where c is defined by the second $f\langle\sqrt{2}\rangle = c \cdot \left(\frac{1}{3}\sqrt{2^3} - 2\sqrt{2}\right)$. The solution is $c = -3/4$, and $f\langle x\rangle = 1.50x - 0.25x^3$.

```
*   (DEFUN F (X) (+ (* 1.5 X) (* -0.25 X X X)))
    ==> F
```

then

```
*   (F-FIXEDPOINT 1)
    1
    1.25
    1.38672
    1.41342
    1.41421
    ==> 1.41421
*   (SETQ R2 (F-FIXEDPOINT 3.0))
    3.0
    -2.25
    -0.52734
```

```
      -0.75435
      -1.02421
      -1.26772
      -1.39224
      -1.41370
      -1.41421
      ==> -1.41421
*     (* R2 R2)
      ==> 2.0   .
```

Example 28:   A general SORT may be defined as the fixed-point of the function F which, given a list of numbers, allows small numbers to "bubble up" past larger numbers. Notice that although we change the definition of the function F whose fixed-point we seek (from a polynomial to a list function), F-FIXEDPOINT and its subfunctions remain the same.

```
*     (DEFUN SORT (NUMBERS)
        (F-FIXEDPOINT NUMBERS) )
                                  ;sorted list is fixed-point
      ==> SORT
*     (DEFUN F (NUMS)
                ;given a list, F moves small numbers left
        (COND
          ((OR (ATOM NUMS) (ATOM (CDR NUMS)))   NUMS)
              ;lists of length 0 or 1 are already sorted
          ((< (CAR NUMS) (CADR NUMS))
                          ;first is smaller than second
          (CONS (CAR NUMS) (F (CDR NUMS))) );so, no switch
          (T    ;first is larger than second, so they switch
          (CONS (CADR NUMS) (F (CONS (CAR NUMS)
                                    (CDDR NUMS))))) )) ))
      ==> F   .
```

Now, F and SORT can be tested:

```
*     (F '(1 9 2 8 3 7 4 6 5))
      ==> (1 2 8 3 7 4 6 5 9)   .
```

Notice that F caused small numbers to bubble past big numbers a bit. The repeated application of F should sort the list.

```
*     (SORT '(1 9 2 8 3 7 4 6 5))
      (1 9 2 8 3 7 4 6 5)
      (1 2 8 3 7 4 6 5 9)
      (1 2 3 7 4 6 5 8 9)
      (1 2 3 4 5 6 7 8 9)
      ==> (1 2 3 4 5 6 7 8 9)   .
```

It does! Notice that since the PRINT in SUB-F-FIXEDPOINT is still in effect, we get to observe the sorting step by step.

Bubble sort is basically an inefficient algorithm. However, the efficiency of this program can be improved by using a Boolean variable (initialized to T, and reset to NIL by F when there is a switch) in place of the (EQUAL...) in SUB-F-FIXEDPOINT.

Exercises

1. Show that root finding (as in Newton's method) is equivalent to finding fixed-points.

2. Improve SORT by replacing (EQUAL...) in SUB-F-FIXEDPOINT by the Boolean variable described in the example.

3. Let F be defined to compute the square root of 2 (as in the previous example).
   ```
   *   (F-FIXEDPOINT 0.0)
       ==> ???
   *   (F-FIXEDPOINT 10.0)
       ==> ???
   ```
   Explain these results.

4. Explain the dynamics of the computation suggested by the illustration titled "fixed-point search."

2.8   Input and Output

In their simplest forms, input and output between a program and the user are expressed in terms of READ, PRINT, PRIN1, PRINC, and TERPRI. If the user input is replaced by a file, then OPEN, CLOSE, and the explicit manipulation of streams are required. We begin by considering communication with the user.

There are two different representations of LISP objects. The printed representation is an s-expression, while the internal representation is a linked data structure. The input/output functions must translate between these representations. READ is generally a 0-ary function:

```
(READ).
```

READ removes an s-expression from the input stream and returns an equivalent internal representation to the listener as its value. PRINT, PRIN1, and PRINC are generally unary functions:

(PRINT arg), (PRIN1 arg), (PRINC arg).

These functions convert an internal representation of their argument's value into an s-expression which is entered into the output stream. PRINT terminates the print line either before printing the text string or after (depending on the implementation). PRIN1 does not terminate the print line. PRINC is used to print strings without the string delimiters, and—like PRIN1—it does not terminate the line. The function TERPRI is generally 0-ary.

(TERPRI)

It is used to terminate print lines.

A *stream* is an object that either produces or consumes LISP data. Streams are usually connected to LISP terms at one end and either a file or the terminal at the other end. A stream can be created by applying OPEN to a string defining the path to a file:

(OPEN path) or (OPEN path :DIRECTION dir)

and an optional direction, dir, equal to either :INPUT or :OUTPUT. A name for the stream is returned. If :DIRECTION is followed by :INPUT, then the stream's name can be used as an optional argument for READ. In

(READ stream),

the value returned by READ is taken from the file attached to the stream. If :DIRECTION is followed by :OUTPUT, then the stream's name can be used as an argument in PRINT.

(PRINT argument stream)

PRINTs the value of its argument into the file or terminal at the end of the stream. Lines in the file at the end of the stream are terminated by

(TERPRI stream).

A stream is undone and its file is saved by

(CLOSE stream).

In using

(READ), (PRINT term), (PRIN1 term), ... , and (TERPRI),

the standard input and output stream are implicitly specified.

Example 29: The stream name returned by OPEN is not a memorable expression, so we use SETQ to bind it to STREAM-OUT (or some other symbol).

```
*   (SETQ STREAM-OUT
      (OPEN "DATA\\TEMP" :DIRECTION :OUTPUT))
    ==> #<CLOSURE 3612:CC01>
```

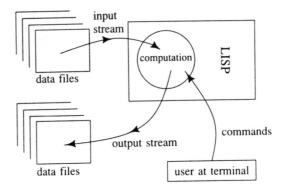

Figure 2.8. Three streams involved in processing data files.

This stream empties into the file TEMP in the DATA directory. An optional second argument to PRINT is the name of a stream into which the PRINTed value is to be entered.

```
*   (PRINT "TEST" STREAM-OUT)
    ==> "TEST"
```

Once values have been entered into a stream, *those values are not saved until the stream has been closed.*

```
*   (CLOSE STREAM-OUT)
    ==> NIL
```

Now, we have entered "TEST" into "DATA\TEMP". So, it should be READable from a stream originating at the file:

```
*   (SETQ STREAM-IN (OPEN "DATA\\TEMP"))
    ==> #<CLOSURE 7546:9870>
*   (READ STREAM-IN)
    ==> "TEST"   .
```

Using streams, the user may control a toolbox of functions which read and write into a variety of files.

Exercises

1. Define an operation FILE-COPY which, given the name of two files, will open the files appropriately, copy the contents of the first file into the second, and then close both.

2. Perform PRINT experiments with IF and AND to determine the order and conditions of subterm evaluation. What does the result of submitting ((PRINT 1) (PRINT 2)) tell you about the way in which functions

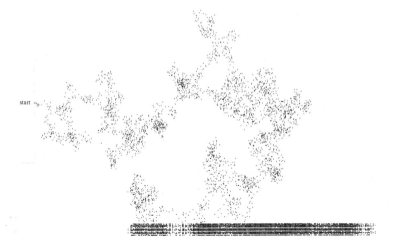

start →

Figure 2.9. Graphics experiment shows random pattern converging to restangle in stripes.

are handled in your LISP? This experiment is especially interesting in early LISPs and SCHEME.

3. Optional problem in graphics: find and experiment with the functions for drawing points, line segments, circles, and ellipses. For example, something of the form

```
(SEND window-name :DRAW-LINE x1 y1 x2 y2)
```

or

```
(%DRAW-LINE x1 y1 x2 y2)
```

draws a line from $(x1, y1)$ to $(x2, y2)$.

4. Optional experiment for those who were successful with problem 3. Sometimes pictures can tell a story that thousands of lines of numbers and symbols could never get across. The following picture, in which a smoky pattern converges into a rectangle with stripes, was created by plotting the points (x_i, y_i), defined from an initial point (x_0, y_0), at midscreen by

$$x_{n+1} = x_n + 5.15 * \sin(x^2) \text{ and } y_{n+1} = y_n + 5.15 * \cos(y^2).$$

Without the picture, a good mathematician might have suspected the convergence to the rectangle (because x and y are not interdependent), but not the existence of the stripes.

2.9   The procedural and functional styles of computation

A programming style in which the order of statement execution or term evaluation has an importance—possibly due to changes in the computational environment—is a *procedural* style. Languages in which assignments play a major role have styles which (due to the effects of their assignments) are procedural. On the other hand, a style based on the application of functions and the evaluation of terms having no effect (on the remote environment) is said to be *functional*. The procedural style of programming is generally associated with languages like FORTRAN, PASCAL, BASIC. The functional style is associated with LISP and SCHEME. However, LISP does have assignments and sequencing, and as a result, it supports a procedural style. This is especially evident in the function PROGN and the functions in which it is implicitly present.

Given arguments $form_1,\dots,form_k$,

(PROGN $form_1 \dots form_k$)

is a form which causes the k subforms to be evaluated in order from left to right. The value returned by this PROGN form is the value of $form_k$. Since no values are saved for the forms before $form_k$, the first $k-1$ forms are evaluated for their effect—say input and output. Effectively, (PROGN $form_1 \dots form_k$) is equivalent to

(LIST $form_1 \dots form_k$).

Contemporary LISPs have built an implicit PROGN into COND and LAMBDA functions. The classical COND syntax is generalized to allow

```
(COND
  (test-term₁ term¹₁... term^j₁ value-term₁)
  (test-term₂ term¹₂... term^k₂ value-term₂)...),
```

which is semantically equivalent to

```
(COND
  (test-term₁ (PROGN term¹₁...term^j₁ value-term₁))
  (test-term₂ (PROGN term¹₂...term^k₂ value-term₂))...).
```

Thus, the usual pair (test-term value-term) is replaced by a list of terms

(test-term effect-term₁ ... effect-term_k value-term)

equivalent to

```
(test-term (PROGN effect-term₁ ... effect-term_k
  value-term )).
```

PROGN is also implicit in the construction of contemporary lambda functions. The function

```
(LAMBDA variable-list term₁ ... termₖ value-term)
```

is semantically equivalent to

```
(LAMBDA variable-list
  (PROGN term₁ ... termₖ value-term) ).
```

Clearly, $term_1, \ldots, term_k$ are present for their effect only.

LET and LET* are like PROGN with a variable binding mechanism at the beginning. These two special forms have the same syntax:

```
(LET
    ((variable₁ value-form₁) ... (variableⱼ value-formⱼ))
    effect-form₁ ... effect-form-k final-value-form);

(LET*
    ((variable₁ value-form₁) ... (variableⱼ value-formⱼ))
  effect-form-1 ... effect-form-k final-value-form).
```

The variable binding is in the list of variable-form pairs following LET and LET*. LET performs the bindings concurrently—this is to say that each variable's value-form is evaluated in the original environment. The bindings of LET* are serial in that the environment used in evaluating $value\text{-}form_{i+1}$ is an extension of that used in evaluating $value\text{-}form_i$.

Example 30: The difference between concurrent and serial binding is shown in the following.

```
*   (SETQ U 0)
    ==> 0
*   (LET   ((U (READ)) (V U)) (LIST U V)) 1
    ==> (1 0)
*   U
    ==> 0
*   (LET* ((U (READ)) (V U)) (LIST U V)) 1
    ==> (1 1)
```

In both cases, the new binding of U is to 1. In the serial LET* binding, V is bound to the new value of U; but in the concurrent LET binding, V is bound to 0—U's original value.

Example 31: The example of MAX1 and MAX2 in 2.5 can be improved by using LET to eliminate the extra function CO-MAX2.

```
*   (DEFUN MAX3 (NUMBERS)
     (IF
      (OR (ATOM NUMBERS) (ATOM (CDR NUMBERS)))
      NUMBERS
      (LET
       ((FIRST (CAR NUMBERS)) (SECOND (CADR NUMBERS)))
       (IF
        (< FIRST SECOND)
        (MAX3 (CDR NUMBERS))
        (MAX3 (CONS FIRST (CDDR NUMBERS)))
    )))))
    ==> MAX3
*   (MAX3 '(9 2 8 3 7 4 -20 -3 67 9 10))
    ==> (67)
```

Exercises

1. In what sense are AND and OR procedural? How does this allow them to be more efficient?

2. Even without the implicit PROGN, COND is procedural. Explain.

3. Which of LET and LET* is procedural in binding its variables? Explain.

4. Does COND evaluate its forms in serial or in parallel environments?

2.10   Additional reading

For moderately sophisticated supplemental material on LISP programming consult McCarthy[1963], [1978], McCarthy and Talcott[1980], and Winston[1984]. Some entertaining recursive functions are described in Knuth[1976]. On the subject of fixed-point computing there is Manna and Vuillemin[1972]. Finally for a discussion of recursion vs. iteration see Saint-James[1984]. Harel[1987] is a pleasant little text with some novel material.

3
Deeper into Essential Structure

In this chapter, we will take a deeper and more careful look at the remaining issues that are fundamental to LISP. The topics include the representation of data; details on EQ, EQUAL, SETF, as well as more familiar functions; the abstract syntax of LISP; examples of self-processing; and approaches to variable binding and scope determination.

3.1 LISP's data

LISP's data objects consist primarily of atoms and other objects created by applying CONS (to simpler objects). Atoms and CONS-constructions are known as s-expressions. The word "atom" suggests an indivisible object, and this is the case when it comes to division by CAR and CDR. However, atoms may have internal structure which is accessible by functions other than CAR and CDR (e.g., LISP's strings, arrays, and structures). Finally, there are nonatomic data objects which *cannot* be constructed by applying CONS. Such creatures are circular data objects created by RPLACA, RPLACD, etc.

This section will deal only with s-expressions, their representation, and a variety of atoms.

ATOMS?

It has been suggested that the word "atom" not be used because it is misleading. "Not of type CONS" could be used in its place if it were not so awkward. It is true that many of the objects that we call atoms have a rich internal structure. However, as long as CAR and CDR play a central role in LISP computing, the program will have to have an appropriate way to filter out inappropriate arguments before applying CAR or CDR.

3.1.1 S-expressions

S-expressions are the fundamental data objects of LISP. They consist of (1) atoms and (2) CONS-cells. An *atom* is any object which is not the value of (CONS ...). This includes numbers, truth-values, strings, arrays, and structures. A *CONS-cell* is any object created by applying CONS to two simpler s-expressions. Thus, all *s-expressions* are either atoms or are built up from simpler s-expressions by CONS.

Example 1:   The value of a term of the form (CONS ...) is a CONS-cell:

```
*   (CONS 1 2)
    ==> (1 . 2)
*   (CONS (CONS 1 2) 3)
    ==> ((1 . 2) . 3)
*   (CONS 1 (CONS 2 '(3)))
    ==> (1 2 3)  .
```

The first two values are expressed in dot notation, the last in list notation. The dot notation equivalent to (1 2 3) is (1 . (2 . (3 . NIL))). One way to think of these objects is as binary trees.

TERMINOLOGY:

> A (finite) tree consists of a set of vertices and a set of directed edges ⟨v w⟩ leading from one vertex v, to another w. The edges must satisfy: (1) for every vertex v there is at most one vertex u having an edge ⟨u v⟩ leading from u to v, and (2) there is exactly one vertex v (known as the "root") for which no edge ⟨u v⟩ leads to v. A tree is binary if (3) for every vertex v there are at most two vertices w for which there is an edge ⟨v w⟩ from v to w.

> It can be shown that a list of consecutive edges in a tree will not return to its starting vertex—in other words, ⟨v1 v2⟩⟨v2 v3⟩...⟨vk v1⟩ is impossible.

> It follows that the number of edges in a tree is one less than the number of vertices.

A *list* is either (1) the atom NIL or (2) the result of CONSing an s-expression onto the beginning of an existing list. Conversely, the CDR of a nonatomic list is a list, and successive CDRing of a list will eventually lead to NIL. Since NIL and every other atom is an s-expression and the set of all s-expressions is closed under CONS, it follows that *all lists are s-expressions*. However, not all s-expressions are lists. Nonlists include atoms other than NIL and CONS-constructions for which successive CDRing terminates in an atom other than NIL.

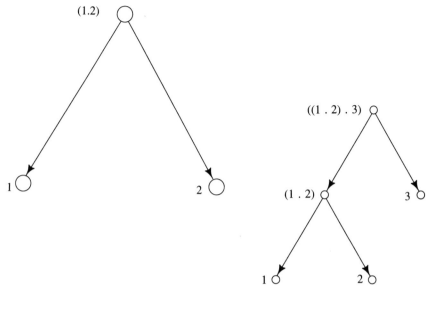

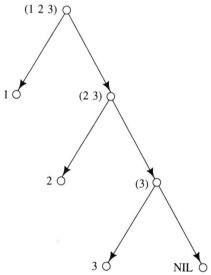

Figure 3.1. Trees.

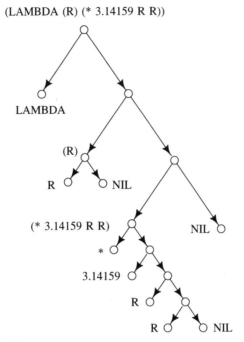

Figure 3.2. (LAMBDA (R) (* 3.14159 R R)) as a tree.

3.1.2 Representations of data

There are two ways of graphically depicting s-expressions. First, as we have just seen, they may be binary trees. In tree notation, atomic objects are terminal nodes and CONS-cells (dotted pairs) are nonterminal branching nodes. Second, there is cell notation. *Cell notation* uses boxes for memory locations and arrows for pointers to locations.

Example 2: We have seen that ordinary LISP data is represented by tree-like s-expressions. Here, we see that LISP functions and terms are represented in the same way. In particular, the unevaluated expressions (LAMBDA (R) (* 3.14159 R R)) and (LIST (CADR X) (CAR X)) are represented by the trees in figures 3.2 and 3.3.

Simple data objects can often be stored in a single memory location, or in a small and limited set of successive locations. Objects, such as s-expressions, whose sizes are highly variable may have to be distributed among memory cells in nonsuccessive locations. In such a distribution, part of an object may be stored in a cell whose address is not a successor of the cells storing preceding parts of the object. To locate the cell containing a subsequent part, its address is stored in the current cell. Such an address is known as a *pointer*. Since this type of

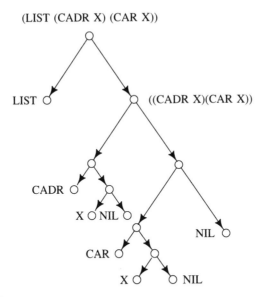

Figure 3.3. (`LIST` (`CADR X`) (`CAR X`)) as a tree.

memory allocation allows data structures to grow indefinitely (limited only by the physical characteristics of the machine), it is said to be *dynamic memory allocation.*

Example 3: The object (`LAMBDA` (`R`) (`* 3.14159 R R`)) isn't large, but we can use it to illustrate this type of distributed storage.

Memory register #1 contains the list as pointers to registers 2 and 3; register 2 contains `LAMBDA`; register 3 is the CDR of the list, it contains pointers to registers 4 and 8; and register 4 contains a pointer to the sublist (`R`).

`NIL` is in register 0000; every time `NIL` is used to end a list there is a pointer to 0000.

HISTORY:

In the IBM704, each memory cell had a capacity of 36 bits, while the addresses required only 15 bits. Thus, each cell could contain the addresses of two other cells and still have a few bits left over. These extra bits were used to identify the type of the register's contents (e.g., to distinguish atoms from `CONS`-constructions).

address	register	contents
0	NIL	
the list 1	2	3
2	LAMBDA	
3	4	100
4	5	0
5	R	
6		
7		
⋮	○ ○ ○	○ ○ ○
100	101	0
101	102	103
102	*	
103	104	105
104	3.14159	
105	106	107
106	R	
107	108	0
108	R	
109		

Figure 3.4. A possible register diagram for (LAMBDA (R) (* 3.14159 R R)).

The *cell notation* is a simplification of the register diagram of the previous example. Registers are replaced by pairs of boxes, and pointers and addresses are replaced by arrows. Cell notation for the preceding register diagram is shown in figure 3.5.

3.1.3 Atoms

In addition to constants like NIL, T, and numbers; LISP's atoms include characters, constants, strings, symbols, vectors, arrays, and structures (i.e., generalizations of PASCAL's records). Each of these objects has substantial internal structure, but they are considered atoms because their internal structure is not accessible by CAR or CDR. Special new functions are required for work with atoms. (Vectors, arrays, and structures are discussed in 5.4.)

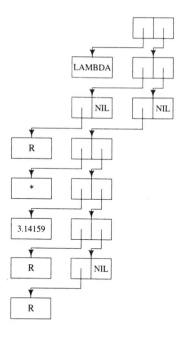

Figure 3.5. A cell diagram representing (LAMBDA (R) (* 3.14159 R R)) in memory.

Roughly speaking, *characters* are internal representations of the elementary symbols

a A b B ... z Z 1 ! 2 @ ... = +... backspace return ... etc.

associated with the keys at your terminal. The characters representing a, A, b, ... are the value of #\a, #\A, #\b, ... The invisible characters are denoted by #\ followed by their name

#\SPACE #\BACKSPACE #\RETURN #\NEWLINE etc.

If this confusing, then experiment with the predicate unary CHARACTERP. You will find that the value of #*character-name* is an internal representation of the given character. This representation can be verified by applying WRITE-CHAR to it.

Example 4: The following experiments explore the triangle of a character's internal representation, its "#\"-notation, and its print name. (This example is implementation dependent and is precisely correct for GCLISP.)

```
*   (SYMBOLP 'A)
    ==> T
*   (CHARACTERP 'A)
```

```
     ==> NIL
*    (SYMBOLP #\A)
     ==> NIL
*    (CHARACTERP #\A)
     ==> T
*    #\A
     ==> 65
*    #\NEWLINE
     ==> 10
*    (WRITE-CHAR 65)A
     ==> 65
*    (WRITE-CHAR 10)

     ==> 10.
```

Notice that WRITE-CHAR had the effect of writing each character before the value was returned. In particular, (WRITE-CHAR 65) caused an "A" to be printed, and (WRITE-CHAR 10) causes a new line to appear.

A *constant* is an atomic data object which is equal to its value. Constants include

```
     T   NIL   0 1 2 ... 3.14159 ... "this is a string" ... etc.
```

According to this definition a string is also a constant, because a string is an atom which evaluates to itself. For example,

```
*    "THIS IS A STRING"
     ==> "THIS IS A STRING"
*    (ATOM "THIS IS A STRING")
     ==> T .
```

Specifically, a *string* is a vector whose elements are characters. (It follows that vectors are atoms.) A string is represented by characters appearing between double quotes. The internal structure for strings is the same as that of vectors. It may be accessed by AREF (see 5.4) and modified by SETF used with AREF (see 3.2.4).

A *symbol* is an atom with a print name whose internal structure is represented in a property list. Symbols such as

```
     CAR   X   FACTORIAL   N   LIST1
```

are used as variables and function names. Others, such as NIL, may be constants. A symbol's *property list* is a list of keys (i.e., property names) and their assigned values. Property lists are of the form

$$(key_1 \; value_1 \; ... \; key_k \; value_k).$$

For each j, the host symbol is assigned $value_j$ as the value of type key_j.
Values are accessed by GET:

    (GET symbol key).

The whole property list is retrieved by

    (SYMBOL-PLIST symbol).

The value associated with a key is changed to $new-value$ by the macro $SETF$:

    (SETF   (GET symbol key) new-value).

A new key and its value can be added to a property list by

    (SETF   (GET symbol new-key) new-value).

Finally, a key and its value are removed by

    (REMPROP symbol key).

Property lists are a convenient way to assign several different types of values
to symbols.

Example 5:   The first shows the fourth character—i—of "string" being accessed by AREF, written by WRITE-CHAR, and changed by SETF.

```
*   (WRITE-CHAR (AREF "string" 3))i
                                ;notice i was written
    ==> 105
*   (SETF X "string")
    ==> "string"
*   (SETF (AREF X 3) #\o)
    ==> 111
*   X
    ==> "strong."
```

The remaining experiments deal with symbols and property lists.

```
*   (SYMBOLP NIL)
    ==> T
*   (SYMBOLP 0)
    ==> NIL
*   (SYMBOL-PLIST 'NUMBERS)
    ==> NIL
*   (SETF (GET 'NUMBERS 'PI) 3.14159)
    ==> 3.14159
```

(This strange behavior of SETF is explained in 3.2.4.)

```
*   (SYMBOL-PLIST 'NUMBERS)
    ==> (PI 3.14159)
*   (GET 'NUMBERS 'PI)
    ==>   3.14159
*   (REMPROP 'NUMBERS 'PI)
    ==> T
*   (SYMBOL-PLIST 'NUMBERS)
    ==> NIL
```

Programming finite irregular functions. There are two approaches to programming irregular functions. First, we have seen that association lists can be used to program functions—such as THULE-TEMP—which are not defined by a simple pattern. When the function's domain is a set of symbols, we have a second option—the use of property lists. The pairs *(symbol$_j$,* value$_j$) such that

$$F\langle symbol_j\rangle = value_j$$

can be recorded in either of two ways, either as properties of F—add the pair

... *symbol$_j$* value$_j$ ...

to F's property list or as properties of symbol$_j$—add

... F *value$_j$* ...

to the property list of *symbol$_j$*. (The second approach would be appropriate if there were several functions with the same small domain.) F$\langle\rangle$ is then defined as either

(LAMBDA (SYMBOL) (GET 'F SYMBOL))

in the first case, or

(LAMBDA (SYMBOL) (GET SYMBOL 'F))

in the second case.

TERMS AND FUNCTIONS:

Given a finite Boolean algebra B, every function $f : B^k \longrightarrow B$ can be defined by a term t⟨x1,...,xk⟩ in the language of the algebra. By "defined" we mean $f\langle x_1, ..., x_k\rangle = t\langle x_1, ..., x_k\rangle$.

However, this is the exception rather than the rule. Let A be the algebra of high school algebra, and f⟨x⟩ be a continuous, infinitely differentiable function satisfying f⟨x⟩=0 for all x≤ 0 and f⟨ x⟩=1 for all x≥1. Functions such as f cannot be represented by terms familiar to high school students.

TERMINOLOGY:

It is the functions f : S-EXPRESSIONS^k ⟶ S-EXPRESSIONS
which cannot be defined in terms of the primitive constants and
functions of LISP that we call *irregular functions*. Notice that a
strict interpretation of this definition requires that we not allow
association lists to be the values of globally bound variables. If we
allow association lists to be values of constants or globally bound
variables, then every finite function is definable in LISP.

3.1.4 Data types

A *data type* is a (generally infinite) set of data objects which share one or more computationally important features. The following Venn diagram shows how some of LISP's more important data types relate to each other.

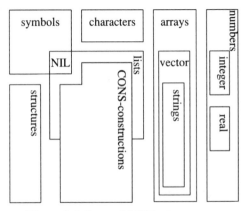

Figure 3.6. Some of LISP's data types.

Structures are complex user-defined data types whose members are constructed without the use of CONS.

Exercises

1. Are there CONS-cells which are not lists? Can a nonlist and a list be CONSed to produce a list? A nonlist? How about two nonlists? Give examples.

2. Period:sentence = ?:list .

3. Depict (LIST (CADR X) (CAR X)) in cell notation.

4. Which of the following are symbols?

```
CAR   X   #\X   2   LIST2   FACTORIAL   NIL   T
"STRING"   STRING
```

Use SYMBOLP as a test.

5. (Optional.) *A comparison of the complexity of two representations or F⟨⟩.*
For F⟨⟩ as defined in 3.1.3, each evaluation of F⟨ symbol⟩ is an assignment
and therefore involves a substantial cost C to reach main memory. However, once we are out there, main memory (being random access) adds an
access cost of only $\log_2(M)$—where M is the size of main memory. The
association-list approach to programming F is different. Association-lists
may be assumed to be local, so the cost to reach them is about 0. However, they have had an access cost (to reach the desired key) on the order
of 1/2D—where D is the number of objects in the domain of F. Under
what circumstances is it more efficient to use property-lists rather than
association-lists? Assume that $M \geq D$.

6. (Optional.) *Strange behavior for* SETF: perform the following experiment
on the string "string".

```
*   (SETQ X "string")
*   (SETF (AREF X 3) #\o)
*   X
```

Explain SETF's strange behavior (hint: look in 3.2.4).

7. How many functions are there from subsets of fingers to subsets of fingers?
Assume that ten fingers are available.

3.2   Another look at familiar functions

In this section, we give alternate semantics for CAR, CDR, CONS; introduce EQ,
the primitive function behind EQUAL; describe new variable types for LAMBDA
functions; and define SETF.

3.2.1   CAR, CDR, CONS: an alternate semantics

HISTORY:

The two 15-bit parts of the IBM704's word were known as the
"address" and the "decrement" CAR and CDR were derived from
IBM acronyms XCAR and XCDR for Contents-of-Address part and
Contents-of-Decrement part of the Register.

CAR, CDR, and CONS may be viewed in two very different—but function-
ally equivalent—ways. First, think of their arguments as lists.

```
*    (CAR ' (A B C D E F G))
     ==> A
*    (CDR ' (A B C D E F G))
     ==> (B C D E F G)
*    (CONS 'A ' (B C D E F G))
     ==> (A B C D E F G)
```

From this point of view, better names for these functions would be FIRST, REST, and ADD-TO. Now, think of the arguments as dotted pairs or as binary trees.

```
*    (CAR ' ((W . X) . (Y . Z)))
     ==> (W . X)
*    (CDR ' ((W . X) . (Y . Z)))
     ==> (Y . Z)
*    (CONS ' (W . X) ' (Y . Z))
     ==> ((W . X) . (Y . Z))
```

From this point of view, the functions could have been LEFT-SUBTREE, RIGHT-SUBTREE, and JOIN-TREES. In comparing these views, we can say that the first is more useful, but the second is more accurate.

Each application of the CONS function consumes a cell of free memory. (Recall from the preceding discussion that this new cell is required to hold the pointers to CONS' two arguments.) However, CAR and CDR have no such cost. The value which they return corresponds to a pointer which already exists. The use of CONS requires a constantly refreshed supply of free memory cells. Linked groups of cells representing CONStructions which are no longer accessible to the computation in progress are periodically identified and collected into a free memory list. This is done automatically by a process known as *garbage collection.*

3.2.2   EQ and EQUAL

The EQUAL that we have been using to compare CONS-type objects is recursively defined from more primitive functions. One of these primitives is EQ. The value returned by

(EQ $object_1$ $object_2$)

is T if the two objects are identical (i.e., have the same address). Since every call to CONS uses a new memory cell to return its value, the values returned by two distinct evaluations of (CONS 1 2) are not exactly the same object. The two values may be equivalent in meaning, but they are represented using different cells in memory. Thus, EQuality is not preserved by CONS. On the other hand, two identical symbols—say the values of ' AMUNDSEN and ' AMUNDSEN—will

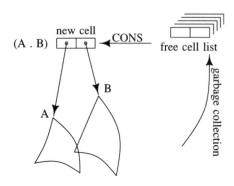

Figure 3.7. A new tree by CONSing.

be EQual. This is because identical symbols are not allowed to exist in more than one location. However, due to variations in the implementation of numbers, two identical numbers may or may not be EQual. All in all, two objects are EQual if and only if they occupy the same locations in memory.

Example 6:   The following experiments illustrate the meaning of EQ and contrast it with EQUAL.

```
*    (EQ 'AMUNDSEN 'AMUNDSEN)
     ==> T
*    (EQ NIL NIL)
     ==> T
*    (EQ 3.14159 3.14159)
     ==> NIL
          or T                    (depending on implementation)
*    (EQUAL 3.14159 3.14159)
     ==> T
*    (EQ 3 3.0)
     ==> NIL
*    (EQUAL 3 3.0)
     ==> NIL
```

For each of the following pairs of arguments, EQUAL will return T.

```
*    (EQ (CONS 1 2) (CONS 1 2))
     ==> NIL
*    (EQ '(1 . 2) '(1 . 2))
     ==> NIL
```

```
*    (SETQ A (CONS 1 2))
     ==> (1 . 2)
*    (SETQ B (CONS 1 2))
     ==> (1 . 2)
*    (EQ A B)
     ==> NIL
```

However, by nesting SETQs, a single construction of (1 . 2) can be given
two names. Since only one object was constructed, the values of A and B are
now EQual.

```
*    (SETQ B (SETQ A (CONS 1 2)))
     ==> (1 . 2)
*    (EQ A B)
     ==> T
```

EQUAL (or at least a version of it) may be defined in terms of EQ and an
equality for numbers (which we represent as =) in approximately the following
way.

```
*    (DEFUN EQUAL (X Y)
     (COND
      ((AND (NUMBERP X) (NUMBERP Y))
       (= X Y) )      ;if X and Y are numbers use = X or Y
      ((OR (ATOM X) (ATOM Y))   (EQ X Y))      ;is an atom
      (T ;otherwise, neither X nor Y are atoms,  so they
       (AND                ;are EQUAL if and only if left
        (EQUAL (CAR X) (CAR Y)) ;subtrees are EQUAL and
        (EQUAL (CDR X) (CDR Y)) ;the right subtrees are
     ))))                                      ;EQUAL
```

(The = above may not be exactly the same as the = in Common LISP.)

TERMINOLOGY:

> The recursion shown in Fig 3.8 is known as *structural recursion*
> because it follows the structure of CONS-objects.

3.2.3 Options for LAMBDA functions

LAMBDA functions have options other than the body's implicit PROGN. An un-
specified number of additional arguments can be handled by an &REST variable.
Functions of the form

$$(\text{LAMBDA}\quad (V_1 \ldots V_k \text{ \&REST}\quad W)\ body)$$

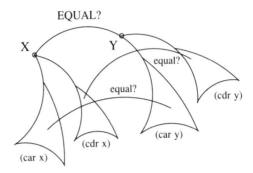

Figure 3.8. Structural recursion in EQUAL.

can be applied to k-or-more arguments. The values of the first k arguments are associated with $V_1,...V_k$, while the values of the remaining arguments make up a list which becomes the value of W. Similar variables are indicated by &OPTIONAL. When a function such as

```
(LAMBDA
    (V₁ ... Vⱼ
     &OPTIONAL (W₁ value-form₁) ... (Wₖ value-formₖ) )
    body )
```

is called, it may have as few as j arguments. As many as k additional arguments are bound to the &OPTIONAL variables. &OPTIONAL variables which do not receive values from external arguments will assume the values of their associated value-forms.

Example 7: The following experiments demonstrate &REST and &OPTION-AL. In FACT, the &OPTIONAL construction was used to keep a variable invisible from the user.

```
*   (DEFUN AND (&REST VAL-LIST)
      (NOT (MEMBER NIL VAL-LIST)) )
    ==> AND
*   (AND T 655 T "STRING" T)
    ==> T
*   (DEFUN FACT (IN &OPTIONAL (OUT 1))
      (IF
       (< IN 2)
       OUT
```

```
        (FACT  (1- IN)  (* IN OUT)  )))
    ==> FACT
*   (FACT 10)
    ==> 3628800
```

In GCLISP, this last evaluation may end with a numerical overflow error. The problem may be corrected by computing in floating point (replace (1- IN) by (- IN 1.0)) and then converting the result to integer.

Example 8: This follow-up on the MAX examples of 2.5 illustrates that &OPTIONAL can be used (1) without any preceding variables, (2) to keep track of variables in a way that is invisible to the user, (3) to make more than one variable optional, (4) so that optional variables are bound serially, and (5) so that the default value-form may be a composite term involving a logical test.

```
*   (DEFUN MAX4
     (&OPTIONAL
      (NUMBERS NIL)
      (BIGGEST (IF (ATOM NUMBERS) NIL (CAR NUMBERS))) )
     (COND
      ((ATOM NUMBERS)  BIGGEST)
      ((< (CAR NUMBERS) BIGGEST)
       (MAX4 (CDR NUMBERS) BIGGEST) )
      (T  (MAX4 (CDR NUMBERS) (CAR NUMBERS))) ))
    ==> MAX4
*   (MAX4 '(1 0 2 9 3 8 4 7 5 6))
    ==> 9
*   (MAX4)
    ==> NIL
```

Notice that we have not CONS this program.

3.2.4 SETF

SETF is a cousin to SETQ and SET in that it assigns and modifies values. Its syntax

```
(SETF place value)
```

is a generalization of (SETQ variable value) in which place may be either a symbol or a form. Given a symbol, SETF is like SETQ. Given a form, place becomes the location of the value of that form. In this case, SETF replaces the value originally stored in that location by the value of its second argument. Thus, SETF processes its first argument to determine the location of its value, then it changes that value.

Example 9: The first use of SETF is the same as SETQ. The second and third uses change the value of places referenced by CADR and AREF.

```
*   (SETF L (LIST 1 22 3 4))
    ==> (1 22 3 4)
*   L
    ==> (1 22 3 4)
*   (SETF (CADR L) 2)
    ==> 2
*   L
    ==> (1 2 3 4)
*   (SETF STRING "STRONG")
    ==> "STRONG"
*   (SETF (AREF STRING 3) #/I)
    ==> 73
*   STRING
    ==> "STRING".
```

Additional applications of SETF are given in Chapter 5, and also in Steele[1984].

Exercises

1. Perform a computation which calls CONS enough to trigger garbage collection (as indicated by your system). How big is the biggest list that you can create in your system?

2. If the internal view of LISP is one of pointer manipulation, then how do we get such a user-meaningful external view of LISP?

3. Do a complexity analysis on MAX4 similar to that given for MAX1 and MAX2 (Section 2.5).

4. Use DO to write an iterative version of MAX.

3.3   LISP syntax in detail

Languages are described by syntax and semantics. The *syntax* is a description of the symbol patterns (i.e., in algebraic talk, the "terms" that make up the expressions of the language). The *semantics* is a description of the meaning of these expressions. Recall the discussion of syntax and semantics given when QUOTE was introduced. Syntax is superficial, while semantics is essential. The syntax of a language is *algebraic* if it consists of terms built up from constants, variables, and functions by the process of function application. LISP is algebraic.

3.3.1 Terms

Simply defined, LISP's *terms* consist of

(1) atomic terms:

    (a) constants—atomic objects which evaluate to themselves, and

    (b) variables—symbols which may have values bound to them; and

(2) composite terms: lists of the form *(function ...)*

    (a) given a k-ary LISP function f and LISP terms $t_1, \ldots, t_k$,

        (f t_1 ... t_k)

    is a LISP term, and

    (b) special forms in which the remaining expressions in the list are not necessarily evaluated, such as

        (QUOTE *s-expression*),
        (SETQ *symbol term*),
        (COND (*test-term*$_1$ *value-term*$_1$)...),

    etc.

3.3.2 Variables and forms

TERMINOLOGY:

Steele[1984, p.54]: "The standard unit of interaction with a Common LISP implementation is the form, which is simply a data object meant to be evaluated as a program to produce one or more values."

Reprinted with permission from *Common LISP: The Language*, by Guy Steele, Jr. @ Digital Press/Digital Equipment Corporation.

In algebra, the syntactically correct expressions of a language are terms. The word "form" was originally used, in an algebraic context by Alonzo Church to mean a term with no unbound variables. This is a slightly stronger notion of "form" than that of Steele. The unbound variable V is a term, but not a form in either sense. The expression (IF T NIL V) is a form in the sense of Steele, but not of Church. Steele's definition is better for us.

However, as it stands, Steele's definition is not precise. Given a LISP expression, it is possible to decide (by algorithm) whether or not an attempted evaluation by a LISP implementation will generate a computation or if it contains syntax error. It is not possible to decide if a value will ultimately be returned (the halting problem, see 4.4) or if there will be a semantic error (exercise 3, 4.4). So, Steele couldn't have intended forms to be terms which ultimately returned values or which do not have semantic errors. Steele must intend forms to be syntactically valid LISP terms which generate computation(s).

First definition: a *form* is a term which could reasonably be expected to generate a computation and which could return a value. This is Steele's definition, and it is still not precise in a way which would allow us to program a form-testing predicate.

Variables occurring in terms are said to be either bound (as in "bound to a value") or free. Assume that v is a variable which occurs in t and is not assigned a value by a function such as SETQ. *V is free in t* if:

1. t is the variable v,

2. t is of the form $(fun\ term_1 ... term_k)$ and, for some j, fun evaluates the term in the jth position and v is free in $term_j$, or

3. v is free in the body of a LAMBDA function but is not included in the function's variable list.

If v occurs in t but it is not free in t, then v *is bound in* t.

Second definition: a term in which all variables are bound is a *form*. This is Church's definition, and it is precise enough to program into a form-testing predicate. It's also a bit more complicated. For the next few pages, Church's definition will be used, then for the remainder of the book, we will relax into the informal *form* of Steele. Both definitions are equivalent in most cases.

The distinction between terms with free variables and forms is motivated by the idea that a term has a meaning or value only when the variables occurring in it are bound. With one exception, the occurrence of variables is just as common English usage of "occur" would suggest. The exception is that variables do not occur in expressions which are not evaluated by their function—for example (QUOTE...), (SETQ...), (SETF...), etc. The motivating idea is almost true.

Example 10: V occurs as a free variable in the terms

```
V,    (CONS NIL (ATOM V)),
((LAMBDA (U) (CONS U V)) 2),
(SET U V), and (IF T 2 V).
```

V does not occur free in

```
((LAMBDA (V) (CONS V V)) 2),
'(CAR V), and (SETQ V 2).
```

In ((LAMBDA (V)...), V occurs and is bound to 2. In the last two terms, V doesn't even occur—at least not as a variable. Thus, the last three (four) terms are forms in the sense of Church (Steele).

An attempt to evaluate a term containing an occurrence of an unbound variable will generally cause an UNBOUND VARIABLE error. On the other hand, forms (no matter what definition we use) can usually be evaluated.

CHURCH VS. STEELE:

Steele's definition is too vague to program. Church's definition is complicated. Both fail as syntactic characterizations of "evaluatable."

3.3.3 Syntax puzzles

When the LISP listener is given an expression, it treats it as a form. In doing this, atomic expressions are assumed to be either constants or bound variables. Lists are assumed to begin with a function and, depending on what the function is, the subsequent elements of the list may be forms, pairs of forms, or (in the case of special forms) s-expressions. The puzzles presented here develop this abstract way of thinking about forms. (We will limit the possibilities to the most basic functions and forms discussed so far.)

Example 11: Suppose that a, b, and c are such that (a b c) is a term. Then what can we deduce about the possible values of a, b, and c? Obviously, a must be a binary function. If a is SETQ, then b is a variable. Otherwise, both b and c are either terms or pairs of terms (in case a is COND).

Example 12: Suppose that we are given the term (e e). What can be said about e? Since it is the first element in the list, e must be a function. However, this makes the second element a function rather than a term or pair of terms. Under these conditions, it is likely that e is QUOTE.

Example 13: Suppose that ((d e f)) is a term. The first element, (d e f), of the list must be a function. So, (d e f) is a LAMBDA function, d=LAMBDA, e is a variable list, and f is a term. Since there is nothing following the function, the function is 0-ary. This makes e=( ) and, since all of the free variables of f can be expected to be in e=( ), f must be a form.

Example 14: (g (h h) (i j)) is a term. G is a function, but it takes two arguments so QUOTE can be excluded. The first argument is not atomic, so SETQ can be excluded. This probably means that (h h) and (i j) are either terms or pairs of

terms. If they are terms, then h=QUOTE, if they are pairs of terms then g=COND
(and i=T is likely).

Analyses such as these have too little information available to them to exhaust
all of the possibilities, but they do cover the main cases.

Exercises

1. Which of the following expressions are terms?

```
NIL,  ( ),  (1+ N),  (COND (NIL NIL) (T T)),
U,  CONS,
(LAMBDA (U) (CONS NIL (ATOM U))),
LAMBDA,  (CONS),
'(1 2), and (CAR (1 2))
```

2. Identify the occurrence of free variables in each of the following terms:

```
NIL,   ( > U V),   (EQUAL U 'V),    (SETQ N 0),
(CAR (CONS U U)),   (COND (NIL U) (T T)).
```

Which of these terms are forms? (Recall that T is a constant.)

3. Let O be (LAMBDA () (O)). Is the term (O) a form in the sense of
Church? Does it have a value? Is (IF T NIL V) a form in the sense
of Church? Does it have a value? Conclude that Church's definition fails
to capture the notion of evaluatable.

4. How does Steele's definition of form fail to capture the notion of evaluatable?

3.4   Self-processing

LISP's ability to process itself is a direct consequence of (1) the representation
of the language in its data structures, (2) the simple algebraic syntax, and (3)
the presence of functions such as QUOTE, DEFUN, FUNCTION, EVAL, and
APPLY.

DEFUN's arguments are unevaluated linguistic objects:

(DEFUN *symbol   variable-list   body*).

It is from the linguistic expressions that the *symbol*'s assigned functional
interpretation—(LAMBDA *variable-list   body*)—is constructed. The
functional interpretation of a given symbol (which names a function) is returned
by

Figure 3.9. Steve Russell, 1960. (Photograph courtesy of the MIT Museum.)

(FUNCTION *function-name*).

In modern LISPs, EVAL takes only one argument,

(EVAL *form*),

whose value is evaluated. In EVAL, the argument must evaluate to a second form whose value is returned by EVAL. APPLY's arguments must evaluate to a function and a list of arguments:

(APPLY *function argument-list*).

The value returned is the result of applying the given function to the argument list. Of these functions, only DEFUN has an effect on the computational environment. (In early LISPs, EVAL and APPLY both had an extra variable for the computational environment.)

HISTORY:

"... Another way to show that LISP is neater than Turing machines was to write a universal LISP function and show that it is briefer and more comprehensible than the description of the universal Turing machine. This was the LISP function eval(e,a), which computes the value of a LISP expression e [in the environment a]. ... Writing eval required inventing a notation representing LISP functions as LISP data, and such a notation was devised for the purposes of the paper [McCarthy[1960]] with no thought that it would be used ... in practice.

> S[teve].R. Russell noticed that eval could serve as an interpreter for
> LISP, promptly hand coded it, and we now had a programming
> language with an interpreter. ... The unexpected appearance of an
> interpreter tended to freeze the form of the language... .

> McCarthy[1981]

Example 15:   Some experiments with EVAL, and APPLY.

```
*    (SETQ INUIT-SCIENTIST 'ETHNOGRAPHER)
     ==> ETHNOGRAPHER
*    (SETQ KNUD-RASMUSSEN 'INUIT-SCIENTIST)
     ==> INUIT-SCIENTIST
*    KNUD-RASMUSSEN
     ==> INUIT-SCIENTIST
*    INUIT-SCIENTIST
     ==> ETHNOGRAPHER
*    (EVAL KNUD-RASMUSSEN)
     ==> ETHNOGRAPHER
*    (EVAL (LIST 'CDR (LIST 'QUOTE '(1 2 3))))
     ==> (2 3).
```

The subform (LIST 'CDR (LIST 'QUOTE '(1 2 3)) has the value (CDR
(QUOTE (1 2 3))) which is evaluated to get (2 3).

```
*    (APPLY 'CONS (LIST 1 '(2 3 4)))
     ==> (1 2 3 4)
```

In the next examples, APPLY's functional arguments are presented as data. We
begin by using SETQ rather than DEFUN to make a data-like assignment of a
program to a function name.

```
*    (SETQ ARCTIC?
       '(LAMBDA (LATITUDE) (< 66.5 LATITUDE)) )
     ==> (LAMBDA (LATITUDE) (< 66.5 LATITUDE))
*    (APPLY ARCTIC? (LIST 70))
     ==> T
*    ((LAMBDA (FUN LAT) (APPLY FUN (LIST LAT)))
       ARCTIC? 70)
     ==> T
*    (ARCTIC? 4)
     ERROR UNDEFINED FUNCTION: ARCTIC?
*    ((LAMBDA (FUN LAT) (FUN LAT)) ARCTIC? 70)
     ERROR UNDEFINED FUNCTION: FUN
```

These examples show that the data-like bindings (either global or local) for FUN
and ARCTIC are invisible when the usual evaluator looks for a function, but
not invisible to APPLY. This disappointing little wrinkle is not present in early

LISPs, SCHEME, or the mathematical foundations for LISP. All three of these would use the data-like bindings to evaluate the last two terms appropriately.

EVAL PLAY:

> "The name of the song is called 'Haddock's Eyes'" "Oh, that's the name of the song is it?" Alice said, trying to feel interested. "No, you don't understand," the Knight said, looking a little vexed. "That's what the name is called. The name is really 'The Aged, Aged Man.'" "Then I ought to have said 'That's what the song is called'?" Alice corrected herself.
>
> "No, you ought'n; that's quite another thing! The song is called 'Ways and Means': but that's only what its called, you know!"
>
> ...
>
> From Lewis Carroll's Through the Looking Glass.

Example 16:   The following experiments with FUNCTION and APPLY illustrate functional interpretation.

```
*   (SETQ CAR-INTERPRETATION (FUNCTION CAR))
    ==> #<COMPILED FUNCTION 07B7:DF9F>
*   (DEFUN NEW-CAR (X)
    (APPLY CAR-INTERPRETATION (LIST X)) )
    ==> NEW-CAR
*   (FUNCTION NEW-CAR)
    ==> (LAMBDA (X)(APPLY CAR-INTERPRETATION (LIST X)))
*   (NEW-CAR '(1 2 3))
    ==> 1
```

MAPCAR is a function which applies a given function to every element of a list and returns the list of values. MAPCAR is built into all LISPs, but using APPLY it can be defined.

```
*   (DEFUN MAPCAR (FUN ARGS)
    (IF
     (NULL ARGS)
     NIL
     (CONS
      (APPLY FUN (LIST (CAR ARGS)))
      (MAPCAR FUN (CDR ARGS))  )))
    ==> MAPCAR
*   (DEFUN SCALAR-PRODUCT (S V)
    (MAPCAR '(LAMBDA (X) (* S X)) V)  )
    ==> SCALAR-PRODUCT
*   (SCALAR-PRODUCT 3 '(1 2 3))
    ==> (3 6 9)
```

Exercises

1. Write a procedure called EVLIS which evaluates each member in a list (e_1 e_2...e_k) of forms and returns the list (EVAL$\langle e_1 \rangle$ EVAL$\langle e_2 \rangle$...EVAL$\langle e_k \rangle$) of values.

2. Identifying LISP language expressions in LISP: Use predicates NULL, EQ< ,T>, NUMBERP, STRINGP, and SYMBOLP to write a predicate CONSTANTP for identifying constants in the LISP language. In some implementations, GET or SYMBOL-PLIST can be used to identify the type of symbol bindings. Use these symbols to develop VARIABLEP. Functions can be identified by FUNCTIONP. Write TERMP to identify s-expressions which are LISP terms (in the most basic sense of "term"). If this was easy, then program a function FREE-VARIABLES for computing the free variables in a LISP term. Finally, program FORMP for identifying s-expressions which correspond to terms with no free variables.

3. Self-mutilation and recovery: We have seen DEFUN's role in LISP's self-processing in its ability, given some variables and terms, to extend the language. However, it can also change built-in functions:

```
*   (DEFUN DEFUN (SM VL TR)
    (SET SM (LIST 'LAMBDA VL TR) )   )
    ==> DEFUN
*   (DEFUN 'SQUARE '(N) '(* N N))
    ==> (LAMBDA (N) (* N N))
*   (SQUARE 4)
    ERROR UNDEFINED FUNCTION: SQUARE
*   (APPLY SQUARE '(4))
    ==> 16   .
```

Explain this error. If possible, find a way to save DEFUN's original code so that, after modifying DEFUN as we did above, it can be restored to its original condition. (Hint: since we cannot use the bad DEFUN to restore DEFUN's original definition, we may succeed with SETF.) Would (APPLY SQUARE (4)) have worked properly if DEFUN had not modified itself before defining SQUARE?

3.5 Bindings, scopes, and environments

DICTIONARY TALK (Webster's New Collegiate Dictionary, @1975 G&C Merriam Co., Springfield, Massachusetts, p.675, p.489.).

local ... 2: of or relating to a particular place : characteristic of a particular place : not general or widespread; 3a: primarily serving

> the needs of a particular limited district; ... **global** ... 2: of, relating to, or involving the entire world; 3: of, relating to, or embracing all or virtually all considerations; ...

Symbols are given meanings by *associating* or *assigning* values, definitions, or properties to them. The computational difference is that associations occur locally while assignments are global. There should also be a difference in the way in which memory is used. We will use the word *binding* to refer to either an association or an assignment. Thus, the binding seen in the term ((LAMBDA ...) ...) would be an association, while that in (SETQ ...) would be an assignment. The segment(s) of LISP text in which a symbol's meaning is determined by a given binding is the scope of the binding. Scope refers to a set of terms and subterms within a series of LISP forms. The scope of a LAMBDA binding is the body of the lambda function. The scope of a SETQ, ..., DEFUN, ..., etc., binding is the set of subsequent terms and is indefinitely large.

A test for determining the scope of a binding to X: the scope is any part of a term, or any set of terms, in which the insertion of (PRINT X) would result in the printing of the value bound to X. This test gives precise meaning to the definition above. In its most general sense, an *environment* is the set of all symbol bindings (both associations and assignments) available for the evaluation of a term in a computation.

Example 17: The scope of a binding is often a segment of text determined by matching parentheses. For example, in evaluating the term

```
((LAMBDA (X) (* X X)) 3)
```

the local variable X is bound to 3 by LAMBDA and its scope is the function's body (i.e., the part between the function's variable-list and right parenthesis closing the function). If the term

```
(SETQ Y 3)
```

is evaluated at the top level, then Y is a global variable and the scope of the resulting binding is potentially unlimited.

Example 18: When we mix local and global, the situation is slightly more complicated (verified on Kyoto Common LISP and SUN Common LISP, but not on GCLISP).

```
*   (SETQ Y 3)
    ==> 3
*   ((LAMBDA (X Y) (PRINT Y) (SETQ Y X) Y) 1 2)
    2
    ==> 1
*   Y
    ==> 3
```

Here, we have the variable Y as both local and global. Y is a local variable within the body of the (LAMBDA ...) function, and in this body, it has the local binding Y=2. Elsewhere, Y is global and has the global binding Y=3. When applied to a local variable, SETQ does not have a global effect, but when applied to a free variable, SETQ does have global effect.

```
*   ((LAMBDA (X) (PRINT Y) (SETQ Y X) Y) 2)
    3
    ==> 2
*   Y
    ==> 2
```

Y is a global variable at all occurrences in the last two evaluations. It is global in the body of the (LAMBDA...) function because it is not in the variable list. Thus, as far as the function is concerned, Y is free.

```
*   (SETQ COUNT 0)
    ==> 0
*   (DEFUN KEEP-COUNT ( ) (SETQ COUNT (1+ COUNT)))
    ==> KEEP-COUNT
*   COUNT
    ==> 0
*   (KEEP-COUNT)
    ==> 1
*   COUNT
    ==> 1
```

Clearly, COUNT is free in KEEP-COUNT, and so it is global throughout. Next, we call KEEP-COUNT from within a function in which COUNT is local.

```
*   (DEFUN TEST-SCOPE (COUNT)
      (PRINT (KEEP-COUNT))              ;COUNT is global
      (PRINT COUNT)                     ;COUNT is  local
      (SETQ COUNT (1- COUNT)) )         ;COUNT is  local
    ==> TEST-SCOPE
*   (TEST-SCOPE 0)
    2
    0
    ==> -1
*   COUNT
    ==> 2
```

This demonstrates that even when KEEP-COUNT is called from within a context in which COUNT is local, the COUNT of KEEP-COUNT is global. In other words, the local COUNT of TEST-SCOPE is strictly local to TEST-SCOPE and cannot be seen from inside KEEP-COUNT. The scope of COUNT in KEEP-COUNT depends only on the definition of KEEP-COUNT, not on the environment in which KEEP-COUNT is used.

The type of scoping just seen—in which a variable's scope depends only on the definition of the function in which it appears, not on the environment in which the function is called—is *lexical scoping*. For the most part, the default binding mechanism for Common LISP is lexical binding. A complementary style of scoping—in which a variable's scope is determined by the most recent environment—is *dynamic scoping*. In GCLISP's dynamic scoping, we would have

```
*   (TEST-SCOPE 0)
    1
    1
    ==> 0    .
```

Dynamic scoping allows variables of one function (say to KEEP -COUNT) to be accessed by other functions (say by TEST-SCOPE).

A SPATIAL VIEW OF LEXICAL SCOPING:

Maybe lexical scoping can be defined in terms of lexical containment. At first, it seems adequate to think of "x is lexically contained in y" as meaning y=axb for some a and b. This is adequate to determine that the body of KEEP-COUNT is not contained in the body of TEST-SCOPE. However, it is not adequate to determine that in

```
(LET ((X 0) (Y X)) ...body...)
```

the scope of the binding X=0 contains (X 0) and ...body... but not (Y X). There would have to be other exclusions, but some definition of this general type would allow us to think of the "lexical scope" of a binding as the text "lexically contained in" the binding expression.

A TEMPORAL VIEW OF DYNAMIC SCOPING:

The general idea of "dynamic scoping" is that a variable's scope is determined by its most recent binding. If V's most recent binding is to e, then the terms whose environment contains this binding as the most recent binding of V compose the dynamic scope of V. Thus, the body of KEEP-COUNT is contained in the dynamic scope of TEST-SCOPE's local variable COUNT. This is because the most recent binding of KEEP-COUNT's COUNT is the binding performed by TEST-SCOPE.

Example 19:   Bindings are also created by LET, SETQ, SET, SETF, DEFUN, LABELS (see 4.2), etc. An assignment of a function's program to its name is created by DEFUN. Thus,

```
(DEFUN FACT (N) (IF (< N 2) 1 (* N (FACT (1- N)))))
```

is a binding for FACT (but not for N), which is in effect until DEFUN is used to reassign FACT's functional value or REMPROP destroys the current assignment. Consider property lists. Symbol:value bindings are stored in a property list by SETF. Thus,

```
(SETF (GET JOHN-FRANKLIN PROFESSION) 'ARCTIC-EXPLORER)
```

binds ARCTIC-EXPLORER to JOHN-FRANKLIN as the value of type PROFES-SION. These property list bindings are similar to the function definition binding created by DEFUN. For these exceptional assignments, the PRINT test is modified to (PRINT (FUNCTION symbol)) or (PRINT (GET symbol indicator)).

DIVERSION:

Sir John Franklin was a famous 19th century British explorer. In 1845, he set off to traverse the Northwest passage through northern Canada. He entered the passage at its eastern end, near Baffin Island, and sailed west for two years. Then, at a point near clear passage to the western end, his ship was frozen into the water and not released for three years.

After a few years, Lady Franklin sold nearly everything she had to finance an expedition, headed by Sir Leopold McClintock, to search for her husband. Entering the passage at its western end, McClintock soon found witnesses to their last days. Local Inuit reported seeing the men die in their tracks as they tried to reach a Hudson Bay Company outpost hundreds of miles to the Southeast.

In 1987, it was found that Franklin and his crew died of lead poisoning resulting from a lead (rather than tin) lining used in their food cans.

The first successful traversal of the Northwest passage by boat was made in 1903 by Ronald Amundsen in his ship the Gjöa.

Example 20: Steele and Sussman[1978] studied the differences between dynamic and lexical scoping and pointed out that they both have a valid place in LISP. However, dynamic scoping is generally thought of as creating problems such as the following. Suppose we have defined MAPCAR as in 3.4, except that we use the variables F and S rather than FUN and ARGS:

```
(DEFUN MAPCAR (F S)
  (IF ... (APPLY F (LIST (CAR S))) ... )),
```

and we have the same

```
(DEFUN SCALAR-PRODUCT (S V) ...).
```

In a lexically scoped LISP, we wouldn't expect this change of variables to have
any effect on the computation, but in a dynamically scoped LISP, the computation will proceed as follows. (The terms are on the left, while the environment
created by the preceding function calls is on the right.)

```
*   (SCALAR-PRODUCT 3 ' (1 2 3))                    ;environment
   => (MAPCAR ' (LAMBDA (X) (* S X)) V)   ;S=3,V=(1 2 3)
   => (IF (NULL S) NIL (APPLY F (LIST (CAR S))) ... )
      ;F=(LAMBDA (X) (* S X)),S=(1 2 3),S=3,V=(1 2 3)
   => (APPLY F (LIST (CAR S)))
      ;F=(LAMBDA (X) (* S X)),S=(1 2 3),S=3,V=(1 2 3)
   => ((LAMBDA (X) (* S X)) 1)
      ;F=(LAMBDA (X) (* S X)),S=(1 2 3),S=3,V=(1 2 3)
   => (* S X)
   ;X=1,F=(LAMBDA (X) (* S X)),S=(1 2 3),S=3,V=(1 2 3)
   ERROR: NONNUMERICAL ARGUMENT FOR *.
```

This error occurs when the value of the S in (* S X) is determined by the
most recent binding to S. In lexical scoping, the meaning of S would have been
determined by the environment created by the call to SCALAR-PRODUCT, and
(* S X) would have had S=3.

The problem illustrated above occurred in early, dynamically scoped LISPs
when functions were used which, like MAPCAR, took another function as an
argument. Consequently, it is known as the *funarg problem*. The funarg problem
can still be seen in Gold Hill's Common LISP.

Special variables. Common LISP allows variables to be dynamically scoped
if they are declared *special*. The existence of special variables complicates the
use of free variables. The value of a free variable in a function is the most recent
binding of either a global variable (of the same name) or a special variable (of
the same name) no matter where the binding occurred. As a matter of style, the
use of special variables should generally be avoided.

Example 21: The previous example of lexical scoping will now be redone with
COUNT declared to be special by TEST-SCOPE. This demonstrates dynamic
scoping. (Verified on Kyoto Common LISP and SUN Common LISP, but not
on GCLISP.)

```
*   (SETQ *COUNT* 0)
   ==> 0
*   (DEFUN KEEP-COUNT ( ) (SETQ *COUNT* (1+ *COUNT*)))
   ==> KEEP-COUNT
*   (PROCLAIM ' (SPECIAL *COUNT*))
                            ;*COUNT* is dynamically scoped
   ==>
*   (DEFUN TEST-SCOPE (*COUNT*)
```

```
    (PRINT (KEEP-COUNT))      ;the local *COUNT* is used
    (PRINT *COUNT*)
    (SETQ *COUNT* (1- *COUNT*))   )
   ==> TEST-SCOPE
*  (TEST-SCOPE 0)                   ;*COUNT* is bound to 0
   1                      ;KEEP-COUNT adds 1 to this *COUNT*
   1
   ==> 0
*  *COUNT*
   ==> 0
```

The asterisks around *COUNT* were used just to make the special variable easy to spot in a crowd. They are not required. (DECLARE (SPECIAL *variable*)) may be used in function bodies to make specific local variables special.

Exercises

1. Show that the scope of X in

       ((LAMBDA (X) (PRINT X) (* X X)) 3)

   is more than just (* X X).

2. What is the scope of the SETQ binding of Y in the following experiment?

   ```
   *   ((LAMBDA (X) (SETQ Y (READ))) (EQUAL X Y)) 3)   4
   *   Y
   ```

   How about the scope and extent of the following SETQ bindings of X?

   ```
   *   (SETQ X 4)
   *   ((LAMBDA (Y) (SETQ X (READ))) (EQUAL X Y)) 3) 4
   ```

3. What do the following experiments indicate about the scopes and extents of conflicting lambda bindings?

   ```
   *   (DEFUN X-TEST (X) (PRINT X) ((LAMBDA (X)
      (PRINT X)) (1+ X) ))
   *   (SETQ X 0)
   *   (X-TEST 2)
   ```

4. What is the scope of X in each of the following?

   ```
   *   (LET ((X 0) (Y X)) ...body...)
   *   (LET* ((X 0) (Y X)) ...body...)
   ```

5. Evaluate the following in your head—not on your machine. Assume lexical scoping, then dynamic scoping.

```
*      (SETQ X 100)
*      ((LAMBDA (X) ((LAMBDA ( ) X))) 0)
*      (DEFUN INNER ( ) X)
*      ((LAMBDA (X) (INNER)) 0)
```

6. Consider function bindings—with DEFUN corresponding to SETQ and LABELS corresponding to LAMBDA. Can the notions of lexical and dynamic scoping be carried from variables bound to data objects over to symbols bound to function objects? Explain.

3.6   Additional reading

The ultimate source when it comes to the essential structure of Common LISP is the reference manual by Steele[1984]. However, it is not easy sailing. Abelson and Sussman[1985] is an outstanding source for a variety of details on SCHEME and LISP. Other well-written general texts on Common LISP include Kessler[1988] and Wilensky[1986]. Dijkstra[1978] also covers garbage collection. The funarg problem is discussed in Moses[1970]. The pros and cons of lexical versus dynamic scoping are examined and lead to a philosophy of interpreters in Steele and Sussman[1978]—beautiful! Some implementation issues are presented in Allen[1978].

4

Computational Philosophy

The essentials of LISP that we have developed so far support some interesting and important computational philosophy. At this point, a little philosophy—like a smile on a friend's face—is an appropriate interruption to the serious study of LISP programming. The objective of this chapter is to introduce some theoretical aspects of functional programming and computing. This will consist of a bit of classical recursion theory, pure LISP, types of recursion, and the folklore of fixed-point computation.

4.1 Models of computation

Figure 4.1. Alan Turing, 1940s.

So, LISP was conceived as both a computer language and as a formalism for recursive function theory. In this section, we will get a glimpse into these theories by studying models of computation.

4.1.1   Mathematical formalisms for computation

Turing machines are mathematical objects that model computation in a very simple and formal way. Other approaches to modeling computation include combinatory algebra (by Moses Schoenfinkel and Haskel Curry), the lambda calculus (Alonzo Church), and the partial recursive functions (Stephen Kleene). These formalisms were developed in the first decades of this century to enable mathematicians to investigate computable functions, algorithms, and computations. They led to the discovery of deep and surprising properties of computation long before the first electronic digital computer.

In the early stages of its development, LISP was viewed as a recursive function theory implemented as a computer language. Like the existing formalisms, it was to allow the creation of new functions from existing functions, allow functions to process appropriately coded algorithms as data, to have a universal function— one which could emulate any other computable function. One particular feature of LISP—the use of lambda abstraction to create new functions from existing variables and terms—was taken from the lambda calculus. Other features are reminiscent of Kleene's partial recursive functions.

The theory of partial recursive functions was developed by Stephen Kleene starting late in the 1930s. It concerns functions whose range and domain are the

Figure 4.2. Stephen Kleene, 1930s.

natural numbers. They are built up from three very simple types of functions by the application of three general operations. The three basic families of functions are

the *successor function,*
$$S\langle n \rangle = n + 1;$$

the *zero constant function,*
$$Z\langle n \rangle = 0;$$

and for every j and k, the *projection function,*
$$P_{jk}\langle n_1, ..., n_k \rangle = n_j \quad 1 \leq j \leq k.$$

The three operations are

composition—given $F\langle n_1, ..., n_j \rangle, G_1\langle n_1, ..., n_k \rangle, ..., G_j\langle n_1, ..., n_k \rangle$, composition creates the function

$$H\langle n_1, ..., n_k \rangle = F\langle G_1\langle n_1, ..., n_k \rangle, ..., G_j\langle n_1, ..., n_k \rangle \rangle;$$

recursion—given $F\langle n_1, ..., n_j \rangle$ and $G\langle m, n_1, ..., n_j \rangle$, recursion creates the function defined by

$$H\langle 0, n_1, ..., n_j \rangle = F\langle n_1, ..., n_j \rangle$$

$$H \langle i + 1, n_1, ..., n_j \rangle = G \langle H \langle i, n_1, ..., n_j \rangle, n_1, ..., n_j \rangle; \text{ and}$$

minimization—given $F \langle m, n_1, ..., n_j \rangle$, minimization creates the function H defined by

$$H \langle n_1, ..., n_j \rangle = \min i [F \langle i, n_1, ..., n_j \rangle = 0].$$

The *partial recursive functions* are the functions that can be built up from the basic functions by applying these operations. In other words, the set of partial recursive functions is the smallest set containing the basic functions and closed under the three operations defined above. (These three operations motivated the computational point of view seen in 2.1, 2.2, and 2.4 (search=minimization). The lambda calculus motivated 2.7.)

On the surface, these basic functions and operations do not seem powerful enough to support interesting computation. But, superficial impressions can be misleading.

4.1.2   Church's thesis and computational completeness

Investigations by the previously mentioned pioneers and others at Princeton during the 1920s and 1930s led to the discovery that the formalisms mentioned at the beginning of this section are all equivalent in their ability to program algorithms. In other words, any function which is computable in one system is computable in the others. Thus, even though the systems are dissimilar in their approach, they all arrive at the same notion of computability. This strongly suggests that the notion is a natural one. Formal computational systems which have this property—that every function computable in one of the systems defined here is computable in them—are said to be *computationally complete*.

A NOTE ON COMPUTATIONAL EQUIVALENCE WITH LISP:

Exercises 3 and 4 (following) show that functions which are computable in the sense of Kleene or Turing are computable in LISP. Similar, although more difficult, arguments show that functions that are computable in LISP are also computable in the sense of Kleene and Turing.

Translate LISP programs to Turing machine programs: the Turing machine (defined in exercise 4) would have to have all of the symbols used in LISP present in its ALPHABET. The partial recursive functions would have to be redefined (as in Kleene above) for words in this ALPHABET. This is done in Machtey and Young[1978]. The easiest solution though is to code the fewer than one hundred characters used in LISP into numbers:) = 40 (= 41, *= 42, ..., Z = 90, ... etc. Then code every list of symbols (which is an s-expression) into its Gödel number (an integer coding a list of

integers). Thus every s-expression corresponds to a unique integer
and every LISP function can be thought of as an integer-valued
function on the integers. The other direction—from the partial
recursive functions into LISP —is no problem because all of the
natural numbers are already in LISP's s-expressions.

Gödel numbers are the products of successive primes raised to
powers which are the numbers in the list. The number-list of $(Z())$
is 41, 90, 41, 40, 40; its Gödel number is
$$2^{41} * 3^{90} * 5^{41} * 7^{40} * 11^{40} = (2.514728...) * 10^{159}.$$

The naturalness of the idea of computation captured by these systems is given
even greater weight by the fact that no one has ever found a function which
is computable by algorithm in any formal/informal sense that is not also computable in these systems. This is despite years of effort by some outstanding
mathematicians. Functions which are common-sense computable but not computable in the formalisms do not seem to exist. This led Alonzo Church to
conjecture that any function which is computable by an algorithm (informally)
is formally computable within each of these systems—*Church's thesis.* Since
we are dealing with an informal notion of "computable by algorithm", Church's
thesis can never be proved, but over the past fifty years, the empirical evidence
has been convincing. In light of this assertion, computational completeness takes
on a new significance. Maybe—in fact, probably—it represents "computable"
in the human sense.

THE LIMITS OF COMPUTATION:

In 4.4, we will prove that the solution to a certain problem about
LISP cannot be computed by any algorithm programmable in LISP.
By Church's thesis, the solution is not computable by algorithm in
any common-sense use of the word "computable". Thus, the
problem is really unsolvable.

Exercises

1. The "partial" in "partial recursive functions" refers to the fact that many of
   the functions are only partially defined. In other words, there may exist n
   for which $f\langle n \rangle$ does not have a value. Give an example of such a function
   in Kleene's system.

2. Construct addition and multiplication as partial recursive functions.

3. Are all partial recursive functions programmable in LISP? The three basic partial recursive functions are obviously programmable in LISP, so

the question becomes "are LISP's functions closed under the three operations?"

4. Simulate a Turing machine in LISP. First, we define Turing machines and their style of computation. A *Turing machine* is represented by four items: a finite alphabet ALPHABET, a finite set of states STATES, an initial state s_0, and a set of instructions PROGRAM. It reads and writes information on a finite but unlimited tape which is represented as a list $(c_1, c_2, c_3, ..., c_k)$ of characters from ALPHABET ∪ {blank}. The machine is thought of as being located at a specific character—say c_j, and in a specific state—say s. In this case, the list

$$(c_1, ..., s, c_j, ..., c_k)$$

is the configuration and the machine is said to be in state s reading c_j. After reading c_j, it may perform any one of four operations: write a new character d_j:

$$(...s, c_j, ...) \text{ becomes } (...s, d_j ...);$$

move left:

$$(...s, c_j ...) \text{ becomes } (...s, c_{j-1} ..) \text{ if } 0 < j;$$

move right:

$$(...s, c_j ...) \text{ becomes } (...s, c_{j+1} ...);$$

or change state:

$$(...s, c_j ...) \text{ becomes } (...t, c_j ...).$$

If c_j is the last character in the configuration and the machine moves right, then c_{j+1} = blank is added. An instruction of the form $[s, c_j, \text{opera-tion}]$ tells the machine what to do in configuration $(...s, c_j ...)$. Assume that the machine is deterministic (i.e., a program does not have more than one instruction beginning with the same s, c_j). A computation begins in a configuration of the form $(s_0, a_1, ..., a_i)$ for some word $a_1 ... a_i$ of ALPHABET and ends when a configuration $(c_1, ..., s, c_j, ..., c_k)$ has been reached for which there is no instruction $[s, c_j, \text{operation}]$ in PROGRAM.

The function computed by this machine is the function on words of ALPHABET which takes $a_1 ... a_i$ to $c_1 ... c_j ... c_k$. Write a LISP program TURING⟨ALPHABET, STATES, s0, PROGRAM, TAPE⟩ which simulates Turing machine computations.

5. Have I got a deal for you! Here, we have a new programming language in which every syntactically correct program is guaranteed to produce a value for every input (i.e., all functions are totally defined). Are you interested?

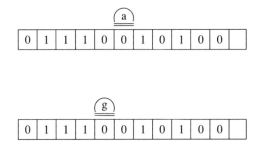

Figure 4.3. A Turing machine executing the instruction (a,0,LEFT,g).

4.2 Pure LISP

Pure LISP is the sublanguage of LISP using only those functions which have
no effect. This eliminates the assignments SETQ, SET, SETF, DEFUN,
PRINT, READ, etc. With the elimination of these functions, there is no need for
the procedural features of PROGN or the implicit PROGNs available in LAMBDA
and LET constructions. However, the procedural aspects of COND, IF, AND,
OR, etc., remain.

The point is that by removing all assignments, the purely functional LISP
that remains is *referentially transparent*. Refer..., what? This means that the
meaning of a symbol, name, or term can be determined from its immediate
context. Lexical scoping contributes to LISP's referential transparency. Neither
English nor FORTRAN consistently exhibit referential transparency. In the case
of English, the variable "she" in

> She brought wild flowers to her Mother.
> Unfortunately, she was allergic to the flowers.

may not refer to the same woman. Similarly, in the case of FORTRAN,

```
    . . .
    n=0
    . . .
    n=n+1
    . . .
```

the value of the term n depends on its place in the computation. Referential
transparency is valuable as an aid to good programming and ease in understanding programs. It is also one of the properties of mathematical languages which
makes it possible to develop formal proofs. In this sense, it is important for the
success of program verification in LISP.

TERMINOLOGY:

[Program] *verification* is the use of formal mathematical techniques to prove the correctness and other properties of programs. The techniques need to be formal (i.e., syntactic) to be carried out automatically. Its success seems to require referential transparency.

HISTORY:

"One mathematical consideration that influenced LISP was to express programs as applicative expressions built up from variables and constants using functions. I considered it important to make these expressions obey the usual mathematical laws allowing replacement of expressions by expressions giving the same value. The motive was to allow proofs of programs using ordinary mathematical methods. This is only possible to the extent that side effects can be avoided. Unfortunately, side effects are often a great convenience when computational efficiency is important and 'functions' with side effects are present in [whole] LISP. However, the so-called pure LISP is free of side effects, and ... Cartwright&McCarthy[1978] show how to represent [it] in first-order logic and prove their properties. This is an additional vindication of the striving for mathematical neatness, because it is now easier to prove that pure LISP programs meet their specifications than it is for any other programming language in extensive use." McCarthy[1981]

LISP axioms and the verification of LISP programs are also presented in chapters III and IV of McCarthy&Talcott[1980].

So, pure LISP is a well-behaved and mathematically tractable sublanguage. The question now is "how powerful is pure LISP?" From a programmer's point of view, a good deal of convenience has been lost with the removal of SETQ, DEFUN, etc. However, from a computational point of view, the only assignments that cannot be replaced by operations available in pure LISP are READ and PRINT. Thus, pure LISP has no input or output. The interesting, and possibly surprising, thing is that every i/o-free function which is computable in full LISP is computable in pure LISP.

LABELS creates local bindings of functions to their names. Its syntax is

```
(LABELS
  ((fun-name₁ var-list₁ body₁)  ... (fun-nameⱼ ...))
  form₁ ... formₖ )
```

where each *fun-name*$_i$ is a symbol locally bound as a function name to (LAMBDA *var-list*$_i$ *body*$_i$) in the environment in which *form*$_1$ . . . *form*$_k$

Figure 4.4. David Park, 1960, MIT.

are to be evaluated. The local binding of functions and the evaluation of the implicit PROGN is done by LABELS. An older approach is to modify the function rather than the term. In this approach, LABEL is used in the function as follows:

(LABEL *function-name* (LAMBDA *variable-list body*)).

Whenever either of these functions are used, the name is bound to the function locally—without an assignment.

Example 1: Now that names can be bound to functions locally, recursive computations can be programmed without resorting to the assignment DEFUN.

```
*   (LABELS
      ((DEPTH (S-EXP)              ;bind DEPTH to function
        (IF (ATOM S-EXP) 0 (1+ (DEPTH-BRANCH S-EXP))) )
       (DEPTH-BRANCH (S-EXP)              ;bind DEPTH-BRANCH
        (MAX (DEPTH (CAR S-EXP)) (DEPTH (CDR S-EXP))) ))
      (DEPTH (FUNCTION DEPTH))
                          ) ;compute the DEPTH of DEPTH
      ==> 11
```

The body, (DEPTH (FUNCTION DEPTH)), of this term is evaluated in an environment in which the mutually recursive DEPTH and DEPTH-BRANCH are locally defined as functions.

> "Logical completeness required that notation used to express
> functions used as functional arguments be extended to provide for
> recursive functions, and the LABEL notation was invented by
> Nathaniel Rochester for that purpose. D.M.R. Park pointed out that
> LABEL was logically unnecessary since the result could be achieved
> using only LAMBDA—by a construction analogous to Church's
> Y-operator, albeit in a more complicated way." McCarthy[1981]

[This method of Church's is described in 7.4.]

Fundamental theorem for pure LISP. Every algorithmically computable (in the informal sense) function can be computed by a program in pure LISP.

Proof sketch 1. By Church's thesis, every such function is computable by a Turing machine. Thus, by the solution to problem 4 of 4.1 they are computable in pure LISP.

Proof sketch 2. By Church's thesis, every such function is computable as a partial recursive function. The proof will be similar to the solution to problem 3, Section 4.1. The three basic partial recursive functions definable without assignments are

```
(LAMBDA (X) (1+ X)), (LAMBDA (X) 0), and
(LAMBDA (X1...Xj) Xi),
```

where $0 < i < j+1$. Thus, they are in pure LISP. If $G1\langle x1, \ldots, xk\rangle, \ldots,$ $Gj \langle x1, \ldots, xk\rangle$ and $H\langle y1, \ldots, yj\rangle$ are programmed in pure LISP, then their composition

```
(LAMBDA (X1...Xk) (H (G1 X1...Xk) ... (Gj X1...Xk)))
```

is in pure LISP. Given $F\langle X1, \ldots, Xj\rangle$ and $G\langle X0, X1, \ldots, Xj\rangle$ in pure LISP, their result by recursion is

```
(LABEL H
 (LAMBDA (W X1...Xj)
  (IF (ZEROP W) (F X1...Xj)
   (G (H (1- W) X1...Xj) X1...Xj) ))).
```

Given that $F<W, X1, \ldots, Xj>$ is programmed in pure LISP, the MIN operation gives us

```
(LABEL MIN-F (LAMBDA (X1...Xj)
  ((LABEL PRE-MIN-F (LAMBDA (W X1...Xj)
    (IF (ZEROP (F W X1...Xj)) W
     (PRE-MIN-F (1+ W) X1...Xj) )))
   0 X1...Xj ))).
```

Thus, pure LISP contains the partial recursive functions.

4.3   Types of recursion

Types of recursion—as reflected in the syntax of their definition—exhibit important and interesting differences in semantics and computational complexity. In this section, we will examine several types of recursion—including tail recursion, structural recursion, nonmonotonic recursion, and compound recursion.

4.3.1   Fat recursion and tail recursion

Recursive definitions in which the call to the recursive function is within the scope of another function call or in the position of a test-form generate "fat computations". These computations tend to be fairly expensive and may be unnecessary. On the other hand, many computations can be translated into a skinny tail recursive form. A definition is *tail recursive* if calls to the recursive function are in the position of value-forms and are not within the scope of another function, nor used as tests.

Example 2:   A fat computation for FIBONACCI is generated by the following definition.

```
*   (DEFUN FIBONACCI (N)
     (IF (<= N 2) 1
       (+ (FIBONACCI (- N 1)) (FIBONACCI (- N 2))) ))
```

In the computations which this program generates, each occurrence of (FIBO-NACCI N) for N>2 is replaced by

```
     (+ (FIBONACCI (- N 1)) (FIBONACCI (- N 2))))).
```

The calls to − in the inner terms can be performed immediately. However, the call to + must be delayed until the recursive calls return their values. This generates a computation that looks something like this.

```
*   (FIBONACCI 100)
     => (+ (FIBONACCI 99) (FIBONACCI 98))
     => (+ (+ (FIBONACCI 98) (FIBONACCI 97))
        (FIBONACCI 98))
     => (+ (+ (+ (FIBONACCI 97) (FIBONACCI 96))
           (FIBONACCI 97)) (FIBONACCI 98))
     => (+ (+ (+ (+ (FIBONACCI 96) (FIBONACCI 95))
              (FIBONACCI 96) ) (FIBONACCI 97) )
        (FIBONACCI 98) )
     . . .
     ==> 3.542 E+20
```

If we look just at the values of N in the calls to FIBONACCI in this computation, we see the following.

```
                        100
                   => 99 98
                  => 98 97 98
                 => 97 96 97 98
                => 96 95 96 97 98
               => 95 94 95 96 97 98
        . . .         . . .        . . .
```

The number of steps in the computation for N=100 is one more than the sum of
the number for N=99 plus the number for N=98. Thus, for our complexity analysis, this computation consists of more than $FIBONACCI\langle 100\rangle = 3.542 * 10^{20}$
lines, with one computational step and about a hundred calls to FIBONACCI
and + (waiting their turn) per line. Obviously, this computation could not be
carried out on a real machine.

FIBONACCI may be given a tail recursive program.

```
*    (DEFUN FIBONACCI (N) (IF (< N 2) 1 (FIB 1 1 2 N)))
*    (DEFUN FIB (FJ- FJ J N)
      (IF (= J N) FJ (FIB FJ (+ FJ- FJ) (1+ J) N)) )
```

The computation which this function generates is obviously skinny and short.

```
*    (FIBONACCI 100)
    => (FIB 1 1 2 100)
    => (FIB 1 2 3 100)
    => (FIB 2 3 4 100)
    => (FIB 3 5 5 100)
    => (FIB 5 8 6 100)
    => (FIB 8 13 7 100)
    => (FIB 13 21 8 100)
    . . .
    ==> 3.542 E+20
```

Complexity: there are about 100 lines, each of which contains only one function
call.

4.3.2 Compound recursion

There are styles of recursive definition which are potentially worse than the
fat definition we had for FIBONACCI. *Compound recursions* involve calls of
the recursive function within a call of the recursive function. This can create
computations whose length grows incredibly fast as a function of the magnitude
of the argument(s). The infamous Ackermann function is defined by a compound
recursion. Another very common and potentially more inscrutable form is the
nonmonotonic recursion (next section).

Example 3:   The Ackermann function is defined for natural numbers by

$$A\langle I, 0\rangle = I+1,$$
$$A\langle 0, J\rangle = A\langle 1, J\text{-}1\rangle$$
$$A\langle I, J\rangle = A\langle A\langle I\text{-}1, J\rangle\ J\text{-}1\rangle.$$

For every I and J, $A\langle I, J\rangle$ actually has a value. However, the sizes and values of the computations grow incredibly fast.

$$A\langle 0, 1\rangle = 2,\quad A\langle 1, 2\rangle = 5,\quad A\langle 2, 3\rangle = 29,$$
$$A\langle 3, 4\rangle = 2^{65536},\ \dots$$

The mathematical significance of this function grows out of two facts: (1) it is a partial recursive function (i.e., can be defined from the three basic function types by applying the three operations), and (2) it cannot be defined without the minimization (i.e., search) operation. The proof of this is based on the fact that A grows faster than any function that can be defined without minimization.

4.3.3   Monotonic and nonmonotonic recursion

A *monotonic recursion* is one in which the changes made to the argument(s) are always in the same "direction". In FACTORIAL, N is changed to (1- N) until 1 is reached. In EQUAL, X and Y are replaced by (CAR X), (CAR Y), (CDR X), and (CDR Y) until atomic values are reached. In MIN-F (Kleene's third operation, programmed in the proof of the fundamental theorem, section 4.1), N is replaced by (1+ N) until the search produces the desired N. Monotonic recursions are also known as *structural recursions* — especially in cases such as EQUAL.

A *nonmonotonic recursion* is one in which the changes made to the argument(s) in the recursive call are not monotonic (i.e., not always in the same direction). C, the Collatz function, and EVAL involve nonmonotonic recursions. Their inscrutability is seen in the open question of C's convergence, and the provably unsolvable halting problem for EVAL (section 4.4). The nonmonotonicity of C is clear in the example of 2.2.2, that of EVAL can be seen in the rewrite rules defining EVAL given in 6.2.1 and in the fact that EVAL can evaluate C. Newton's (search) method for finding the zeros of a function is also nonmonotonic.

Exercises

1. The usual definition for FACTORIAL is fat. Give a tail recursive definition for it. Compare the complexity of the two for N=100.

2. What kind of recursion do we see in the usual definition of SUBST?

3. Program A, the Ackermann function, in LISP and evaluate as many values of A<I,J> as possible.

4. Given that A does not have a tail recursive definition, prove that the interpreter (i.e., EVAL, APPLY,. . .) does not have tail recursive definitions for all of its functions.

5. Hofstadter[1980, p.137] defines the following chaotic function:

$$Q\langle 0 \rangle = Q\langle 1 \rangle = 1, \text{ and } Q\langle N \rangle = Q\langle N - Q\langle N - 1 \rangle \rangle + Q\langle N - Q\langle N - 2 \rangle \rangle$$

$$\text{for } 1 \leq N.$$

Program Q in LISP and experiment with it. Is Q<M> defined for every natural number M? Is Q monotonic? How does Q<M>/M behave?

6. A short and wide recursion. The following compound recursive function was originally defined by Ikuo Takeuchi. For X>Y,

$$\text{TAK}\langle X,Y,Z \rangle = \text{TAK}\langle \text{TAK}\langle X\text{-}1,Y,Z \rangle, \text{TAK}\langle Y\text{-}1,Z,X \rangle, \text{TAK}\langle Z\text{-}1,X,Y \rangle \rangle,$$

otherwise

$$\text{TAK}\langle X,Y,Z \rangle = Z.$$

Program this function in LISP and explore its properties.

```
(DEFUN TAK (X Y Z)
  (IF
   (NOT (< Y X))
   Z
   (TAK (TAK (1- X) Y Z) (TAK (1- Y) Z X)
     (TAK (1- Z) X Y)) ))
```

Using this program, the computation of TAK$\langle 18,12,6 \rangle$ makes $63,609$ calls to TAK, performs $47,706$ subtractions by 1, and still never has a depth of recursion greater than 18 (Gabriel[1985, page 81-92]).

7. The end of the world. There is a story that the world will end when Buddhist monks living in Hanoi complete the following process. There are three pegs with sixty-four punctured gold disks of different sizes stacked on them. Initially, they are stacked on the first peg with all larger disks below all smaller disks. The monks may move one disk at a time from the top of one peg's stack to the top of another. In these moves, a disk may never be placed on a smaller disk. The objective is to move all of the disks from the first peg to the second.

Meanwhile, astronomers have their own story leading to the end of the world. They believe that the sun will become a red giant and engulf the earth in about 3,000,000,000 years. Assuming that the monks move one disk per second without interruption, who predicts an earlier end to the earth? Program a LISP simulation of the monk's process.

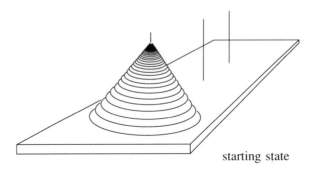

starting state

Figure 4.5. The towers of Hanoi in its starting state.

4.4   The limits of LISP: an unsolvable problem

In the 1930s, mathematicians working in recursion theory made the amazing
discovery that there exist problems which are clearly stated, which have answers,
but which can never be solved. This is to say an algorithm which will generate
the answers to the problems cannot exist. The halting problem, famous as the
simplest and most meaningful of these unsolvable problems, is easily recast in
LISP. (In light of the fact that LISP was created in the image of recursion theory,
this is not surprising.) In the following presentation and proof of unsolvability,
we'll use pure LISP.

First, an informal look at the problem. If

`UM<program, arguments>`

is a universal computing machine (e.g., programmable digital computer, Turing
machine, `APPLY`) which performs the computation defined by the given *program* on the *arguments*, we may ask "Does the machine ever halt for the
given program and arguments?" In other words, "Does the computation ever terminate for the given program and arguments?" The problem of answering this
question is the *halting problem*. A simple diagonalization argument proves that
in general this question is not solvable. Of course, for many if not most choices

of program and arguments, the problem can be answered correctly. However, by a "solution", we mean an algorithm

    HP-SOLUTION<*program,arguments*>

which takes the *program* and the *arguments* as parameters and always returns the answers (T or F) to the problem. In saying that the problem is *unsolvable*, we are saying that no such algorithm exists.

In recasting this problem

    (APPLY *function arguments*)

plays the role of UM<*program,arguments*>. We'll prove that an algorithm for solving this halting problem cannot be programmed in LISP. Assume, for the sake of contradiction, that a function HP-SOLUTION such that

    (HP-SOLUTION *function arguments*)
    ⇒T if (APPLY *function arguments*) returns a value,
    ⇒NIL, otherwise

exists in LISP. Without making any additional assumptions, we'll prove that this leads to a contradiction.

Since HP-SOLTUION is assumed to be defined by a lambda expression, we can use it to define a diagonalizing function. Let DIAGONAL be the name of

```
(LAMBDA (X)
 (IF
  (LABELS
   ((HP-SOLUTION (FUN ARGS)...))
   (HP-SOLUTION X (LIST X)) )
  (CONS (APPLY X (LIST X)) NIL)
  NIL )).
```

According to our discussion of HP-SOLUTION, DIAGONAL's test term is nonNIL if and only if (APPLY X (LIST X)) returns a value (call it *s-expression*). In this case, the value returned is the list (*s-expression*). Otherwise, (APPLY X (LIST X)) has no value and DIAGONAL returns NIL. In other words,

```
*    (LABELS ((DIAGONAL (X)...)) argument)
     ==> (value)
             if (APPLY argument (LIST argument)) ==> value
     ==> NIL
             if (APPLY argument (LIST argument)) has no value.
```

Since HP-SOLUTION always returns a value, DIAGONAL will always return a value.

Now for the contradiction. First, observe that since DIAGONAL always returns a value, the form

```
* (APPLY DIAGONAL (LIST DIAGONAL))
```

will return a value—call it DV. Second, we will explore the computation resulting from applying DIAGONAL to itself.

```
* (DIAGONAL DIAGONAL)
  => (IF
       (LABELS ((HP-SOLUTION...)) (DIAGONAL
        (LIST DIAGONAL) ))
       (CONS (APPLY DIAGONAL (LIST DIAGONAL)) NIL)
       NIL )
```

The test term is the same as HP-SOLUTION<DIAGONAL>, which is T (because DIAGONAL always returns a value). Thus, we continue with

```
  => (CONS (APPLY DIAGONAL (LIST DIAGONAL)) NIL)
  ...
  => (DV) .
```

On the other hand,

```
(APPLY DIAGONAL (LIST DIAGONAL)) = (DIAGONAL DIAGONAL),
```

so

```
  DV = (DV) .
```

Contradiction, an s-expression cannot be a list and an element of that list (itself) at the same time.

The key to the contradiction was not the assertion that an algorithm could tell us if another algorithm halted, but the another algorithm could tell us when it didn't halt.

When a computational system such as LISP is a source of problems that can't be solved within the system, there are two ways to interpret this unsolvability phenomenon. One is that the system is too weak to solve its own problems. The other is that it presents such a strong notion of computability that deep and unsolvable questions can arise. Either interpretation could be true. However, in this case, we believe (from Church's thesis and the computational completeness of LISP) that the strong interpretation is correct.

Example 4: Counter-example: Let the set TOTALD consist of all totally defined (i.e., always halting to return a value) functions

$f : D^n \rightarrow D$, where n is a nonnegative integer.

(D may be the set of s-expressions, of nonnegative integers, or of anything else. D^n is the nth Cartesian product of D.) The function HP-SOLUTIONTOTALD : $D^2 \rightarrow D$ is defined by

HP-SOLUTIONTOTALD<FUN,ARGS> = T,

and is in TOTALD. Thus, the halting problem is solvable in TOTALD.

TOTALD isn't important for three reasons. First, TOTALD is not computationally complete (the absence of partial functions indicates that functions defined from nontrivial searches are not in TOTALD). Second, there cannot exist a computer language whose programmable functions are precisely those of TOTALD (see exercise 4). Finally, the halting problem is trivial for TOTALD, we knew from the beginning that everything halts.

Exercises

1. An affirmative answer to "(APPLY *function arguments*) halts?" is computable (i.e., decidable). Write a LISP program which returns T precisely when this computation halts.

2. The decision problem for semantic equality. Two terms, t_1 and t_2, in a term algebra are *semantically equal* if for any environment function *env* $\langle \rangle$ and *eval* $\langle \rangle$, we have

$$eval \langle t_1 \rangle = eval \langle t_2 \rangle$$

   For example, the terms $(if \; x \; 0 \; 0), (- \; v1 \; v1)$, and 0 are all semantically equal. Use the undecidability of the halting problem and the answer to problem 1 to prove that semantic equality is undecidable for LISP terms.

3. Semantic errors are errors which result from the evaluation of a syntactically correct term as a result of inappropriate values for variables, terms, or computed functions. Show that the question of the existence of semantic errors in a LISP form is undecidable. Hint: consider (IF *term* V V), where V is an unbound variable.

4. The Halting Problem. Carefully compute the following. Assume that FACTORIAL is programmed as usual, O is (LAMBDA () (0)), HP-SOLUTION and DIAGONAL are as described in the text.

   a. (HP-SOLUTION 'FACTORIAL '(5))

   b. (HP-SOLUTION 'O NIL)

   c. (HP-SOLUTION 'DIAGONAL '(DIAGONAL))

   d. (DIAGONAL 'QUOTE)

   e. (DIAGONAL '(LAMBDA (X) (CAR X)))

   f. (DIAGONAL 123)

   g. (DIAGONAL 'O)

h. (DIAGONAL 'FACTORIAL)

i. Given that the value returned in c above is T, will

(DIAGONAL 'DIAGONAL)

create a loop resulting in stack overflow? Explain.

4.5   The folklore of fixed-point computation

Among technical folk, there are strange stories that circulate about recursive and, especially, fixed-point processes. In this section, we'll take a look at them. Examples in 2.8 show that a fixed-point computation is a form of recursion— probably tail recursion. In 7.4, we will show that recursion is a special case of fixed-point computation. So, the two types of processes are really one.

Introductory calculus courses often prove the following fixed-point theorems along with the mean-value and intermediate-value theorems.

One-dimensional fixed-point theorem. If $f:[0,1] \rightarrow [0,1]$ is a continuous function, then there exists a point p for which $f<p>=p$.

The proof is easy, just show that the graph of $y=f<x>$ intersects the diagonal $y=x$.

This theorem may never become a part of your tavern conversation, but its three-dimensional cousin may.

The coffee cup theorem. If your spoon enters the coffee without cutting it (just denting it), you stir the coffee without splashing it, and it is removed without any coffee sticking to it, then when the coffee comes to rest, at least one molecule will have returned exactly to its starting position.

Analytical fixed-point theorems such as these are actually related to existence theorems for fixed-point computations [see 7.3].

FOR THE MATHEMATICALLY INCLINED READER

The coffee cup anecdote illustrates another fixed-point theorem from mathematical analysis. Specifically, the coffee corresponds to a nonvoid, closed, bounded, simply connected subset of C of R^3 (Euclidean 3-space). The stirring is a continuous function $s:C \rightarrow C$, where the continuity of s corresponds to the coffee being neither cut nor splashed by the spoon. It is true in the mathematical contex that there exists a point m in C which is returned to its original location by s, specifically $s<m>=m$. In terms of the idealized coffee, there is a molecule that returns to its original position.

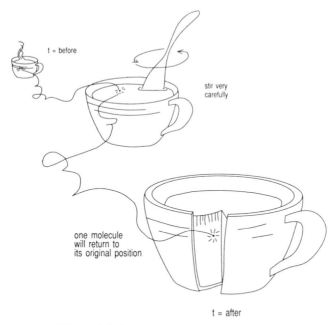

t = before

stir very
carefully

one molecule
will return to
its original position

t = after

Figure 4.6. A fixed-point in your coffee.

John VonNeumann died in 1957, before he could complete his theory of self-reproducing automata. But, he made a good start—see VonNeumann[1966]. Others, including Arthur Burkes and John Myhill continued, refined, and abstracted his ideas on self-reproducing machines until they landed in recursion theory. There, the idea of self-reproduction had boiled down to the point that it could be recognized as a fundamental computational procedure. The existence of self-reproducing computations was seen to be a consequence of a fixed-point theorem similar to that given in 7.3.

Example 5 from McCarthy & Talcott[1980]: A simple self-reproducing program in LISP is given by

```
*  ((LAMBDA (X)  (LIST X (LIST (QUOTE QUOTE) X)))
   (QUOTE
    (LAMBDA (X)  (LIST X (LIST (QUOTE QUOTE) X)))) ))
 ==>  ((LAMBDA (X)  (LIST X (LIST (QUOTE QUOTE) X)))
      (QUOTE
       (LAMBDA (X)  (LIST X (LIST (QUOTE QUOTE) X)))) )).
```

A much more sophisticated and dangerous self-reproducing program—termed a "Trojan horse" by Thompson and a "virus" by the popular press—is described in

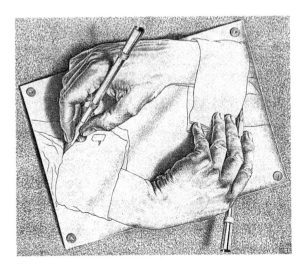

Figure 4.7. Drawing hands. M.C. Escher, 1948. ©1989 M.C. Escher Heirs, Cordon Art-Baarn-Holland.

Reflections on Trusting Trust, Ken Thompson's Turing Award Lecture, Thompson[1984]. The analogy between life and computation is used to discuss theories of the origin of life (life = reproduction + metabolism) in chapters 4 and 5 of *Infinite in All Directions*, Dyson[1988]. The analogy between distributed processes as seen in social systems and distributed computation is explored from a mathematical point of view in Stark & Kotin[1989]. The June 1986 issue of the *Communications of the ACM* is devoted to the famous internet worm—check it out.

Finally, there is Kurt Gödel's famous incompleteness theorem. It shows that any computational system, which is at least as complicated as arithmetic, can never be completely described axiomatically. Thus, in the formalist sense, no such system can ever be completely understood. Since Gödel's theorem applies to predicate logic with LISP's axioms, it clearly limits the scope of program verification. The theorem's proof is probably the most beautiful fixed-point argument in existence. For more on the relevance of this theorem, see Kolata[1982] and Rogers[1967, page 96].

Exercises

1. McCarthy[1963, page 34] gives a definition of consciousness. How could LISP be modified (at least in theory) to achieve consciousness (in McCarthy's sense)?

2. A "working mathematician" is considered to be a pretty far-out creature. But, is he/she far-out enough to ever encounter the consequence of Gödel's theorem? The answer deals with Ackermann-like functions and is given in Kolata[1982]. Find it.

3. Write a LISP form which under successive evaluation generates a series of distinct forms. In other words, $form_0$ is a form for which

$$form_0 ==> form_1 ==> \ldots ==> form_m ==> form_{m+1} ==> \ldots$$

are distinct forms generated by (EVAL $form_m$) ==> $form_{m+1}$.

4.6 Additional reading

For more on strange recursions, see Conway[1972]. Fixed-point computing is discussed from a rather sophisticated point of view in Manna & Viullemini[1972]. An important criticism of the VonNeumann/assignment-oriented style of computing, as opposed to the functional style, is given by John Backus in his Turing Award speech. In Backus[1978], a functional style and an algebra of programs is described. Glassner, Hankin & Till[1984] and Henderson[1980] give a thorough development of functional programming. Finally, for some fantastic and Nobel-Prize-winning short stories with themes straight out of the dreams of an overworked student of this chapter, see Borges [1962]. Gregory Chaitin's work [1987] develops consequences of Gödel's theorem and related undecidability phenomena in LISP. Chaitin's work ends with speculation on biological evaluation as a computational process and its computational complexity.

5

LISP Functions for Powerful Programming

This chapter introduces major topics not developed in chapters 1 or 3. The first section covers the basics of debugging. The second presents applicative operators (APPLY, FUNCALL, MAPCAR, and MAPLIST) and their programming style. Section three deals with macros—functions which perform syntactic preprocessing on unevaluated arguments. Four discusses structures and vectors—objects not described in 3.1. As an application, structures are used to represent chemical atoms and fragments of molecules which are linked into desired molecules by a macro called BOND. In section five, function closures are explained. Finally, the last section introduces functions which surgically reconfigure pointers in data structures.

5.1 Debugging tools

Debugging tools have the effect of allowing the programmer to look into the detailed workings of a computation generated by their program. The debugging tools that we will examine include BREAK, BACKTRACE, STEP, TIME, and DRIBBLE.

When an error causes a computation to BREAK at a listener level other than the top level, locally bound variables can be directly evaluated and functions such as BACKTRACE make it possible to examine the steps which lead to the error. Even without a BREAK in a computation, the functions TRACE and STEP allow you to follow a computation forward from the step at which they are invoked. Explicit use of the BREAK function makes it possible to interrupt a computation at any point. After such an interruption, STEP, TRACE, or BACKTRACE can be used. If STEP, TRACE, or programmer experimentation create a large body of information that requires close examination, then DRIBBLE can be used to record (in a file) a segment of an interactive session.

5.1.1 The listener, access to local bindings, and BACKTRACE

By now, we've all seen an error cause the LISP listener to move to a deeper level (i.e., a level indicated by a prompt of the form 1>, 2>, etc.). When an error is encountered, the listener calls BREAK. This creates a temporary listener level in which the environment of the error is preserved along with the steps that lead to the error. At this point, local bindings can be examined by simply evaluating local variables, or BACKTRACE (or :b) can be used to trace back through the steps that lead to the error.

Example 1: In the following example, an error in a FACTORIAL computation moves the listener from its top level (indicated by *) to its first sublevel (indicated by 1>). While at level 1>, the local binding of N is examined and BACKTRACE is used to step back through the computation which led to the error.

```
*   (DEFUN FACTORIAL (N)
     (IF (EQ N 0) 1 (* N (FACTORAIL (1- N))))) )
    ==> FACTORIAL
*   (FACTORIAL 3)
    ERROR: UNDEFINED FUNCTION FACTORAIL
1> N
    ==> 3
1> (BACKTRACE)
    (BACKTRACE)
    (FACTORAIL (1- N))
    (* N (FACTORAIL (1- N)))
    (FACTORIAL 3)
    ==> NIL
```

In some LISPs :b is used in place of (BACKTRACE). Now move back to the top level.

```
*   N
    ERROR UNBOUND VARIABLE: N
```

Even though N may not be bound at the top level, it will have a (local) binding at the deeper levels of this computation. The fact that N is still bound to 3 tells us that the error occurred at or before the recursive call (which would have bound N to 2). The list of forms following (BACKTRACE) is the reverse of the computation:

$$(FACTORIAL\ 3)\ => \ ... \ => \ ... \ (BACKTRACE).$$

Thus, it includes the reverse of the computation that led to the error of FACTORI-AL. In the second step back, we see the error: ...IA... was transposed to ...AI... in the recursive term in the original definition.

While BACKTRACE was not really necessary in this case, it can be very helpful in debugging complex programs. If FACTORIAL had been defined by mutual recursion in terms of several other functions, then the misspelling might have occurred in any number of function definitions.

Computations may start to go wrong before an error is evident to the listener. To interrupt a computation in such a situation, the user may add a conditional call to the 0-ary function BREAK. When the computation strays enough to trigger the condition, (BREAK) is evaluated and the process is stopped and preserved in a lower level of the listener. In debugging a program in which a large number of functions are calling each other, it may be helpful to simply add a (BREAK) at the beginning of a few of the function bodies. Then, at each break, the programmer can examine bindings. (CONTINUE) restarts the computation after a break.

Example 2: The following program for FACTORIAL works in some implementations of LISP but causes a stack overflow error in others.

```
*   (DEFUN FACTORIAL (N)
     (IF (EQ N 0) 1 (* N (FACTORIAL (1- N))))) )
    ==> FACTORIAL
*   (FACTORIAL 3)
    ERROR: STACK OVERFLOW.
```

The error suggests that more than four calls to FACTORIAL are being made. To explore this possibility, we add a conditional call to BREAK. The condition for BREAK is (< N 0).

```
*   (DEFUN FACTORIAL (N)
     (IF   (< N 0)   (BREAK)
       (IF   (EQ N 0)   1   (* N (FACTORIAL (1- N))))) ))
*   (FACTORIAL 3)
    BREAK, ENTER (CONTINUE) TO CONTINUE
1> N
    ==> -1
```

This value for N indicates that (EQ N 0) evaluates to NIL for N=0 in this implementation of LISP. An experiment

```
1> (EQ 0 0)
    ==> NIL
```

confirms it. We have come up against the inconsistency of EQ when applied to numbers. The problem can be corrected by using (ZEROP N) or, better yet, (< N 1) in place of (EQ N 0).

The procedure for returning to the top level of the listener is implementation dependent. Enter ? for help from your implementation, or consult the manual.

5.1.2 STEP and TRACE

STEP causes all of the intermediate steps in the interpreter's evaluation of a
term to be displayed, as well as the bindings of local and global variables. In
terms of our computation notation

> form => intermediate₁ => ... => intermediateₖ
>   => value,

it is the intermediates that are displayed. In the case of forms which evaluate
properly, STEP can be used to keep the programmer in touch with the actual
details of a computation. In cases of improper evaluation, STEP provides an
easy and natural means of finding errors. STEP is invoked, for a given form, as

> (STEP form).

The user can control the resulting process from the terminal. For details on
controlling STEP in your implementation, enter ? after STEP has been invoked.

Example 3:   The first few steps in a computation of FACTORIAL can be
observed by evaluating the form within STEP.

```
*   (DEFUN FACTORIAL (N)
     (IF (EQUAL N 0) 1 (* N (FACTORIAL (1- N)))) )
    ==> FACTORIAL
*   (FACTORIAL 2.0)
    ERROR: STACK OVERFLOW
```

In this case, we probably do not want to use BACKTRACE because the computation doesn't end in an identifiable error. So, we'll try it again inside STEP.

```
*   (STEP (FACTORIAL 2.0))
    (FACTORIAL 2.0)
      2.0
        2.0=2.0
      (IF (EQUAL N 0) 1 (* N (FACTORIAL (1- N))))
        (EQUAL N 0)
          N
            N=2.0
          0
            0=0
          (EQUAL N 0)=NIL
        (* N (FACTORIAL (1- N)))

          . . .

          (EQUAL N 0)
            N
              N=0.0
            0
```

```
     0=0
     (EQUAL N 0)=NIL
        .  .  .
```

Eventually, we will see that the problem is a failure to exit because (EQUAL
0.0 0)= NIL. This may be considered an error in applying FACTORIAL to
an argument of the wrong type (i.e., not an integer) or a programming error
corrected by replacing the inappropriate exit clause by (ZEROP N) or (< N
1).

Several patterns surface in the steps of the preceding example. First, steps
corresponding to the evaluation of subforms are indented. Second, STEP breaks
each nonatomic form into subforms and steps through their evaluation, with
their values being expressed by an indented equation at the end:

```
(fun form1 form2)
 form1
 . . .
 form1=value1
 form2
 . . .
 form2=value2
 . . .
(fun form1 form2)=value.
```

Third, variables and constants (being atomic) are locally the most deeply
indented steps. Finally, when the main function is defined (DEFUN   fun
variable-list value-term) the value-term of the definition follows
the last subform.

```
(fun form1 form2)
 form1
 . . .
 form2
 . . .
value-term
 . . .
(form form1 form2)=value.
```

TRACE is similar to STEP in that it displays intermediate steps in the interpreter's evaluation of a form. However, TRACE is restricted to steps in which
certain user-specified functions are being applied. Intermediate steps in which
other functions are being applied are not displayed. Thus, tracing is more nar-
rowly focused in the way it explores a computation. TRACE is invoked by

```
(TRACE 1st-function-name ... kth-function-name).
```

All subsequent computations will be traced until the process is terminated by

(UNTRACE 1st-function-name ... kth-function-name).

Example 4: The previous problems with FACTORIAL can be located by tracing EQUAL.

```
*   (TRACE EQUAL FACTORIAL)
    ==> T
*   (TRACE
    ==> (EQUAL FACTORIAL)
*   (FACTORIAL 2.0)
    Entering FACTORIAL with arguments: (2.0)
    Entering EQUAL with arguments: (2.0 0)
    Exiting EQUAL with value: NIL
     Entering FACTORIAL with arguments: (1.0)
     Entering EQUAL with arguments: (1.0 0)
     Exiting EQUAL with value: NIL
      Entering FACTORIAL with arguments (0.0)
      Entering EQUAL with arguments: (0.0 0)
      Exiting EQUAL with the value: NIL
     .  .  .
*   (UNTRACE EQUAL FACTORIAL)
    ==> (EQUAL FACTORIAL)
```

In debugging interesting programs, TRACE may produce hundreds of lines of output. DRIBBLE may be used to save this in an external file.

5.1.3 Other tools for debugging

TIME and DRIBBLE can be useful in certain circumstances. The evaluation of the *form*

(TIME *form*)

causes the form's evaluation to be timed. The time required for evaluation is displayed at the terminal just before the value of the form is returned. The effect of

(DRIBBLE *path-to-file*)

is to open the indicated file and record the following exchange between the user and the listener into that file. The variable *path-to-file* is string valued. The process is ended, and the file is closed by (DRIBBLE).

Example 5: Suppose we are doing a government study on the efficiency of various Fibonacci algorithms. The simplest definition of FIBONACCI uses a simple form of recursion which a timing experiment shows to be inefficient. A record of these timing experiments will be created by DRIBBLE.

```
*   (DRIBBLE "FIBONACCI.TIMES")
    ==> T
*   (DEFUN FIBONACCI1 (N)
     (IF (< N 2) 1
      (+ (FIBONACCI1 (1- N)) (FIBONACCI1 (- N 2)))) )
    ==> FIBONACCI
*   (TIME (FIBONACCI1 10))
    Elapsed time: 0.00.20
    ==> 89
*   (TIME (FIBONACCI1 20))
    Elapsed time: 0.28.70
    ==> 10946
```

The times shown here are for GCLISP on an AT&T6300; for TI's Explorer
LISP, they were 718,910 and 88,400,173 microseconds. The TI statistics are
mentioned here for later comparison with compiled code. In both cases, the
experiment was actually performed without DRIBBLE. Another definition of
FIBONACCI may have different time requirements.

```
*   (DEFUN FIBONACCI2
     (N &OPTIONAL (I 1) (FI- 1) (FI 1))
                                   ;I increases from 1 to N
     (IF          ;FI- and FI are values at I-1 and I.
      (EQUAL N I)
      FI
      (FIBONACCI2 N (1+ I) FI (+ FI- FI)) ))
    ==> FIBONACCI2
*   (TIME (FIBONACCI2 10))
    Elapsed time: 0.00.00
    ==> 89
*   (TIME (FIBONACCI2 20))
    Elapsed time: 0.00.10
    ==> 10946
*   (DRIBBLE)
    ==> NIL
```

The TI Explorer® times for the last two were 69,225 and 164,484 microseconds. With respect to evaluation time, FIBONACCI2 is substantially better than
FIBONACCI. Further improvements can be achieved by compiling the functions
(see 6.3).

By using DRIBBLE, we have created a file containing the details of the
experiment which may be included in our final report to the government. This
file may be printed without leaving LISP by using the appropriate LISP function
to submit the print command to the operating system. In GCLISP, the DOS
operator would be used in (DOS "PRINT file-name").

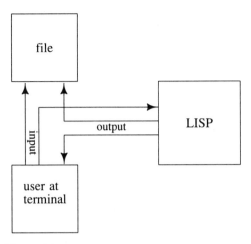

Figure 5.1. DRIBBLE's input and output streams.

Exercises

1. Use STEP to examine the computation of (SET (READ) (PRINT (*
4 5))) N.

2. We have tried to define a function ATOML which returns a list of atoms
occurring (at any level) in its argument.

```
*   (DEFUN ATOML (S)
    (IF (ATOM S) S
      (APPEND (ATOML (CAR S)) (ATOML (CDR S))) ))
    ==> ATOML
*   (ATOML '((1 A) (2 B)))
    ==> NIL
```

We wanted the value (1 A NIL 2 B) . Use one of the debugging tools
to find the error in ATOML's definition.

3. Bright idea! Define APPEND by

```
*   (DEFUN APPEND (L1 L2) (SUBST L2 NIL L1))
    ==> APPEND
*   (APPEND '(0 1 2 3 4) '(5 6 7 8 9))
    ==> (0 1 2 3 4 5 6 7 8 9)
*   (APPEND '(0 1 (2 3 4)) '(5 6 7 8 9))
    ==> ???
```

Use (IF (NULL L1) (BREAK) (SUBST ...)) in the definition of
APPEND to find the error in the program.

4. Get an idea of the average time required for the garbage collector. In GCLISP, the form (GC) triggers a run of the garbage collector. Thus, something of the form

```
(/ (LIST (GC) (GC) (GC) (GC) (GC) (GC) (GC) (GC) (GC) (GC))
   10 )
```

would evaluate to the average time. Perform another experiment to demonstrate the degree of variation in times for (GC).

5.1.4 Application: debugging a LISP text (optional)

The examples in this text were developed in a variety of LISP implementations, but in the end all of the examples (except those involving closures) were verified in GCLISP® . The following examples illustrate the functions used to extract and verify the examples as well as the verification process.

DETAILS:

The manuscript for this text was created in an AT&T PC6300® (an IBM® compatible), using Lotus Manuscript® (for text processing), Lotus Freelance® (for graphics), and GCLISP® (a popular version of Common LISP for IBM®-style PCs). Since (1) the manuscript and Common LISP existed in the same machine and (2) LISP is a nonnumerical language, it was possible to have a machine-verifcation of the text's examples as a part of the final editing. Unfortunately, it was subsequently formatted by hand.

Example 6: First, a formatted text file, say,

```
C:\MS\LISP\FIVE.DOC ,
```

is stripped of everything except LISP expressions occurring in the context

```
*    LISP-expression .
```

In other words, if READ-CHAR found an asterisk followed by two blanks, then the next value of READ (i.e., a LISP expression) was saved in a second file, say,

```
C:\LISP\LISPLIB\VERIFY\FIVE.LSP .
```

Second, this file was visually checked and edited by hand. Third, the function VERIFY initiates DRIBBLE to a third output file, say,

```
C:\LISP\LISPLIB\VERIFY\FIVE ,
```

then reads and evaluates the lisp expressions from the second file. This results in a complete record of code evaluation of the third file. STRIP is defined in the file C:LISP\LISPLIB\STRIP.LSP which follows.

```
(TERPRI)(TERPRI)
(PRINC "Enter input-stream: ")
(SETQ INPUT-STREAM (OPEN (READ)))
(TERPRI)
(PRINC "Enter output-file: ")
(SETQ OUTPUT-FILE (READ))
(TERPRI)(TERPRI)

(SETQ ASTERISK 42)
(SETQ BLANK 32)
(SETQ M1 "When the evaluation process is interrupted
 by an error, enter (S) to continue.")

(DEFUN EXAMPLE? (CHAR)
; This function READ-CHARs through the INPUT-STREAM
; until it finds * BLANK BLANK , then it stops and
; returns T.
 (AND
  (= CHAR ASTERISK)
  (= (READ-CHAR INPUT-STREAM) BLANK)
  (= (READ-CHAR INPUT-STREAM) BLANK) ))

(DEFUN NEXT-FORM ()
; After each T from EXAMPLE?, NEXT-FORM returns the
; next value of (READ INPUT-STREAM). This value is
; a LISP-expression being evaluated in an example.
 (DO
  ((CHAR 0 (READ-CHAR INPUT-STREAM)))
  ((EXAMPLE? CHAR)
   (READ INPUT-STREAM) )))

(DEFUN S ( )
; S used DO to apply (NEXT-FORM) repeatedly and to
; PRINT the LISP-expressions returned. DRIBBLE will
; record every PRINTed LISP-expression in the
; OUTPUT-FILE.
 (DO
  ((FORM NIL (PRINT (NEXT-FORM)))) ))

(DEFUN STRIP ( )
; STRIP opens DRIBBLE to OUTPUT-FILE, then calls S.
 (TERPRI)
 (PRINC M1)      ;M1 is a message defined in line 10.
```

```
(TERPRI)
(DRIBBLE OUTPUT-FILE)
(S) )
```

Due to the large number of times that READ-CHAR must be called, the recursive version of these functions may cause a STACK-OVERFLOW. Consequently, these functions were programmed iteratively using DO. The use of this file is illustrated by the following.

```
*   (LOAD "LISPLIB\STRIP")
ENTER INPUT-STREAM: "c:\ms\lisp\five.doc"
ENTER OUTPUT-FILE: "c:\lisp\lisplib\verify\five.lsp"
# (PATHNAME "C:LISPLIB\STRIP.LSP")


*   (STRIP)

When the evaluation process is interrupted by an
error, enter (S) to continue.
(DEFUN FACTORIAL (N) (IF (EQ N 0) ...)))
(FACTORIAL 3)
N
(DEFUN FACTORIAL (N) (IF (< N 0) ...)))
 .  .  .    .
```

After all of the LISP forms used in examples have been stripped of the surrounding text, the output file is closed.

```
*   (DRIBBLE)
==> NIL.
```

Example 7: The stripped LISP forms are read from the input file, printed in the output file, evaluated, and their values printed in the output file by VERIFY. The file C:\lisp\lisplib\verify.lsp follows.

```
(TERPRI)(TERPRI)
(PRINC "Enter INPUT-STREAM: ")
(SETQ INPUT-STREAM (OPEN (READ)))(TERPRI)
(PRINC "Enter OUTPUT-FILE: ")
(SETQ OUTPUT-FILE (READ))(TERPRI)
(TERPRI)(TERPRI)

(DEFUN V ( )
 (SETQ FORM (READ INPUT-STREAM))(TERPRI)
 (PRINC "* ")(PRIN1 FORM)(TERPRI)
 (PRINC "   ==> ")(PRIN1 (EVAL FORM))(TERPRI)
 (V) )
```

```
(DEFUN VERIFY ( )
 (DRIBBLE OUTPUT-FILE)
 (PRINC "DRIBBLE is open to: ") (PRINC OUTPUT-FILE)
 (TERPRI)
 (PRINC "Close DRIBBLE and INPUT-STREAM at end of
  session.")
 (TERPRI)
 (V)  )

(PRINC "Type (VERIFY) to begin verification, (V) to
 continue after an error.) (TERPRI) (TERPRI)
```

A sample of the verification of this chapter's stripped LISP code follows.

```
*   (LOAD "LISPLIB\VERIFY")
;Reading file: C:LISP\LISPLIB\VERIFY.LSP
```
Enter INPUT-STREAM:"c:\lisp\lisplib\verify\five.lsp"
Enter OUTPUT-FILE:"c:\lisp\lisplib\verify\five"

Type (VERIFY) to begin verification, (V) to continue
after an error.
 # (PATHNAME "C:LISP\LISPLIB\VERIFY.LSP")

```
*   (VERIFY)

*   (DEFUN FACTORIAL (N) (IF (EQ N 0) ...))
```
==> FACTORIAL

```
*   (FACTORIAL 3)
```
ERROR UNDEFINED FUNCTION: FACTORIAL

```
1> (V)

*   N
 .  .  .

*   (DRIBBLE)
```
==> NIL

The bold lines are output from VERIFY or the LOADing operation.

5.2 Applicative operators

In chapter three's section on self-processing, we met APPLY and MAPCAR.
These functions, together with MAPLIST, FUNCALL, and others, are known

as *applicative operators* because of their similarity to APPLY. All of the operators take a function argument followed by data arguments.

5.2.1 APPLY, FUNCALL, MAPCAR, and MAPLIST

The functions listed in the title are built into all LISPs. Their syntax and semantics are defined as follows. The value of

(APPLY *k-arg-function list-of-k-arguments*)

is *function*⟨*argument*$_1$...*argument*$_k$⟩. A sibling of APPLY is FUNCALL.

(FUNCALL *k-arg-function arg*$_1$ ... *arg*$_k$)

returns the same value as (APPLY *k-arg-function* (LIST *arg*$_1$...*arg*$_k$)). MAPCAR is an iterated version of APPLY.

(MAPCAR *k-arg-function arg-list*$_1$ ... *arg-list*$_k$)

returns a list of values, *k-arg-function*⟨a$_1$,...,a$_k$⟩, where each a$_i$ is an element of *arg-list*$_i$. MAPLIST is similar to MAPCAR. The value of

(MAPLIST *k-arg-function arg-list*$_1$ ... *arg-list*$_k$)

is a list of values, *k-arg-function*⟨cd$_1$, . . . , cd$_k$⟩, where each cd$_j$ is a CD..DR of the *arg-list*$_j$;. The MAPping operations involve multiple applications of their function argument. MAPping functions apply their function arguments serially (i.e., the environments accumulate effects). All applicative operators can apply functions presented to them as data. However, the function argument may not be a macro or a special form.

Example 8: The following evaluations illustrate how applicative operators are applied to k (k $\geq$ 0) lists of arguments and the variety of the functions that they can handle.

```
*   (FUNCALL 'CONS 2 5)
    ==> (2 . 5)
*   (APPLY 'CONS '(2 5))
    ==> (2 . 5)
*   (APPLY (FUNCTION CONS) '(2 5))
    ==> (2 . 5)
*   (FUNCALL #'CONS 2 5)
    ==> (2 . 5)
*   (APPLY #'CONS '(2 5))
    ==> (2 . 5)
```

The use of 'CONS illustrates FUNCALL and APPLY handling functions presented in the way that we usually present data. The use of (FUNCTION CONS)

and its abbreviation #'CONS illustrate that FUNCALL and APPLY handle functions presented as function objects (as opposed to data objects). The error in the
following experiment indicates that FUNCALL and APPLY evaluate their first
argument as if it were data.

```
*   (APPLY CONS '(2 5))
    ERROR: UNBOUND VARIABLE CONS
*   (APPLY 'READ NIL) 3.14159
    ==> 3.14159
```

Function arguments may be computed data.

```
*   (SETQ DATA-FUN-LIST
      (LIST '(LAMBDA (V) ( )) '(LAMBDA (V) (CAR V))) )
    ==> ((LAMBDA (V) ( )) (LAMBDA (V) (CAR V)))
*   (FUNCALL (CADR DATA-FUN-LIST) (LIST 4 5))
    ==> 4
```

An important operation in programming with MAPCAR and MAPLIST is the use
of APPLY 'APPEND. A first experience with this operation follows.

```
*   (APPLY 'APPEND
    '(( ) (1) ( ) (2 3) ( ) ( ) (4 5 6) (7 8 9 0)))
    ==> (1 2 3 4 5 6 7 8 9 0)
```

These experiments illustrate how function arguments must be presented to APPLY
and the relation between APPLY and FUNCALL. The basics of MAPCAR and
MAPLIST are seen in the following.

```
*   (MAPCAR 'CONS '(1 2 3) '(A B))
    ==> ((1 . A) (2 . B))
*   (MAPLIST 'CONS '(1 2 3) '(A B))
    ==> (((1 2 3) A B) ((2 3) B))
*   (MAPCAR 'LIST '(1 2 3 4) '(A B) '(7 8 9))
    ==> ((1 A 7) (2 B 8))
*   (SETQ APP (FUNCTION APPEND))
    ==> #<COMPILED FUNCTION ...>
*   (MAPLIST APP '(1 2 3 4) '(A B))
    ==> ((1 2 3 4 A B) (2 3 4 B))
```

The last evaluation illustrates again that the function arguments for applicative
functions may have data-like bindings to their names. The following shows that
these MAPping functions apply their function argument in serial environments.

```
*   (SETQ C 0)
    ==> 0
*   (MAPCAR '(LAMBDA (X) (SETQ C (+ X C))) '(1 2 0 1))
    ==> (1 3 3 4)
```

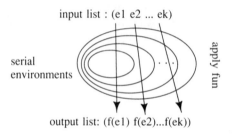

input list : (e1 e2 ... ek)

serial
environments

apply fun

output list: (f(e1) f(e2)...f(ek))

Figure 5.2. Nested environments in an evaluation of (MAPCAR fun input-list).

A NOTE ON HANDLING FUNCTION ARGUMENTS:

We have used quoted functions as arguments to applicative
operators to emphasize that this is a case of LISP processing
LISP-code as data. All of these examples work for GCLISP 1.01.
However, users of other dialects may encounter problems when
QUOTE or ' is used on function arguments rather than FUNCTION
or #' . In particular, function arguments with free variables bound
in the applicative operator's environment may not be bound unless
a closure FUNCTION or #' is used (this is a result of the fact that
FUNCTION and #' create closures).

Recursive functions can frequently be defined *iteratively* in terms of MAPping
functions. This approach allows a more incremental approach to program development than is possible with recursive definitions.

Example 9: The recursive function REDUCE (defined in exercise 10 of 2.2)
removes duplicate elements from a list. For example,

```
*    (REDUCE '(M I S S I P P I))
     ==> (M S P I)  .
```

A nonrecursive program for REDUCE can be developed incrementally as follows.

```
*    ((LAMBDA (TAIL)
       (IF                                    ;Elements that
        (MEMBER (CAR TAIL) (CDR TAIL))  ;come again later
        NIL                                   ;are forgotten,
        (LIST (CAR TAIL)) ))           ;all others are saved.
     '(S S I P P I) )
     ==> NIL
*    (MAPLIST
     '(LAMBDA (TAIL)
       (IF (MEMBER (CAR TAIL) (CDR TAIL)) NIL
        (LIST (CAR TAIL)) )
```

```
    '(M I S S I P P I) )
    ==> ((M) NIL NIL (S) NIL NIL (P) (I))
*   (APPLY 'APPEND '((M) NIL NIL (S) NIL NIL (P) (I)))
    ==> (M S P I)
```

Notice the use of APPLY 'APPEND and its relation to the operations of the MAPping functions. We put these pieces together to get REDUCE.

```
*   (DEFUN REDUCE (LST)
      (APPLY 'APPEND
       (MAPLIST
        '(LAMBDA (TAIL)
          (IF (MEMBER (CAR TAIL)(CDR TAIL))
            NIL (LIST(CAR TAIL))) )
        LST )))
*   (REDUCE '(M I S S I P P I))
    ==> (M S P I)
```

This REDUCE is not the same as the one built into common LISP.

ANOTHER TRICK:

> In addition to (APPLY 'APPEND (MAP... , there are times when
> we would like to use (APPLY 'OR (MAP... or (APPLY 'AND
> (MAP... . However, OR and AND are macros, so APPLY cannot
> apply them. In this case, the same result is achieved by using
> (EVAL (CONS 'OR (MAP... or (EVAL (CONS 'AND (MAP....

5.2.2 Application: symbolic differentiation

HISTORY:

> "I spent the summer of 1958 at the IBM Information Research
> Department at the invitation of Nathaniel Rochester and chose
> differentiating algebraic expressions as a sample problem. It lead to
> the following innovations ...

> The MAPLIST [now MAPCAR] function ... was obviously wanted
> for differentiating sums of arbitrarily many terms, and ... products.

> To use functions as arguments, one needs a notation for functions,
> and it seemed natural to use the lambda-notation of Church[1941].

> The recursive definition of differentiation made no provision for
> [the] erasure of abandoned list structure. No solution was apparent
> at the time, but the idea of complicating the elegant definition of
> differentiation with [the inclusion of instructions for] explicit
> erasure was unattractive. [This wrinkle eventually lead to the
> invention of automatically invoked garbage collection.]

Needless to say, the point of the exercise was not the differentiation program itself, several of which had already been written, but rather clarification of the operations involved in symbolic computing."

McCarthy[1981]

Example 10:   In the following, we have an approximation to McCarthy's original symbolic differentiation algorithm. Given a term

$$Z = term <var_1, ..., var_k>,$$

and a specified variable var_i, the algorithm will return the derivative

$$\frac{\partial}{\partial var_i} Z.$$

The terms are defined by (1) constants = numbers; (2) variables = symbols; (3) composite terms: given $term_1$, $term_2$, ..., the following are terms:

(+ $term_1$, $term_2$, ...),
(- $term_1$, $term_2$),
(* $term_1$, $term_2$, ...), and
(/ $term_1$, $term_2$) .

Thus, the terms include polynomials and rational functions.

```
*   (DEFUN DIFF (TERM VAR)
      "The derivative of TERM w.r.t. VAR is computed."
      (COND
        ((ATOM TERM) ;If TERM is atomic, then it is either
         (IF (EQ TERM VAR) 1 0) )       ; V, variable, or a
        ((OR                 ;constant. The derivative of
          (EQ (CAR TERM) '+)                        ;a sum
          (EQ (CAR TERM) '-) )       ;or difference is the
         (CONS                 ;sum or difference of the
          (CAR TERM)                          ;derivatives
          (DIFF-LIST (CDR TERM) VAR) ))  of subterms. The
        ((EQ (CAR TERM) '*)    ;derivative of a product is
         (CONS                 ;is the sum of the products
          '+                 ;of a differentiated subterm
          (DIFF* (CDR TERM) VAR) ))    ;times the others.
        ((EQ (CAR TERM) '/) ;The derivative of a quotient
         (LIST '/                 ;is the quotient of the
          (CONS '-                  ;difference between
           (DIFF* (CDR TERM) VAR) ) ;two products and the
          (CONS '*                 ;square of the denominator.
           (APPEND (CDDR TERM) (CDDR TERM)) ))))
      ))
```

```
==> DIFF
```

```
*   (DEFUN DIFF-LIST (TERM-LIST VAR)
    "Given a list of terms, the list of derivatives
    of those terms with respect to VAR is returned."
    (MAPCAR
    '(LAMBDA (TRM) (DIFF TRM VAR))
    TERM-LIST ))
    ==> DIFF-LIST.
```

```
*   (DEFUN DIFF* (TERM-LIST VAR)
    "Differentiation for products. If (t1 t2...tk) is
    the value TERM-LIST, then
    ((* dt1 t2...tk)(* t1 dt2...tk)...(...dtk))
    is the value returned."
    (MAPLIST
    '(LAMBDA (TL1)
       (CONS '*
        (MAPLIST
        '(LAMBDA (TL2)
          (IF
           (EQUAL (LENGTH TL1) (LENGTH TL2))
           (DIFF (CAR TL1) VAR)
           (CAR TL2) ))
         TERM-LIST )))
      TERM-LIST ))
    ==> DIFF*
```

We can now test DIFF on some elementary problems from first semester calculus.

```
*   (DIFF 'X 'X)
    ==> 1
*   (DIFF 'X 'Y)
    ==> 0
*   (DIFF '(* X Y) 'Y)
    ==> (+ (* 0 Y) (* X 1))
```

This last calculation is of

$$\frac{\partial Z}{\partial X}, \quad \text{where} \quad Z = \frac{X+Y}{X-Y}.$$

```
*   (DIFF '(/ (+ X Y) (- X Y)) 'X)
    ==> (/ (- (* (+ 1 0) (- X 1)) (* (+ X 1) (- 1 0)))
        (* (- X 1) (- X 1)) ).
```

Clearly, some work remains to be done. At the very least, we need to add an algebraic simplifier which will perform algebraic evaluations such as

```
(+ term 0)  => term,   (* 0 term)  => 0,
(comm-oper term 0) => (comm-oper term 0),
(* term 1)  => term,   (* 1 term)  => term,
(- term 0)  => term,   (/ term 1)  => term,   etc.,
```

where *comm-oper* is either + or *. It would also help if DIFF could be defined so that the terms didn't have to be quoted (see the introduction to 5.3).

Exercises

Use applicative operators to write nonrecursive programs for the functions defined in the exercises 2,4,5,6.

1. Use (MAPLIST 'PRINT '(1 2 3 4 5 6 7 8 9 0)) to explore the workings of MAPLIST.

2. EVLIS evaluates the members of a given list of forms. For example,

   ```
   *   (EVLIS
       '((SETQ C (READ))(SETQ C (1+ C))(PRINT C)) ) 9
       10
       ==> (9 10 10)
   ```

   Program EVLIS using MAPCAR.

3. Program the MEMBER function (without options such as :TEST) using MAPLIST. The (EVAL (CONS 'OR (MAP... trick may be useful.

4. The SUBSET function, given two lists, returns T if the members of the first are members of the second. Use SUBSET to define EQUAL-SETS.

5. The INTERSECT function, given two lists, returns their intersection. Also program the UNION function.

6. The CARTESIAN-PRODUCT function, given two lists, returns the list of all possible pairs of elements from the first list and the second list. For example,

   ```
   *   (CARTESIAN-PRODUCT '(A B C) (LIST 1 2 3 4))
       ==> ((A 1) (A 2) (A 3) (A 4) (B 1) ... (C 4))
   ```

7. *Parallel LISP*. The serial environment property of the MAPping operators is not necessary for any of the preceding functions. Each one would work just as well if the environments for the application of the function argument were concurrent (i.e., started out the same). Does this imply that

these function programs could be efficiently implemented on a parallel computer? Explain.

8. Define MAX, the function which computes the maximum of a list of numbers in the nonrecursive style developed here. To what extent is MAX less concurrent than the previous functions?

9. Implement DIFF and evaluate (DIFF (/ (* 3 X Y) (- X Y))).

10. Extend DIFF to cover the cases

$$term = \exp(term), = \ln(term), = trig(term),$$

where *trig* is a trig function.

11. The APPLY'APPEND operation allows MAPping functions to make decisions. Explain.

12. Read the discussion of computer algebra given in Pavelle, et.al.[1981].

5.3   Macros

A *macro* is a procedure which takes unevaluated expressions, often LISP terms or functions, as its arguments. These unevaluated expressions are then processed syntactically to produce a new term (or terms) known as an *expansion*. Finally, the expansion is evaluated, and that value is returned as the value of the macro. This process is appropriate for procedures which take a short user-friendly expression and expand it into several lines of more technical code before evaluation or which check their arguments' syntax before evaluation.

TYPICAL APPLICATION:

The computational features of a macro could be used to improve DIFF. If DIFF had been defined as a macro, then it would not be necessary to quote the arguments.

```
*   (DIFF (* X Y) Y)
    ==> (+ (* 0 Y) (* X 1)).
```

5.3.1   The basic idea

In Common LISP, the syntax for creating a macro is

(*DEFMACRO macro−name variable−list body*),

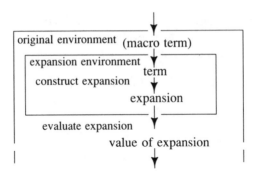

Figure 5.3. Macro environments.

where the body is an implicit PROGN. Like DEFUN, the value returned is the *macro-name*. The value of the last form in the *body* is the expansion. The value of the expansion is then the value of the macro.

The macro input-expansion-evaluation process is illustrated above. The outer box represents the environment in which the macro was called, while the inner box represents the environment created by the macro's call. The expansion is created in the inner environment, but it is evaluated in the outer environment.

Example 11:   The basic mechanisms of macros in Common LISP are illustrated by the following.

```
*   (DEFMACRO M1 (X) (PRINT X))
    ==> M1
*   (M1 (LIST 1 2 3))
    (LIST 1 2 3)
    ==> (1 2 3).
```

X is bound to the unevaluated expression (LIST 1 2 3). (PRINT X) is evaluated (in this expansion environment), and the value (LIST 1 2 3) of (PRINT X) becomes the expansion. Finally, the expansion is evaluated (in the original environment) and that value is returned.

```
*   (DEFMACRO M2 (X) (PRINT X) (CONS '+ (CDR X)))
    ==> M2
*   (M2 (LIST 1 2 3))
    (LIST 1 2 3)
    ==> 6
```

Again, X is bound to the expression (LIST 1 2 3) and printed. In this environment, the last expression of the body is evaluated to get the expansion (+ 1 2 3). Finally, the expansion is evaluated and the value returned.

In Common LISP, there is a mechanism for evaluating forms within the scope of a QUOTE. This mechanism uses the *back-quote*—denoted '—in place of QUOTE and the comma—denoted , —for its inverse. This can shorten and simplify the construction of expansions. For example,

```
*    (SETQ X '(1 2 3))
     ==> (1 2 3)
*    '(EQUAL (CAR X) (CADR X))
     ==> (EQUAL (CAR X) (CADR X))
*    '(EQUAL ,(CAR X) ,(CADR X))
     ==> (EQUAL 1 2) .
```

In the last form only, (CAR X) and (CADR X) are evaluated. General rule: in situations where you would normally use QUOTE but need to use , for an evaluation within the scope of the QUOTE, replace QUOTE by the back-quote then use the comma within the scope of the back-quote.

Example 12:   A macro similar to M2 can be defined using back-quote.

```
*    (DEFMACRO M3 (X) (PRINT X)
     '(APPLY '+ (QUOTE ,(CDR X))) )
     ==> M3
*    (M3 (LIST 1 2 3))
     (LIST 1 2 3)
     ==> 6
```

Since X is bound to (LIST 1 2 3) and ,(CDR X) is evaluated, the expansion is (APPLY '+ (QUOTE (1 2 3))).

IMPLEMENTATION:

> Some LISPs handle these expressions by a macro which rewrites the LISP expression. The rewriting moves QUOTE and the back-quote from the outside of a term into its subexpressions,
>
> ```
>               '(EQUAL (CAR X) (CADR X)) =>
> (LIST 'EQUAL (LIST 'CAR 'X) (LIST 'CADR 'X))
> ```
>
> However, when this macro encounters a back-quote immediately followed by a comma, both are annihilated,
>
> ```
>               '(EQUAL ,(CAR X) ,(CADR X))
> => (LIST 'EQUAL (CAR X) (CADR X)) => ....
> ```
>
> After this sort of rewriting, the results are evaluated as usual.

5.3.2   Application: INFIX and EVAL&TIME

Example 13:   Terms such as (9 + (8 * u)) in which binary operators appear
between arguments are infix terms. INFIX is a macro which treats two-argument
terms as infix terms and converts them to prefix before evaluation.

To easily separate the bad coding ideas from the good, we do some experimentation in the macro's inner environment. We must create the appropriate
expansion. For example, the argument (9 + U) should expand into (+ 9 U).

```
*   (DEFMACRO INFIX (I) (BREAK))
    ==> INFIX
*   (INFIX (9 + U))
    BREAK: enter (CONTINUE) to continue
1> I
    ==> (9 + U)
1> (APPLY
    (CADR I)
    (LIST (CAR I) (CADDR I)) )
    ERROR: FUNCTION + APPLIED TO NONNUMERIC ARGUMENT U
    . . .
1> '(APPLY
    (QUOTE ,(CADR I))
    (LIST ,(CAR I) ,(CADDR I)) )
    ==> (APPLY (QUOTE +) (LIST 9 U))
1> (SETQ U 2)
    ==> 2
1> (APPLY (QUOTE +) (LIST 9 U))
    ==> 11
    . . .
```

Eventually, we figure out how to do it and write the final definition.

```
*   (DEFMACRO INFIX (I)
    (COND
    ((ATOM I) I)                        ;atomic terms
    ((= (LENGTH I) 3)              ;terms with two arguments
    '(APPLY
    (QUOTE ,(CADR I))
```

```
        (LIST (INFIX ,(CAR I)) (INFIX ,(CADDR I))) ))
    ((= (LENGTH I) 2)              ;terms with one argument
     '(APPLY
       (QUOTE ,(CAR I))
       (LIST (INFIX ,(CADR I))) ))
    (T I) ))                                     ;other terms.
==> INFIX

*   (SETQ U 2)
    ==> 2
*   (INFIX (9 + (U * 8)))
    ==> 25
```

The next evaluation shows that infix notation works just as well when applied to nonnumerical expressions—notice the position of CONS.

```
*   (INFIX
     (CAR (1 CONS (LIST 2))) )
    ==> 1
```

Example 14:   EVAL&TIME is a front-end to the listener which automatically times the evaluation of forms.

```
*   (DEFMACRO EVAL&TIME (IN)
     (TERPRI)
     (EVAL '(TIME ,IN))
     (PRINC "Value: ")
     (PRIN1 (EVAL IN))
     (TERPRI)(TERPRI)
     (PRINC "LITHP ith lithening: ")
     (EVAL&TIME (READ) )
    ==> EVAL&TIME

    (EVAL&TIME NIL)
    Elapsed time: 0:00.0
    Value: NIL

    LITHP ith lithening: (DEFUN FIBONACCI (N) ...)
    Elapsed time: 0:00.0
    Value: FIBONACCI

    LITHP ith lithening: (FIBONACCI 20)
    Elapsed time: 0:29.70
    Value: 10946
```

Since there is no exit clause in EVAL&TIME, it continues until it redefines itself to be nonrecursive, or until an error occurs.

```
LITHP ith lithening: (DEFUN EVAL&TIME ( ) ( ))
Elapsed time: 0:00.0
Value: EVAL&TIME

LITHP ith lithening: (EVAL&TIME)
Elapsed time: 0:00.0
Value: NIL
```
*

PROGRAMMING NOTE:

Macros DEFMACRO, DEFUN, DEFSTRUCT, DO, SETF, STEP, TIME, TRACE, UNTRACE, etc., cannot be used by applicative operators.

Exercises

1. A classical use of macros is to give a binary function an extension which can take any number of arguments. For example, the usual binary +, *, OR, and AND can be extended to the n-ary versions that we have in LISP. Extend CONS so that

   ```
   *    (CONS form1 form2 form3 ...)
   =>   (CONS form1 (CONS form2 (CONS form3 ...)))
   =>   ....
   ```

2. Write a front-end to the listener which turns your EVAL LISP into an EVALQUOTE LISP. An EVALQUOTE LISP takes two expressions, the first is a LISP function and the second is a list of terms which are not evaluated. Thus, for example, the inputs CAR and ((LIST 1 2 3)) would return the value LIST.

3. Write a macro which tests its input for having the syntax of a LISP term, then returns either a list containing the input (if the syntax was correct) or the empty list (if the input was not a LISP term).

4. The recursive macro problem. Suppose we program FACTORIAL as a macro:

   ```
   *    (DEFMACRO FACTORIAL (N)
          (IF (ZEROP N) 1 (* N ((FACTORIAL (1- N))))) )
   ==> FACTORIAL.
   ```

   Our first attempt to use FACTORIAL returns an error. What is wrong? How do we write FACTORIAL as a macro? What is a general approach to creating recursion in a macro?

5.4   Structures, vectors, and arrays

Basic data types were introduced in section 3.1. The remaining important data types are structures, vectors, and arrays. Structures are arbitrarily complex data structures similar to the records of PASCAL. The ATOM predicate will return T for objects of each of these types, indicating that they are not of type CONS.

5.4.1   Vectors and arrays

An array of given dimensions and initial values can be created by MAKE-ARRAY:

```
(MAKE-ARRAY dimensions
 :INITIAL-CONTENTS initial-values ).
```

The value of *dimensions* is a list of integers, the value of *initial-values* is a list of (...lists of...) values. The last two arguments are optional and are used only if the new array is initialized. Of course, this generalizes to create arrays of more than two dimensions. A vector can be created by VECTOR

```
(VECTOR e1 ... em ).
```

Since a vector is just a one-dimensional array, an equivalent creation is possible using MAKE-ARRAY. Vector and array entries are retrieved by AREF. The entry in a two-dimensional *array* with coordinates i, j is the value of

```
(AREF array (i j)).
```

After the array is created, these entries can be set to the value of a given form by SETF and AREF:

```
(SETF (AREF array (i j)) value-form).
```

SETF's strange behavior is explained in 5.7. The rank (i.e., number of dimensions) of an array is the value of

```
(ARRAY-RANK array),
```

and the list of dimensions by

```
(ARRAY-DIMENSION array axis-number).
```

Example 15:   Basic vector functions such as DOT-PRODUCT⟨v1,v2⟩ and VECTOR-SUM⟨v1,v2⟩ are programmed using the preceding functions.

```
*    (SETQ A (VECTOR 1 2 3 4))
     ==> #<VECTOR T 4 1234:5678>
*    (SETQ B (VECTOR 2 3 4 5))
     ==> #<VECTOR T 4 1234:6000>
*    (DEFUN D-P
      (V1 V2 I SUM DIM)    ;DIM is the vector's dimension
```

```
  (IF            ;I is our position in the vector, and
  (< I DIM)                                ;D-P   recurs
  (D-P V1 V2 (1+ I)
   (+ SUM (* (AREF V1 I) (AREF V2 I))) DIM )
  SUM ))                                   ;until I=D-P.
==> D-P
* (DEFUN DOT-PRODUCT (V1 V2)
  (LET
   ((D1(ARRAY-DIMENSIONS V1))(D2(ARRAY-DIMENSIONS V2)))
   (IF
    (EQUAL D1 D2)
    (D-P V1 V2 0 0 D1)
    NIL )))
==> DOT-PRODUCT
```

CODE PATCH:

In many LISPs, LENGTH may be used in place of
ARRAY-DIMENSION when dealing with vectors.

```
*  (DOT-PRODUCT A B)
   ==> 40
*  (DEFUN S (V1 V2 I DIM VSUM)
   (SETF                              ;Now we set
    (AREF VSUM I)              ;the ith element of VSUM
    (+ (AREF V1 I) (AREF V2 I)) )     ;to V1<I>+V2<I>.
   (IF
    (< I (1- DIM))
    (S V1 V2 (1+ I) DIM VSUM)
    VSUM) )
   ==> S
*  (DEFUN VECTOR-SUM (V1 V2)
   (LET
    ((D1 (ARRAY-DIMENSIONS V1))
     (D2 (ARRAY-DIMENSIONS V2)) )
    (IF (EQUAL D1 D2) (S V1 V2 0 D1 (MAKE-ARRAY 4))
    NIL )))
   ==> VECTOR-SUM
*  (SETQ C (VECTOR-SUM A B))
   ==> #<VECTOR T 5 1111:2222>
*  (AREF C 2)
   ==> 7
```

Exercises

1. Write the function VECTOR-NORM which, given a vector, returns the length of the vector.

2. Write and test MATRIX-MULTIPLY—a matrix multiplication function.

3. LISP keeps a record of symbols in OBLISP, OBARRAY, *OBARRAY*, or a package (see Steele[1984], chapter 11). If your system uses an array, then READ your name, and use AREF to investigate the contents of OBARRAY or *OBARRAY* until your name is found. What happens to the system if you SETQ the array to NIL? OBLIST, OBARRAY, *OBARRAY*, or the package catalog symbols under their PRINT name and are used to keep track of existing symbols and to prevent the construction of more than one symbol with a given print name.

5.4.2 Structures

A good approach to computing on complex objects is to treat them as cohesive individuals (rather than as a set of simpler components) and to simplify their manipulation by providing appropriate new functions which operate at their level (rather than at the level of their components). This isolates the user from unnecessary and inappropriate details. The internal structure of these complex objects should not detract from their manipulation. DEFSTRUCT makes this process easy.

EXAMPLE:

This approach was not used in the way that FORTRAN handles arrays. Consequently, such simple expressions as

```
READ(W)
X = I
UNTIL (NEWX .EQ. X) DO
  X = NEWX
  NEWX = I+(X*W)
ENDDO
```

are not supported for array-valued (variables) W, X, NEWX, and (constants) I. The advocated approach allows this sort of computing.

The power of abstraction is illustrated in the way in which we process visual images. The image of this page that you see now is not processed as an array of values reported by the rods and cones in your retna (as a FORTRAN-programmed mind would process it),

but as a single high-level entity. The high-level entity that contains
this page is an example of data abstraction. The operations that your
mind performs on it can be interpreted as examples of procedural
abstraction.

A *structure* is a user-defined data type whose elements (i.e., individual data
items) have user-specified internal structure. Associated with this data type are
new *data constructor* and *data selector* functions. A structure and its functions
are created by DEFSTRUCT according to the syntax

```
(DEFSTRUCT structure-name
  (field-name₁ default-value₁)
    . . .
  (field-nameₖ default-valueₖ) ).
```

The effect is to create the new data type = *structure-name*, with
structure-name-functions:

```
(structure-name-P object)
(structure-name-field-nameⱼ object)
(MAKE-structure-name)
(COPY-structure-name object)
```

for the given *structure-name* and each *field-name*ⱼ. The first function
is a predicate to test whether or not the object is of the type indicated by
structure-name. The second function is a selector. It returns the value
of the indicated field in an object of the appropriate type. The last two are
constructors which make and copy objects of the type = *structure-name*.

Example 16:   Suppose that we plan to be working with organic molecules. A
data type for organic molecules is created as follows.

```
*   (DEFSTRUCT MOLECULE
      (C (C)) (H (H)) (O (O)) (N (N)) (BONDS (BONDS)) )
    ==> MOLECULE ,
```

where C, H, O, N, and BONDS are fields whose values represent atoms and
bonds between atoms. Initial values for these fields are given by 0-ary functions
of the same name. For example,

```
*   (DEFUN C ( )
      (TERPRI) (PRINC "ENTER CARBON ATOMS: ") (COLLECT) )
    ==> C .
```

Then, follow the same pattern in creating functions H, O, N, and BONDS.
The function COLLECT is defined in section 2.5.

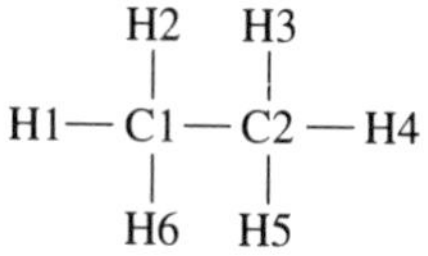

```
        H2    H3
        |     |
H1 — C1 — C2 — H4
        |     |
        H6    H5
```

Figure 5.4. A chemists' diagram for ethane.

```
*   (DEFUN H ( ) ...)
    ==> H ,
*   (DEFUN O ( ) ...)
    ==> O ,
*   (DEFUN N ( ) ...)
    ==> N ,
*   (DEFUN BONDS ( ) ...)
    ==> BONDS
```

Besides creating a data type named MOLECULE, this application of DEFSTRUCT creates the functions

```
MOLECULE-P, MAKE-MOLECULE, COPY-MOLECULE,
MOLECULE-C, ..., MOLECULE-N, and MOLECULE-BONDS.
```

Until MAKE-MOLECULE is applied, there are no objects of type MOLECULE.

Example 17: After creating the data type and the functions as above, a representation of ethane can be created as an object of type MOLECULE.

```
*   (SETQ ETHANE (MAKE-MOLECULE))
    ENTER CARBON ATOMS: C1 C2 NIL
    ENTER HYDROGEN ATOMS: H1 H2 H3 H4 H5 H6 NIL
    ENTER OXYGEN ATOMS: NIL
    ENTER NITROGEN ATOMS: NIL
    ENTER BONDS: (C1 H1) (C1 H2) (C1 H6) (C2 H3)
      (C2 H4) (C2 H5) (C1 C2) NIL
    ==> #<MOLECULE 621C:57B3>
```

The evaluation of (MAKE-MOLECULE) displays each of the "ENTER...ATOMS:" prompts. The user's response to each prompt includes the delimiter "...NIL" with the atoms or bonds being given in between. These atoms or bonds are recorded in the object being created as the initial values of the corresponding fields. The value returned by (MAKE-MOLECULE) is the unmemorable #<MOLECULE...>. Finally, this is bound to the descriptive symbol ETHANE by SETQ. We now have a data structure in the type MOLECULE which represents ethane.

Example 18: Now, we can experiment with the new functions and object.

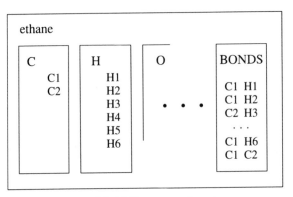

Figure 5.5. LISP structure for ethane.

```
*   (MOLECULE-P ETHANE)
    ==> T
*   (MOLECULE-P '(C1 C2 H1 H2 H3 H4 H5 H6))
    ==> NIL
```

MOLECULE-P tests objects for being of type MOLECULE. These experiments show us that there is a difference between MOLECULEs and LISTs.

```
*   (CAR ETHANE)
    ERROR: ATTEMPT TO TAKE CAR OF AN ATOM
*   (ATOM ETHANE)
    ==> T
```

Yes, all structures are atoms (i.e., not of type CONS).

```
*   (MOLECULE-H ETHANE)
    ==> (H1 H2 H3 H4 H5 H6)
*   (MOLECULE-BONDS ETHANE)
    ==> ((C1 H1)...(C1 C2))
```

Since ETHANE is a MOLECULE, these functions return the values of its fields.

CAR and CDR are the selector functions and CONS is the constructor function for objects of type CONS. Structures are created to have their own selector and constructor functions. In the preceding case, the selectors MOLECULE-H, ..., MOLECULE-BONDS are the analogs of CAR and CDR, and MAKE-MOLECULE the analog of CONS.

5.4.3   Application: working with organic molecules

Example 19:   It's Friday afternoon, so let's change our ETHANE into ETHANOL.

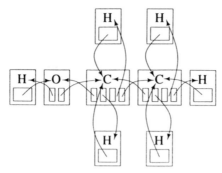

Figure 5.6. Ethanol represented as a group of linked structures.

```
*    (SETQ ETHANOL (COPY-MOLECULE ETHANE))
==> #<MOLECULE 631C:59BB>
```

CODE COMMENTS:

Some LISPs do not have COPY-MOLECULE. In this example, we
could get by without COPY-MOLECULE by using
(SETF ETHANOL (MAKE-MOLECULE))
and then re-enter the description of ethane. This is tedious, but, by
creating two distinct objects, we can change the second object into
ETHANOL without changing the original ETHANE. Another
approach, since there is a fixed set of field names, is to define
COPY-MOLECULE.

In Steele[1984, 19.1], another approach to field initialization is
described. DEFSTRUCT makes each field name into a key word
which can be used to identify initial values. For example,
```
*    (SETQ H2
     (MAKE-MOLECULE
      :C () :H '(H1 H2) :O '() :N ()
      :BONDS '((H1 H2)) )).
```

But, just calling it ethanol doesn't make it so.

```
*    (EQUAL ETHANE ETHANOL)
     ==> T
*    (EQ ETHANE ETHANOL)
     ==> NIL
```

This experiment shows that we have two distinct copies of the same structure.

```
*    (MOLECULE-O ETHANOL)
     ==> NIL
```

The oxygen that distinguishes ethanol from ethane is not present. We can use SETF to add an oxygen, break the bond between C1 and B1, and replace it by new bonds to the oxygen. In other words, H1–C1 will become H1–O–C1.

```
*   (SETF (MOLECULE-O ETHANOL) '(O1))    ;oxygen is added
    ==> (O1)
*   (SETF (MOLECULE-BONDS ETHANOL)    ;BONDS to ETHANOL,
       (APPEND '((H1 O1) (O1 C1)) ;add a H1--O1--C1 bond,
        (CDR (MOLECULE-BONDS ETHANOL)) ))    ;remove H1-C1
    ==> ((H1 O1) (O1 C1) (C1 H2)...(C1 C2))
*   (MOLECULE-O ETHANOL)
    ==> (O1)
*   (EQUAL ETHANE ETHANOL)
    ==> NIL.
```

Success! [Reckless conclusion.] Now, the weekend can begin.

DEFSTRUCT MAINTAINS GENERIC FUNCTIONS:

Functions which have a meaning for objects of any data type are said to be *generic*. EQUAL is a generic function. The preceding example shows us that DEFSTRUCT has had an effect on EQUAL in that it has extended the definition of EQUAL to cover objects of type MOLECULE. This can't be said for CONS eventhough CONS is defined for objects of type MOLECULE. The difference is that EQUAL must know how to look inside of two molecules to determine if they have the same structure, while CONS doesn't need to know anything about MOLECULEs.

A more sophisticated approach to building molecules would be to begin by representing atoms as structures. Then, build up molecules by operations linking groups of structures representing atoms or fragments of molecules.

Example 20: We will create the hydrogen molecule H_2 by bonding two structures representing hydrogen atoms. Although we will not use it yet, the structure for carbon atoms is defined to establish the pattern involved.

```
*   (DEFSTRUCT H (B1 ( )))
    ==> H
*   (DEFSTRUCT C (B1 ( )) (B2 ( )) (B3 ( )) (B4 ( )))
    ==> C
*   (DEFSTRUCT O (B1 ( )) (B2 ( )))
    ==> O
*   (SETQ H (MAKE-H))
    ==> #<H 7229:3103>
*   (SETF (H-B1 H) (MAKE-H))
    ==> #<H 7229:311A>
```

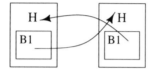

Figure 5.7. The hydrogen molecule, H_2, as a linked group

Now, we have two hydrogens. H is the first, the second appears in the BOND field of the first. It remains to put the first into the BOND field of the second. The second hydrogen is the value of (H-B1 H).

```
*   (SETF (H-B1 (H-B1 H)) H)
                            ;bind the first H to the second
    ==> #<H 7229:3103>.
```

Verify that we have two hydrogens which are bonded to each other as follows.

```
*   H
    ==> #<H 7229:3103>
*   (H-B1 H)
    ==> #<H 7229:311A>
*   (EQ H (H-B1 (H-B1 H)))
    ==> T
```

IMPLEMENTATION VARIATIONS IN SETF:

SETQ and SETF generally describe the values that they bind, and a SETF that returns #<H 7229:3103> is not being very descriptive. In most implementations, SETF will try to describe the structure it binds. Unfortunately, many of the description mechanisms are not able to handle recursively linked structures without producing an unbounded output. If your SETF has this defect, then call it from within another function—e.g.,

```
(NULL (SETF (H-B1 (H-B1 H)) H)).
```

The representation of H_2 just created is not a structure itself. It is a linked group of structures. A *linked group* is a set of structures such that the field values for every structure in the group are either NIL or another structure in the group. If the value of the Bi field of structure X is the structure Y, then X *is linked to* Y *at* Bi. The group has a *free bond* at field Bi in X if the value of that field is NIL. In the current example, X is linked to Y and Y is linked to X.

Example 21: The tedious process of bonding structures into linked groups can be wrapped up in a macro called BOND. The BOND macro is designed to link given structures S1 and S2 at fields F1 and F2.

```
*    (DEFMACRO BOND (MAKE1 FIELD1 MAKE2 FIELD2)
       (SETQ STRUCTURE1 (EVAL MAKE1))
                              ;make & bind 1st structure,
       (SETQ STRUCTURE2 (EVAL MAKE2))
                              ;make & bind 2nd structure,
       (EVAL '(SETF (,FIELD1 STRUCTURE1) STRUCTURE2))
             ;STRUCTURE1 linked to STRUCTURE2 in FIELD1,
       (EVAL '(SETF (,FIELD2 STRUCTURE2) STRUCTURE1))
             ;STRUCTURE2 linked to STRUCTURE1 in FIELD2,
       'STRUCTURE1
             ;the first structure is the value returned.
     )
     ==> BOND
```

Actually, MAKE1 and MAKE2 are forms which create structures or linked groups. Thus, in order to make only one copy of each structure, they can be evaluated only once. Since the structures may have to be used more than once, we'll bind the creations to the symbols STRUCTURE1 and STRUCTURE2. Further, FIELD1 and FIELD2 are field selector functions rather than just fields.

BOND is tested by using it to make linked groups representing water (H_2O) and the oxygen molecule (O_2).

```
*    (SETQ WATER                       ;To make water,
       (BOND
        (BOND                          ;make O and H
         (MAKE-O)                           ;and
         O-B2                          ;bond them,
         (MAKE-H)
         H-B1 )                             ;then
        O-B1                           ;make another H
        (MAKE-H)                       ;and bond it.
        H-B1) )
     ==> WATER.

*    WATER
     ==> <O 7C04:A3BB>
*    (O-B1 WATER)
     ==> <H 260E:345C>
*    (O-B2 WATER)
     ==> <H 7C04:9658>
*    (H-B1 (O-B1 WATER))
     ==> <O 7C04:A3BB>.
```

Yes! We've really got water. Now, for the oxygen:

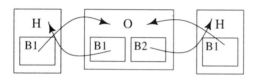

Figure 5.8. Water as created by BOND.

```
*   (SETQ O2
      (BOND
        (BOND (MAKE-O) O-B1 (SETQ TEMP (MAKE-O)) O-B1)
    ;two oxygens are created and linked in the B1 fields.
     ;The second is saved in TEMP, the first is returned.
        O-B2    ;The B2 field of the first oxygen is bound
        TEMP                        ;to the second oxygen,
        O-B2                            ;and vice versa.
      ))
    ==> #<O 7C06:7865>
*   (O-B1 O2)
    ==> #<O 7C06:9899>
*   (O-B2 O2)
    ==> #<O 7C06:9899>
*   (O-B1 (O-B1 O2))
    ==> #<O 7C06:7865> .
```

The preceding examples illustrate simple computational methods for building and representing molecules. Since our only empirical constraint was having the correct number of bonding positions for each atom, we have not been solving problems in chemistry. In order to do that, some intelligence will have to be added. This could be done by extending linked groups to structures representing molecules and their fragments and adding data on bond-type and polarity. Then, operations (corresponding to simple chemical reactions) could be defined on these new structures. Such operations might represent families of reactions such as $RCH_2OH + K_2Cr_2O_7 \Longrightarrow RCHO$, where R is a variable.

Exercises

1. The value of HYDROXYL as defined below is a linked group, molecule, structure of type O, or other (pick one).

    ```
    *   (SETQ HYDROXYL
          (BOND (MAKE-O) O-B1 (MAKE-H) H-B1))
    ```

2. Verify that the following H2O does / does not represent water.

```
*   (SETQ H2O (BOND HYDROXYL O-B2 (MAKE-H) H-B1))
```

3. Use BOND to construct METHANE (CH$_4$) as a linked group.

4. Use BOND to create ETHANOL as a linked group of structures (as shown in the first illustration in this section).

5. Generic functions. The bond values of an oxygen are obtained by using O-B1 and O-B2, the bond values of a hydrogen are obtained with the help of H-B1, those of carbon ... . The action of these functions can be unified and generalized by BOND-VALUES which applies to all structures representing an atom and returns the value of all bonds for that atom— regardless of which atom it is given. One approach would be

```
*   (DEFUN BOND-VALUES (ATOM)
     (COND
       ((H-P ATOM) (LIST (H-B1 ATOM)))
       ((O-P ATOM) (LIST (O-B1 ATOM) (O-B2 ATOM)))
       ((C-P ATOM) (LIST (C-B1 ATOM) (C-B2 ATOM)
        (C-B3 ATOM) (C-B4 ATOM) ))
       ((N-P ATOM) ...
        ... )) .
```

A better approach (described in Winston&Horn[1988], Chapter 14) is to use DEFMETHOD to extend BOND-VALUES' definition as new types of atoms are introduced. An approximate idea of DEFMETHOD follows:

```
*      (DEFMETHOD BOND-VALUES (H-P ATOM)
        (LIST (H-B1 ATOM)) )
*      (DEFMETHOD BOND-VALUES (O-P ATOM)
        (LIST (O-B1 ATOM) (O-B2 ATOM)) ) .
```

Then later, as other atoms begin to be used,

```
*      (DEFMETHOD BOND-VALUES (N-P ATOM)
        (LIST (N-B1 ATOM) (N-B2 ATOM) (N-B3 ATOM)) )
*      (DEFMETHOD BOND-VALUES (C-P ATOM)
        (LIST (C-B1 ATOM) (C-B2 ATOM) (C-B3 ATOM)
        (C-B4 ATOM) )) ,
```

etc. Write DEFMETHOD as a macro which creates (in the first case) or enlarges (in all subsequent cases) the existing definition of BOND-VALUES (or whichever function name is given) to contain new test and value terms. Use DEFMETHOD to build BOND-VALUES.

This style of programming leads into object-oriented programming—for a development of this important subject see Keene[1989].

5.5   Function closures

A *closure* is a function with its own private environment. The environment's
bindings may not be used or modified—except by the associated function. The
environment is used to define the values of free variables (i.e., variables in the
function body which are not in the variable list). Closures are created from
LAMBDA-*functions* by FUNCTION or CLOSURE. The value returned by

>   (FUNCTION (LAMBDA *variable-list body*))

or

>   (CLOSURE *variable-list body*)

is a closure in which the function's free variables are given values from the
environment in which FUNCTION or CLOSURE were used to create the function.
Without the closure-creating mechanism, free variables are given values from
the environment in which the function is applied.

If a variable is bound in both the public environment and the private environment of a closure, then the closure function can only access the binding in
its environment. In this situation, the closure's environment is said to shadow
the public environment.

PROGRAMMING NOTE:

(FUNCTION arg) may be abbreviated #'arg .   Closures may
be named by DEFUN, LABELS, SETQ, etc.

Some LISPs may use CLOSURE in place of FUNCTION.
Consequently, the following examples using FUNCTION may not
work in GCLISP.

5.5.1   Creating and using closures

Example 22:   We'll define a function ADDER which given a number—say 3
—returns a new function which remembers the given number. This new function
is the closure ADD3.

```
*   (DEFUN ADDER (X) (FUNCTION (LAMBDA (Y) (+ X Y))))
    ==> ADDER
*   (SETQ ADD3 (ADDER 3))
    ==> #<LEXICAL CLOSURE ...>
*   (MAPCAR ADD3 '(1 2 3 4 5))
    ==> (4 5 6 7 8)
*   X
    ERROR: UNBOUND VARIABLE X
```

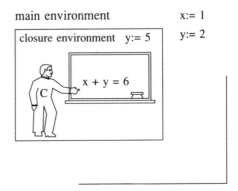

Figure 5.9. A closure's private environment.

X is a free variable in (LAMBDA (Y) (+ X Y)). The environment which determines the value of X is the one in effect after ADDER is applied to 3. ADD3 is a closure whose environment binds X to 3. FUNCTION may be abbreviated #', so ADDER could have been defined.

```
*   (DEFUN ADDER (X) #'(LAMBDA (Y) (+ X Y)))
    ==> ADDER
```

The preceding is from Steele[1984]. In LISPs using CLOSURE, we would have the following.

```
*   (SETQ X 3)
    ==> 3
*   (SETQ ADDER
      (CLOSURE '(X) '(LAMBDA (Y) (+ X Y))) )
    ==> #<CLOSURE ...>
*   (SETQ X 0)
    ==> 0
*   (APPLY ADDER '(10))
    ==> 13
```

Example 23: A closure may use SETQ to modify its private environment. Here, we will construct a counter function which is immune to outside manipulation. The first assignment is present just to show that previously existing values are, in this case, invisible to FUNCTION.

```
*   (SETQ C 3.14159)
    ==> 3.14159
*   (DEFUN PREPRECOUNT (C)
      (FUNCTION (LAMBDA ( ) (SETQ C (1+ C)))) )
    ==> PREPRECOUNT
*   (SETQ PRECOUNT (PREPRECOUNT 0))
```

```
   ==>  #<LEXICAL CLOSURE ...>
*   C
   ==>  3.14159
*   (FUNCALL PRECOUNT)
   ==>  1
*   (DEFUN COUNT ( )  (FUNCALL PRECOUNT))
   ==>  COUNT
*   (COUNT)
   ==>  2
*   (SETQ C 0)
   ==>  0
*   (COUNT)
   ==>  3.
```

(Franz LISP responds differently in the fourth and fifth entry. Kyoto Common LISP warns that the sixth entry is redefining COUNT.)

These experiments illustrate that external evaluation and assignments to C have no relation to the C maintained in PRECOUNT (the closure) and COUNT (PRECOUNT's boss). Further, the second DEFUN shows one way by which closures can become functions recognized by the listener.

HISTORY:

"In all innocence, James R. Slagle programmed the following LISP function and complained that it didn't work.

```
testr(x,p,f,u) =
if p(x) then f(x)
else if atom(x) then u()
else testr(cdr(x),p,f,
   lambda.testr(car(x),p,f,u))
```

The object of the function is to find a subexpression of x satisfying $p(x$ and return $f(x)$. If the search is unsuccessful, then ...u()...is returned. The difficulty was that when an inner recursion occurred, the value of x in $car(x)$ wanted was the outer value, but the inner value was actually used. In modern terminology, lexical scoping was wanted, and dynamic scoping was obtained.

I must confess that I regarded this difficulty as just a bug and expressed confidence that Steve Russell would soon fix it. He [and Patrick Fischer] did fix it, but by inventing the so-called FUNARG device that took the lexical environment along with the functional environment. Similar difficulties showed up later in ALGOL 60, and [this] turned out to be one of the more comprehensive solutions to the problem. ..[For] a history of the problem, the interested reader is referred to Moses[1970]... ." McCarthy[1981].

5.5.2   Examples: COMPOSE and Currying CONS

Example 24:   COMPOSE is a function which takes two unary functions—say f
and g—as arguments and returns a new function which is their composition—
f∘g. COMPOSE will be a closure in which the private environment defines the
bindings of f and g.

```
*   (DEFUN COMPOSE (F &OPTIONAL(G F))
      (FUNCTION (LAMBDA (X) (FUNCALL F (FUNCALL G X)))))
    ==> COMPOSE
```

This simple composition operation works only on unary functions. The variable
G is declared to be optional so that COMPOSE itself can be treated as a unary
function (exercise 1).

```
*   (SETQ PRE-CADR
      (COMPOSE (FUNCTION CAR) (FUNCTION CDR)) )
    ==> #<LEXICAL CLOSURE ...>
*   (DEFUN CADR* (L)       ;We define a version of CADR.
      (IF (OR (ATOM L) (ATOM (CDR L))) NIL
        (FUNCALL PRE-CADR L) ))
    ==> CADR*
*   (CADR* '(1 2 3))
    ==> 2
*   (SETQ A2 (COMPOSE '1+ '1+))
    ==> #<LEXICAL CLOSURE ...>
*   (DEFUN ADD2 (N) (FUNCALL A2 N))
    ==> ADD2
*   (ADD2 25)
    ==> 27
```

The process of converting k-ary functions ($1<k$) into unary functions is known
as *Currying* (after Haskel Curry). Certain models of functional computation have
the interesting and important property that all functions are unary. For example,
a Curried + is a function which given 13 returns another function p13, which
given 8 returns 21 or p21. Since this implies that 21=p21, the business of all
functions having unary interpretations is related to there being only one type of
object — data=procedures.

Example 25:   Here a closure is used to Curry CONS.

```
*   (DEFUN CONS-1 (X)
      (SETQ       ;A data-like binding attaches a closure
      CONS-2            ;of CONS with this X environment
      (CLOSURE '(X) '(LAMBDA (Y) (CONS X Y))) )       ;to
      'CONS-2 )                            ;CONS-2.
    ==> CONS-1
```

```
*   (DEFUN CONS-2 (Y)     ;A function binding to  CONS-2.
    (FUNCALL CONS-2 Y) )
    ==> CONS-2
```

The definition of CONS-2 creates a function which is bound as a function to CONS-2. A subsequent application of CONS-1 creates a closure which is bound as data to CONS-2. The function binding and the data binding may coexist on CONS-2 because they are stored differently.

```
*   (CONS-1 2345)             ;After the first argument, the
    ==> CONS-2                ;next function is returned.
*   (CONS-2 6789)
    ==> (2345 . 6789)
```

The final value is the same as would have been returned by CONS. Thus, we have Curried CONS into CONS-1 and CONS-2. The preceding construction works in GCLISP®, the following construction works in all other Common LISPs.

```
*   (DEFUN CONS-1 (X)
    (SETQ CONS-2 (FUNCTION (LAMBDA (Y) (CONS X Y))))
    'CONS-2 )
    ==> CONS-1
```

Exercises

1. Create COMPOSE then perform the following experiment. Explain what is happening.

    ```
    *   (SETQ WHAT? (COMPOSE 'COMPOSE' COMPOSE))
    ==> #<LEXICAL CLOSURE ...>
    *   (FUNCALL (FUNCALL WHAT? '1+) 0)
    ==> 4
    (==> 3 in GCLISP+®)
    ```

2. Why does the ability to Curry any function imply that there is no distinction between data and procedures?

3. McCarthy[1963] discusses ambiguous functions such as AMBIG Given arg_1 and arg_2,

    ```
    *   (AMBIG arg₁ arg₂)
    ==> ???
    ```

    nondeterministically returns either the value of arg_1 or arg_2. Using closures, define AMBIG. Computationally interesting features of AMBIG are discussed on pages 48 and 63 of this paper by McCarthy. Use AMBIG to define a unary function LESS which, given a nonnegative integer k, returns as its value a relatively unpredictable integer between 0 and k.

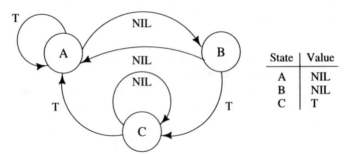

Figure 5.10. A finite-state automaton.

4. The finite-state automaton illustrated here has an output function AUTO-MATON which can be defined as a closure. If AUTOMATON has not been previously used, then it should behave as follows:

```
*    (AUTOMATON NIL)
     ==> NIL                    ;as it enters state=A
*    (AUTOMATON NIL)
     ==> NIL                    ;as it enters state=B
*    (AUTOMATON T)
     ==> T                      ;as it enters state=C
*    (AUTOMATON T)
     ==> NIL                    ;as it returns to state=A.
```

The input to AUTOMATON determined the arrow to be traversed. The value of the state reached by the transition is the value returned.

5. Mortal functions. Write a version of a factorial which self-destructs after exactly 10 top-level applications (no matter how large the arguments for the 10 applications). Use a closure to hide the LIFE-TIME-REMAINING variable.

6. Strictly speaking CONS-1 is not exactly the Curried version of CONS. Explain.

5.6 COERCion

Many objects which are not of type CONS (e.g., strings, structures, symbols, and vectors) have internal structure. The function COERCE can be used to translate these objects from one type to another and to provide access to that structure by the mainstream of LISP. The syntax for this function is

(COERCE *object new-type*).

If the *object* is of type STRING and *new-type* is LIST, then a list of the characters in the string is returned (we denote this "*STRING* ⟶ *LIST*"). It may not be possible to translate between all types, but the following conversions are common:

> *character* ⟶ *symbol*,
> *integer* ⟶ *character*,
> *integer* ⟶ *floating –point*,
> *list* ⟶ *string*,
> *list* ⟶ *vector*,
> *string* ⟶ *list*,
> *string* ⟶ *vector*,
> *symbol* ⟶ *character*,
> *vector* ⟶ *list*,
> *vector* ⟶ *string*.

For more complete information, consult Steele[1984] or the manual for your implementation.

Example 26:   The following is from GCLISP®, Symbolics® Common LISP, TI® Explorer Common LISP, and Sun® Common LISP.

```
*   (COERCE "help" 'LIST)
    ==> (104 101 108 112)                              ;GCLISP
    ==> (#\H #\E #\L #\P)                         ;in TI's LISP
*   (COERCE (LIST 104 101 108 112) 'STRING)      ;GCLISP
*   (COERCE (LIST #\h #\e #\l #\p) 'STRING) ;in TI LISP
    ==> "help"
*   (SETQ V2 (COERCE (LIST 1 2 3 4 5 6) 'VECTOR))
    ==> #<VECTOR ...>
*   (AREF V2 2)
    ==> 3
*   (COERCE V2 'LIST)
    ==> (1 2 3 4 5 6)
```

With lists as the middle ground, we can use the constructors and selectors created by DEFSTRUCT on one hand and COERCE on the other to convert between arbitrary structures and strings, vectors, etc.

Exercises

1. EXPLODE expands a symbol into a list of (print names) of its characters, while IMPLODE does just the opposite.

    ```
    *   (EXPLODE BOMB)
        ==> (B O M B)
    ```

Program EXPLODE.

2. Use COERCE to extend < to symbols. Call the extension LEXICOGRAPHIC-
   ORDER.

   *   (LEXICOGRAPHIC-ORDER '(FRANKLIN NANSEN AMUNDSEN))
        ==> (AMUNDSEN FRANKLIN NANSEN)

3. Use COERCE, AREF, 1+, etc., to write a CODE and DECODE function
   of the following type.

   *   (CODE "I LOVE LUCY")
        ==> "J MPWF KVEZ"
   *   (DECODE "J MPWF KVEZ")
        ==> "I LOVE LUCY"

5.7   Surgical operations

Surgical operations are operations which move pointers directly in their
arguments—not just in copies of their arguments. Since a single pointer may
be a part of several objects, a surgical operation on one object may have an effect on others. Also, these operations may create objects which are not (strictly
speaking) s-expressions. The formal syntax of these functions follows the examples.

Example 27:   An endless "list" can be created by using RPLACD (for RePLAce
CDr) as follows.

```
*    (SETQ SEASONS '(SPRING SUMMER FALL WINTER))
     ==> (SPRING SUMMER FALL WINTER)
*    (SETQ AFTER-LABOR-DAY (CDDR SEASONS))
     ==> (FALL WINTER)
*    (RPLACD (LAST SEASONS) SEASONS)
     ==> (WINTER SPRING SUMMER FALL WINTER SPRING ...)
```

In the second operation, (LAST SEASONS) => (WINTER), the CDR pointer
of (WINTER) initially points to NIL; RPLACD moves this pointer from NIL
back to the head of SEASONS. The resulting circular structure is not, strictly
speaking, an s-expression. Consequently, it has the interesting property that it
looks like an infinite list to many LISP functions.

```
*    SEASONS
     ==> (SPRING SUMMER FALL WINTER SPRING SUMMER FALL
             WINTER ...)
*    (NTH 100 SEASONS)
     ==> SPRING
```

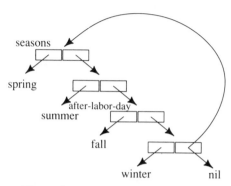

Figure 5.11. Changing SEASONS.

```
*   (EQUAL (CDDR (CDDR SEASONS)) SEASONS)
    ==> T
*   (LENGTH SEASONS)
    . . .
```

RPLACD has the dangerous property that it alters the original data structure rather than a copy of it. This can be seen in the following experiment.

```
*   AFTER-LABOR-DAY
    ==> (FALL WINTER SPRING SUMMER FALL WINTER ...)
```

How did AFTER-LABOR-DAY get changed when we didn't do anything to it?

Most LISP functions protect the user from such unexpected changes in variable bindings by copying arguments when necessary. However, the copying is costly—especially when space is severely limited and the garbage collector is thrashing around. Functions such as RPLACD, RPLACA, NCONC, and SETF can be used to perform list operations by surgically moving pointers in their original arguments rather than by copying and changing.

Example 28: In the following example, SETF replaces a part of the list (1 2 3) by 0.

```
*   (SETQ LIST (LIST 1 2 3))
    ==> (1 2 3)
*   (SETF (CADR LIST) 0)
    ==> 0
*   LIST
    ==> (1 0 3)
*   (SETF (CDDDR LIST) LIST)
    ==> (1 0 3 1 0 3 1 0 3 1 0 3 ...).
```

Their syntax and approximate semantics are as follows. Given a cons-cell and any other *object*,

    (RPLACA *cons-cell* *object*)

moves the car-pointer of the *cons-cell* to the *object*, while

    (RPLACD *cons-cell* *object*)

moves the cdr-pointer of *cons-cell* to the *object*. NCONC is like APPEND in that it joins two lists. Given *list₁* and *list₂*,

    (NCONC *list₁* *list₂*)

moves the pointer from the last element of *list₁* from NIL to the head of *list₂*. APPEND would have copied the first list before moving the last pointer to *list₂*.

Example 29:   APPEND and NCONC can be understood by experiments which compare them.

```
*   (SETQ LIST1 ' (1 3 5))
    ==> (1 3 5)
*   (SETQ LIST2 ' (7 9))
    ==> (7 9)
*   (SETQ LIST3 LIST1)
    ==> (1 3 5)
*   (APPEND LIST1 LIST2)
    ==> (1 3 5 7 9)
*   LIST1
    ==> (1 3 5)
*   (NCONC LIST1 LIST2)
    ==> (1 3 5 7 9)
*   LIST1
    ==> (1 3 5 7 9)
*   LIST3
    ==> (1 3 5 7 9)
```

APPEND copied LISP1 before attaching LIST2. Consequently, there were no aftereffects. NCONC simply moved the last pointer from LIST1 to the beginning of LIST2. LIST3 was changed by the operation performed on LIST1. Continuing, we see that now that LIST1 and LIST2 share the elements of LIST2, certain changes to LIST1 will be reflected in LIST2.

```
*   LIST2
    ==> (7 9)
*   (RPLACD (LAST LIST1) ' (11 13 15 17 19))
    ==> (1 3 5 7 9 11 13 15 17 19)
*   LIST2
    ==> (7 9 11 13 15 17 19)
```

Example 30:   List processing without CONS is possible in cases where the total number of (and size of) the elements involved does not increase. Suppose that we have a large list SOURCE of objects which we wish to sort into lists GOOD and BAD according to some TEST. If SOURCE is not empty, then the value returned by (TEST) is either GOOD or BAD—determining the destination of the first element of SOURCE. The following functions allow us to sort SOURCE into GOOD and BAD without a single CONS.

```
*    (SETQ SOURCE '(A B C D E F G))
     ==> (A B C D E F G)
*    (SETQ GOOD (SETQ BAD NIL))
     ==> NIL
```

Now, the crux of the business: we will define functions GOOD (and BAD) which move the first element of SOURCE to the list GOOD (respectively, BAD) without copying or using CONS.

```
*    (DEFUN GOOD ( )
       (SETQ TEMP SOURCE)     ;All of SOURCE saved in TEMP,
       (SETQ SOURCE (CDR SOURCE))
                       ;top element of SOURCE removed,
       (RPLACD TEMP GOOD) ;rest of TEMP replaced by GOOD,
       (SETQ GOOD TEMP) )     ;element from SOURCE to GOOD.
     ==> GOOD
*    (DEFUN BAD ( )
       (SETQ TEMP SOURCE)
       (SETQ SOURCE (CDR SOURCE))
       (RPLACD TEMP BAD)
       (SETQ BAD TEMP) )
     ==> BAD

*    (GOOD)
     ==> (A)
*    (BAD)
     ==> (B)
*    (GOOD)
     ==> (C A)
*    SOURCE
     ==> (D E F G)
*    GOOD
     ==> (C A)
*    BAD
     ==> (B)
```

Now, we can define our TEST and SORT functions.

```
*    (DEFUN TEST ( )
```

```
      (COND
       ((ATOM SOURCE) NIL)    ;Return NIL if SOURCE is NIL,
       ((MEMBER (CAR SOURCE) '(B A D)) (BAD))         ;move
       (T (GOOD)) ))                    ;object to BAD, move
      ==> TEST                          ;object to GOOD.
*     (DEFUN SORT ( )
       (IF
        (APPLY 'TEST NIL)               ;Sort top element, and
        (SORT)             ;continue sorting until SOURCE=( ).
        GOOD ))                         ;Return GOOD at end.
*     (SORT)
      ==> (G F E C)
*     SOURCE
      ==> NIL
*     BAD
      ==> (D B A)
```

The fact that list processing of this kind can be performed sans CONSing is not surprising when you realize that memory cells need only be moved—not added.

Exercises

1. How did AFTER-LABOR-DAY get changed when we didn't do anything to it?

2. In light of the last example, in what kind of processing is CONS really necessary?

3. Use surgical functions to create the convoluted structure ON-AND-ON.

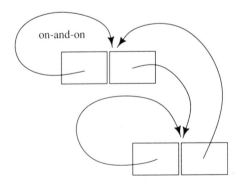

Figure 5.12. Convoluted structure, ON-AND-ON.

4. PUSH and POP are surgical functions which treat lists like stack memory.

```
*   (SETQ LIST '(S B C D E))
    ==> (S B C D E)
*   (POP LIST)
    ==> (B C D E)
*   LIST
    ==> (B C D E)
*   (PUSH 'A LIST)
    ==> (A B C D E)
*   LIST
    ==> (A B C D E).
```

Rephrase the last example (i.e., list processing without CONS) in terms of POP and PUSH in place of RPLACD.

5. Use SETF to define PUSH and POP.

6. LISP seemed like a very simple language after Chapter 2, but not it is complicated. Simplicity, elegance, and faithfulness to mathematical laws have, until recently, been the celebrated virtues of LISP. The loss of LISP's virginity, especially in the very large language defined in Steele[1984], is mourned in Allen[1987] and Brooks&Gabriel[1984]. Do these authors present a practical disadvantage to LISP's increased complexity and deviation from mathematical laws?

6

Interpreters: From Algebra to LISP

The interpretive style of computing is founded in abstract algebra and applied in implementations of computer languages from BASIC to LISP and PROLOG. This chapter begins with the abstract algebra of the subject, continues with interpreters for LISP, and concludes by mentioning the LISP compiler.

6.1   Algebras and interpreting: an abstract view

The idea of algebraic computing is rooted in the languages of mathematics. It is a syntactic style of computing based on repeatedly applying rules to rewrite terms and subterms—just as a student solves equations in high school algebra or differentiates a function in calculus. This syntactic style is known as *interpretive computing*. In this section, the basics of interpretive computing are developed. This includes object algebras, term algebras, the interpretations that connect the two, and the rewrite rules that define the interpreters.

Example 1:   Given the problem of evaluating the term $(x - 2) \cdot (y + 1) - (x - 2)$ for $x = 2$ and $y = 1$, a high school student, acting as an interpreter, will perform something like the following (essentially numerical) computation.

$$
\begin{array}{ll}
(x - 2)(y + 1) - (x - 2) & \text{substitute 2 for } x \\
\rightarrow (2 - 2)(y + 1) - (2 - 2) & \text{apply rule } (c - c) \rightarrow 0 \\
\rightarrow 0(y + 1) - 0 & \text{substitute 1 for } y \\
\rightarrow 0(1 + 1) - 0 & \text{apply } 1 + 1 \rightarrow 2 \\
\rightarrow 0 \cdot 2 - 0 & \text{apply rule } 0 \cdot c \rightarrow 0 \\
\rightarrow 0 - 0 & \text{appl } (c - c) \rightarrow 0 \\
\rightarrow 0 &
\end{array}
$$

If the instructions give no values but require simplification, then the rules and the computation will be term oriented.

$$(x - 2)(y + 1) - (x - 2) \qquad \text{apply rewrite rule } -t_1 \to (-1) \cdot t_1$$
$$\to (x - 2)(y + 1) + (-1)(x - 2) \qquad \text{apply rule } t_1 \cdot t_2 \to t_2 \cdot t_1$$
$$\to (x - 2)(y + 1) + (x - 2)(-1) \qquad \text{apply rule } (t_1 \cdot t_2 + t_1 \cdot t_3) \to t_1 \cdot (t_2 + t_3)$$
$$\to (x - 2)((y + 1) + (-1)) \qquad \text{apply rule } ((t_1 + t_2) + t_3) \to (t_1 + (t_2 + t_3))$$
$$\to (x - 2)(y + (1 + (-1))) \qquad \text{apply rule } (t_1 + (-t_1)) \to 0$$
$$\to (x - 2)(y + 0) \qquad \text{apply rule } (t_1 + 0) \to t_1$$
$$\to (x - 2)y$$

In these rules, t_1, t_2, and t_3 were used as high-level variables to represent arbitrary terms.

6.1.1   Algebras of objects and algebras of terms

Algebras are discrete mathematical systems which formalize the behavior of functions and relations over a domain. In the abstract, algebras are of the form

$$(domain, c_1, c_2, ..., f_1, f_2, ..., r_1, r_2, ...),$$

where the c's are constants, the f's are functions, and the r's are relations. An algebra may have any number (0 or more) of constants, functions, and relations. Each constant is an object in the domain

$$c_i \in domain,$$

each function is from (a product of) the domain into the domain

$$f_j : domain^m \to domain,$$

and each relation corresponds to a subset of (some product of) the domain

$$r_k \subseteq domain^n.$$

Often structures with relations are called *models*, while structures with only constants, variables and functions are called *algebras*.

Example 2:   Boolean algebras are basic to logic and computer science. For a nonvoid set X, let $P(X)$ be the set of all subsets of X, 0 be the empty set, $\cup$ be the set-theoretic union function, $\cap$ be the intersection function, $\sim$ be the complement function, and $\subseteq$ be the subset relation. Then,

$$(P(X); 0, X; \cup, \cap, \sim; \subseteq)$$

is a Boolean algebra with $P(X)$ as the domain, 0 and X as constants, etc. In case X contains only one element, then we have the usual two-element algebra, $P(X) = \{0, X\}$. The two-element algebra, $B\{0, 1\}$, is frequently denoted

$$(\{0, 1\}; 0, 1; +, \cdot, -; \leq),$$

where 0 is the empty set, 1 is X, $+$ is addition except that $1 + 1 = 1$, $\cdot$ is multiplication, $-$ is defined by $-0 = 1$ and $-1 = 0$, and $\leq$ is less than or equal; or

$$(\{F, T\}; F, T; \vee, \wedge, \neg; \Rightarrow),$$

where T (true) corresponds to X, F (false) to 0, and the functions ($\vee$, $\wedge$, $\neg$, respectively) correspond to $+$, $*$, and $-$.

The objects, functions, and relations of an algebra are analogous to the objects, functions, and relations that exist as actual data structures in a computer. In both cases, we need a language to discuss them. The language associated with an algebra is composed of *terms* built up from constants $C_1, C_2, \ldots$ (representing the objects $c_1, c_2, \ldots$), variables $V_1, V_2, \ldots$ (representing variable objects from the domain), and function symbols $F_1, F_2, \ldots$ (representing $f_1, f_2, \ldots$). If there are relations, then symbols $R_1, R_2, \ldots$ (for $r_1, r_2, \ldots$) are applied to terms to produce *formulas*. The language used to discuss an algebra is composed of the terms and formulas.

Example 3:   The terms of the algebra on the real numbers consist of expressions such as $(3x^2 - 2x + 1)$ and $\sin(x + \log(x))$, while the formulas include $\log(7) = 0.8451$ and $x^2 \leq (x + k)$. For $B\{0, 1\}$, the terms and formulas come in many different styles. There are the set-theoretical

$$(A \cap B) \subseteq (A \cup B), \ldots$$

and the corresponding logical formulas

$$(A \wedge B) \Rightarrow (A \vee B), \ldots.$$

The terms corresponding to an algebra of objects can be viewed as making up an algebra of terms. The domain is the set of all terms and the functions are interpretations of the action of the function symbols. In this case, a function symbol F_i operates on terms $t_1, t_2, \ldots$ to create a new term $F_i(t_1, t_2, \ldots)$. For example, given terms $(x + 2)$ and $(3 - x)$ the term function $+$ returns the term $((x + 2) + (3 - x))$ — not the value 5. The algebras

$$(terms; C_1, C_2, \ldots; F_1, F_2, \ldots; R_1, R_2, \ldots)$$

produced in this way are known as *term algebras*. For contrast, we'll call the original algebras *object algebras*. Term algebras are important as the languages of computation for the corresponding object algebras. They stand in relation to their object algebras as English to the real world, as our scribblings in high school algebra to the "world" of real numbers, and as a computer language to the circuit states that exist in a machine.

Example 4:   *PC*, propositional logic, is a term algebra for the two-element Boolean object algebra. Given propositional variables, $A, B, C, \ldots$, the domain

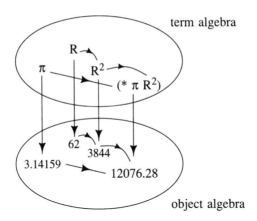

Figure 6.1. ANALOGY: Term algebra is to object algebra as syntax is to semantics.

of this term algebra consists of the propositional terms built from these variables. Propositional terms consist of (1) variables

$$A, B, C, \ldots$$

and constants
$$T, F,$$

and (2) given terms t_1 and t_2, composites of the form

$$(t_1 \wedge t_2), \quad (t_1 \vee t_2), \quad \text{and} \quad (\neg t_1).$$

Although the constants T and F are perfectly good terms for logic, they are rarely used.

6.1.2 Interpretation and computation

One approach to computing objects from terms is to use an interpreter. Strictly speaking, an *interpretation* is a function

$$value : term\text{-}algebra \to object\text{-}algebra$$

which computes the intended value of a term. If variables are present in the term algebra, then the interpretation is partially determined by an environment:

$$env : variables \to object\text{-}algebra$$

which associates objects with variables. An interpretation may be defined inductively by rewrite rules such as

(1) $value\langle C_i \rangle \Rightarrow c_i$,

(2) $value\langle V_i \rangle \Rightarrow env\langle V_i \rangle$, and

(3) $value\langle F_i(t_1, ..., t_j) \rangle \Rightarrow f_i\langle value\langle t_1 \rangle, ..., value\langle t_j \rangle \rangle$

for each constant C_i, variable V_i, and compound term $F_i(t_1, ..., t_j)$. The notation $f_i\langle value\langle t_1 \rangle, ..., value\langle t_j \rangle \rangle$ indicates that rewriting is to be continued at the $value\langle \rangle$'s, and that f_i is to be applied when the values are returned. An *interpreter* is a program or algorithm for computing the interpretation function.

Interpreters such as this, in which $value\langle \rangle$ recurs on subterms so that functions can be applied to the values of their arguments, are said to be *call-by-value*. A call-by-value interpreter seeks to move evaluation to the lowest, or innermost, levels in the term structure. For the most part, LISP is *call-by-value*. Other interpreters may recur at the top level (e.g., the interpreter for combinatory algebra defined in exercise 5).

As we saw in the first example, rewrite rules are used by interpreters. *Rewrite rules* are of the form

$$left\text{-}hand\text{-}pattern \;\Rightarrow\; right\text{-}hand\text{-}pattern,$$

where all of the high-level variables (i.e., term-valued variables) on the right are also on the left. The patterns represent sets of terms with similar syntax. These rules are applied to terms by pattern matching on the left and substitution on the right. Specifically, a rewrite rule is applied by

(1) matching the left-hand pattern to a given term,

(2) using the resulting variable-to-term bindings to construct a new term from the right-hand pattern, and

(3) replacing the given term by the new term.

The interpreters we have just described

$$value : term\text{-}algebra \rightarrow object\text{-}algebra$$

are object-valued interpreters (this version of the word "interpreter" is used by both mathematicians and computer scientists). A similar notion (used by computer scientists) involves computing term values:

$$reduce : term\text{-}algebra \rightarrow term\text{-}algebra.$$

The *reduce* interpreters are used to simplify linguistic expressions. The rules for such an interpreter make up a *grammar* or *production system*. The example given in 6.1 contained a computation for an object-valued interpreter (first) and a term-valued interpreter (second). The following example of $error\langle \rangle$ and exercise 7 for $CAreduce\langle \rangle$ show term-valued interpreters.

Example 5: Suppose that PARENTHESES* is the algebra of all strings of parentheses, with $\sim$ as a constant for the empty string and concatenation as the only function. We can compute balancing errors in these strings by $error\langle\,\rangle$—an interpretation defined for strings x, y, and z of PARENTHESES* as follows:

$$error\langle x()y\rangle \Rightarrow error\langle xy\rangle, \text{ and}$$

$$error\langle z\rangle \Rightarrow z \text{ if } z \text{ is not of the form } x()y.$$

By removing balanced pairs (first rule), the string of parentheses is reduced to its unbalanced members. The second rule is an exit from $error\langle\,\rangle$. In particular, the errors in the string $(()(()())($ are computed by applying the first rule four times and then the second rule:

$$error\langle(()(()())()\rangle \Rightarrow error\langle((()())()\rangle \Rightarrow error\langle((())()\rangle$$
$$\Rightarrow error\langle(()()\rangle \Rightarrow error\langle(()\rangle \Rightarrow ((.$$

A *computation* for value$\langle\,\rangle$ or reduce$\langle\,\rangle$ is a series of expressions

$$expr_1, \Rightarrow expr_2, \Rightarrow \ldots \Rightarrow expr_i, \Rightarrow \ldots$$

in which $expr_1$ is a given term and each successive $expr_{j+1}$ is the result of applying one of the rewrite rules to $expr_j$. If, as in the case of LISP, the interpreter can modify its environment, then a computation is a series of pairs

$$(expr_1, env_1) \Rightarrow \ldots \Rightarrow (expr_i, env_i) \Rightarrow \ldots.$$

Example 6: *Value*$\langle\,\rangle$ can be used to interpret terms of PC into $BA\{T,F\}$. Let A, B, C be variables in PC, with

$$env\langle A\rangle = env\langle B\rangle = T, \text{ and } env\langle C\rangle = F.$$

Value$\langle\,\rangle$ interprets a term such as

$$(\neg(A \wedge C) \vee B)$$

by the repeated application of the rewrite rules.

$$
\begin{array}{ll}
(\neg(A \wedge C) \vee B), & (A = T, B = T, C = F)\\
\Rightarrow \vee\langle(\neg(A \wedge C)), B\rangle, & (A = T, B = T, C = F)\\
\Rightarrow \vee\langle\neg\langle(A \wedge C)\rangle, T\rangle, & (A = T, \ldots)\\
\Rightarrow \vee\langle\neg\langle\wedge\langle A, C\rangle\rangle, T\rangle, & (\ldots)\\
\Rightarrow \vee\langle\neg\langle\wedge\langle T, F\rangle\rangle, T\rangle, & (\ldots)\\
\Rightarrow \vee\langle\neg\langle F\rangle, T\rangle, & (\ldots)\\
\Rightarrow \vee\langle T, T\rangle, & (\ldots)\\
\Rightarrow T.
\end{array}
$$

The interpreters of this chapter deal with functions but not with relations (unless the presence of truth values allows the relations to be represented by functions). Thus, it defines a *functional* style of computing. A *relational* style is given by an interpreter which attempts to satisfy a relation or formula by constructing an environment in which the formula is true. This may be done by searching various environment extensions until one is found in which the given formula evaluates to T. In this relational style of computing, the input consists of formulas which define a relation between variables and constants along with some initial environment bindings. The output is an extension of the given environment which satisfies the conditions expressed in the given formulas. This procedure is used in PROLOG interpreters (along with unification and other mechanisms).

Exercises

1. Describe the algebra corresponding to the strings of balanced parentheses and the associated constant(s) and function(s). The objects in this algebra should include (), (( )( )(( )( ))),)))))(, the empty string $\sim$, and the concatenation operation $\wedge$. Give rewrite rules which reduce every string of parentheses to its maximal balanced string.

2. Let OA be an object algebra and TA be the corresponding term algebra. Is there a relation between the number of objects in OA and the number of terms in TA? Hint: consider term algebras for $OA = B\{0, 1\}$ and $OA = $ Reals.

3. Functions can be constructed in pure LISP. Does this go beyond what can be done in the term algebras discussed here? Consider the construction of recursive functions.

4. If the LISP language is thought of as a term algebra and the s-expressions as an object algebra, then what do QUOTE, READ, and PRINT, do?

5. *Combinatory algebra* $(CA; K, S; *)$ is a term algebra similar to the lambda calculus. Its terms are generated from two constants, K and S, and the binary operator $*$ (called apply). For example,

$$((S * K) * K)$$

is a term that corresponds to the identity function. Given terms t_1 and t_2 in CA, $(t_1 * t_2)$ is a term in CA. In this term algebra, there is no distinction between functions and their arguments—except that * interprets the first expression as a function and the second as the function's argument. There are no variables in *CA*. *CAreduce* is defined for terms w, x, y, and z of *CA* by

$$CAreduce\langle((K * x) * y)\rangle \Rightarrow CAreduce\langle x \rangle,$$
$$CAreduce\langle(((S * x) * y) * z)\rangle \Rightarrow CAreduce\langle((x * z) * (y * z))\rangle,$$
$$CAreduce\langle w \rangle \Rightarrow w \qquad \text{for } w \text{ not of the above forms.}$$

CAreduce is applied at the top level. In other words, *CAreduce* is applied to the left-most occurrence of w..., with $w = ((K * x) * y)$ or $w = (((S * x) * y) * z)$. Show that $((S * K) * K)$ is actually an identity function.

HISTORY:
This algebra originated in 1920 with
Moses Schoenfinkel, see vanHeijenoort[1967],
but was subsequently extensively
developed by Haskell Curry.

6. Program an interpreter for propositional logic in LISP. Hint: define $\neg$, $\wedge$, and $\vee$ as LISP functions, then use INFIX.

7. In what ways is LISP's EVAL a call-by-value interpreter? In what ways does it differ from call-by-value?

8. Assume that functions cannot be created in the term algebra. Can the *value*$\langle\rangle$ handle recursive computations? searches? Are all functions totally defined in this system?

9. Explain why the *value*$\langle\rangle$ defined above cannot be a function in its own algebra. Conclude that the occurrence of LISP's interpreter EVAL within LISP requires something beyond the ideas developed in this chapter.

10. Are operations on functions possible in algebraic computing?

11. Is *CAreduce*$\langle\rangle$ call-by-value? Explain.

12. Intelligent interpreter. Could a call-by-value interpreter give us

$$value\langle(V_i - V_i)\rangle \Rightarrow 0, \quad value\langle(V_i * 0)\rangle \Rightarrow 0, \text{ etc.,}$$

even though *env*$\langle V_i \rangle$ is undefined? How does this sort of intelligence occur in LISP's handling of AND and OR?

6.2 LISP interpreters

Some of LISP's computational characteristics are based on algebraic features covered in the last chapter and others are based on the underlying algebra's

ability to create new functions. A detailed view of LISP's foundations will
be developed in the next chapter. However, since the basic ideas of LISP's
interpreter are not very far beyond the ideas seen in the previous interpreters,
we can explore the interpreters now.

6.2.1   A sketch of the usual LISP interpreter

The following interpreter is, in many respects, similar to the

EVAL⟨*form*, *environment*⟩ and APPLY⟨*function*, *argument-list*, *environment*⟩

interpreter presented in McCarthy et.al[1965]. In this interpreter, EVAL and
APPLY work hand in hand. EVAL processes terms, while APPLY processes
functions. This EVAL⟨⟩ interpreter differs from *value*⟨⟩ in that it must be able
to handle algebraically constructed functions. It handles these functions by extra
rules for EVAL⟨⟩ and most of APPLY⟨⟩. Interpreters are programs which process
syntactic patterns. As such, we need to define these patterns before getting
involved in EVAL⟨⟩ and APPLY⟨⟩.

The *terms* in our LISP consist of

>   atoms
>
>>   constants: NIL, T, numbers;
>>
>>   variable or function-name
>>
>>>   (bound to data, bound to functions, unbound);
>
>   lists
>
>>   special forms:
>>
>>>   (QUOTE *object*), (COND (*term*$_1$ *term*$_2$)...), (COND);
>>
>>   usual forms:
>>
>>>   (*function-name term*$_1$ ...),
>>>
>>>   (*function term*$_1$ ...).

Variables and *function-names* are symbols. An *object* is a constant, symbol, or
an s-expression. A *function* is one of the following types:

>   (LAMBDA *variable-list term*),
>
>   (FUNCTION *function environment*),
>
>   (LABEL *function-name function*).

Bindings exist only in an environment. An *environment* is an association list
containing elements of the form

>   (*variable object*),

(*function-name* LAMBDA *variable-list term*), and

(*function-name* FUNCTION *function environment*).

The interpreter must be programmed in a system with

(1) dynamically allocated memory;

(2) data structures to represent numbers, symbols, and s-expressions of arbitrary size;

(3) high-level variables: *arg-list, env, form, fun,* and constants:
COND, FUNCTION, IF, LABEL, LAMBDA, NIL, QUOTE, T, *numbers*;

(4) primitive functions:
ATOM, CAR, CDR, CONS, EQ, IF, LIST, NUMBERP, PRIM-FUN, =, +, −, *; and

(5) the ability to compute from recursive programs.

We assume that

(1) the variables *arg-list, env, form,* and *fun* represent lists of terms, environments, terms, and either function-names or functions, respectively;

(2) the constants evaluate (as data) to themselves
COND $\Rightarrow$ COND, ..., NIL $\Rightarrow$ NIL, QUOTE $\Rightarrow$ QUOTE;

(3) EQ$\langle$NIL, NIL$\rangle$ = EQ$\langle$(), NIL$\rangle$ = T;

(4) PRIM-FUN identifies the names of primitive functions (given above), in particular
PRIM-FUN$\langle$ATOM$\rangle$ = ... = PRIM-FUN$\langle$PRIM-FUN$\rangle$ = ... = T,
otherwise
PRIM-FUN$\langle$*symbol*$\rangle$ = NIL;

(5) data-assignments and function-assignments for the dual-purpose symbols QUOTE and COND are distinct;

(6) the functions
APPEND$\langle$ $\rangle$, ASSOC$\langle$ $\rangle$, CDDR$\langle$ $\rangle$, LENGTH$\langle$ $\rangle$, NTH$\langle$ $\rangle$, NULL$\langle$ $\rangle$, OR$\langle$ $\rangle$, and PAIRLIS$\langle$ $\rangle$,
are defined from primitive functions; and

(7) CDR$\langle$ $\rangle$ and PAIRLIS$\langle$ $\rangle$ satisfy
CDR$\langle$NIL$\rangle$ = NIL,
and given *symbols* = ($sym_1...sym_j$), *values* = ($val_1...val_j$), and *env* = ($sv_1...sv_k$), we have
PAIRLIS$\langle$*symbols*, *values*, *env*$\rangle$ = (($sym_1 val_1$)...($sym_j val_j$) $sv_1...sv_k$).

EVAL$\langle$*form*, *environment*$\rangle$,APPLY$\langle$*function*, *argument-list*, *environment*$\rangle$and
EVLIS$\langle$*list-of-forms*, *environment*$\rangle$ are defined by the following rules.

```
EVAL<form, env>
  if ATOM<form> then
    if OR<EQ<form,T>,NUMBERP<form>> then
      => form                                            (1)
    if ASSOC<form,env> then
      if ATOM<CDDR<ASSOC<form,env>>>
        => NTH<2, ASSOC<form,env>>                       (2a)
      otherwise
        => CDR<ASSOC<form, env>>                         (2b)
    otherwise
      => NIL                                             (2c)
  if EQ<CAR<form>,COND> then
    if NULL<CDR<form>> then
      => NIL                                             (3a)
    if EVAL<CAR<NTH<2,form>>,env> then
      => EVAL<NTH<2,NTH<2,form>>, env>                   (3b)
    otherwise
      => EVAL<CONS<COND,CDDR<form>>, env>                (3c)
  if EQ<CAR<form>,QUOTE> then
      => NTH<2,form>                                     (4)
  if ATOM<CAR<form>> then
    if PRIM-FUN<CAR<form>>
      => APPLY<CAR<form>, EVLIS<CDR<form>,env>, env>(5)
    otherwise
      => APPLY<CDR<ASSOC<CAR<form>,env>>,
              CDR<form>, env>                            (6)
  otherwise
    => APPLY<CAR<form>, CDR<form>, env>                  (7)
```

NOTE ON IMPLEMENTATIONS IN LISP:

If this interpreter is implemented in another LISP, then the expression
$APPLY\langle CAR\langle form\rangle, ...\rangle$ of rule 5 may not handle the case
$EQ\langle CAR\langle form\rangle, IF\rangle$ properly.
In this case, some additional tests will be required ending in

$\Rightarrow$ if $EVAL\langle NTH\langle 1,form\rangle,env\rangle$
then
$EVAL\langle NTH\langle 2,form\rangle,env\rangle$
otherwise
$EVAL\langle NTH\langle 3,form\rangle,env\rangle$.

```
APPLY<fun, arg-list, env>
  if ATOM<fun> then
    if PRIM-FUN<fun> then
      => fun<NTH<1,arg-list>,...,
```

```
                    NTH<k,arg-list>>                         (8)
               where k = LENGTH<arg-list>
          if ASSOC<fun, env>
            => APPLY<CDR<ASSOC<fun, env>>, arg-list, env> (9)
          otherwise
            => NIL                                          (10)
        if EQ<CAR<fun>,LAMBDA> then
          => EVAL<NTH<3,fun>, env+>                         (11)
             env+ = PAIRLIS<NTH<2,fun>, EVLIS<arg-list>,env>
        if EQ<CAR<fun>,LABEL> then
          => APPLY<NTH<2,fun>, arg-list, env+>              (12)
             where env+ = CONS<CONS<NTH<2,fun>,
                                     NTH<3,fun>>, env>
        if EQ<CAR<fun>,FUNCTION>
          => APPLY<NTH<2,fun>, arg-list, env+>              (13)
             where env+ = APPEND<NTH<3,fun>,env>
        otherwise
          => APPLY<EVAL<fun,env>, arg-list, env>.           (14)

EVLIS<form-list,env>
    if NULL<form-list>
      => NIL                                                (15)
    otherwise
      => CONS<
          EVAL<CAR<form-list>,env>,
          EVLIS<CDR<form-list, env> > .                     (16)
```

Comments on EVAL⟨⟩: Rules 1, 2, and 5 for EVAL⟨⟩ are analogous to 1, 2, and 3 for value⟨⟩ in section 6.1.2. 2a recovers data-bindings from the environment, 2b recovers function-bindings, and 2c returns NIL for NIL and unbound symbols. Rules 3 and 4 handle special forms (COND...) and (QUOTE...). Rule 6 is a generalization of rule 5 (which dealt only with terms beginning with primitive functions) to forms (*function-name* ...) where *function-name* is bound in the environment. Two types of name-to-definition bindings, (*function-name* LAMBDA *variable-list term*), and (*function-name* FUNCTION *function environment*) exist in the environment. Rule 7 handles forms of the form ((LAMBDA...)...), ((LABEL...)...), or ((FUNCTION...)...). Notice that functions are bound to their names only by LABEL, and values are bound to symbols by LAMBDA or FUNC- TION only.

The rules defining APPLY⟨⟩: Rule 8 invokes the primitive functions when their names are called from LISP. Rule 9 replaces user-defined function-names by their definition. Rule 10 returns NIL when an unbound function-name or the NIL function appears. (The origin of a NIL function is rule 14.) Rule 11 handles lambda functions. Rule 12 binds functions to function-names when LABEL is used. Rule 13 handles closures, and rule 14 handles functions computed in LISP.

Example 7:   There are no DEFUNs in this interpreter, so every recursive function must be LABELed. EVAL⟨⟩'s computation of 3! is sketched. The factorial function used is

```
( (LABEL FACT
   (LAMBDA (N)  (IF  (< N 2)  1  (* FACT  (- N 1))))  )  3) .
```

$\Rightarrow$ EVAL⟨ ((LABEL FACT (LAMBDA (N)...)) 3), () ⟩   apply rule 7

$\Rightarrow$ APPLY⟨ (LABEL FACT (LAMBDA...)), (3), () ⟩   rule 12

$\Rightarrow$ APPLY⟨ FACT, (3), ((FACT LAMBDA (N) (IF...))) ⟩   rule 9

$\Rightarrow$ APPLY⟨ (LAMBDA (N) (IF...)), (3), ((FACT LAMBDA...)) ⟩   11

$\Rightarrow$ EVAL⟨ (IF (< N 2)...), ((N 3) (FACT LAMBDA...)) ⟩   5

$\Rightarrow$ EVAL⟨ (* N (FACT (- N 1))), ((N 3) (FACT ...)) ⟩   5

$\Rightarrow$ APPLY⟨ *, EVLIS⟨(N (FACT (- N 1))), ((N 3)(FACT...))⟩, (...)⟩

apply rule 16 twice

$\Rightarrow$ ...CONS⟨EVAL⟨N,...⟩,

CONS⟨EVAL⟨(FACT (- N 1)),...⟩,EVAL⟨NIL,...⟩⟩⟩...

apply rules 2a, 6

$\Rightarrow$ ...CONS⟨3,

CONS⟨APPLY⟨(LAMBDA(N)...),EVLIS⟨((- N 1)),..⟩,NIL⟩

. . . etc. . . .

$\Rightarrow$ APPLY⟨ *, (3 2 1), ((N 1)...)⟩

$\Rightarrow$ 6

Example 8:   The previous interpreter was implemented in GCLISP to interpret a language we'll call toyLISP. The constants and primitive functions were from GCLISP (except for PRIM-FUNS). All nonprimitive functions of toyLISP were distinguished from functions with the same name in GCLISP by adding an asterisk to the end of the name – e.g., COND* in toyLISP is distinguished from COND of GCLISP. The same thing was done with other symbols – e.g., LAMBDA* in toyLISP is distinguished from the LAMBDA of GCLISP. By distinguishing the symbols of the two languages in this way, we can guarantee that toyLISP uses only the indicated rules (i.e., the constants and functions without asterisks) from GCLISP. The following evaluations test the EVAL*⟨⟩ of toyLISP.

```
* (EVAL* () ())
  NIL
* (EVAL* T ())
  T
* (EVAL* 9876 ())
```

```
    9876
*  (EVAL* V ((V 9876)))
    9876
```

The value of ENV0 is an environment in which the definitions for toyLISP's own constants and functions – e.g., COND*, ..., EVAL*, APPLY*, etc. – are defined.

```
*  ENV0
    ((COND* COND*) (FUNCTION* FUNCTION*) (LABEL* LABEL*)
     (QUOTE* QUOTE*) (EVAL* LAMBDA* (FORM ENV) (IF (ATOM
         FORM) (IF ... NIL ...) (IF ...) ...)
     (APPLY* LAMBDA* (FUN ARG-LIST) (IF...)) ... )
*  (EVAL* EVAL* ENV0)
    (LAMBDA* (FORM ENV) (IF (ATOM FORM) (IF (NULL* FORM)
      NIL #)))
*  (EVAL* (* 2 3 4 5 (+ 6 7)) ())
    1560
*  ((EVAL* (QUOTE* (1 2)) ())
    (1 2)
*  (EVAL* (CONS 1 3) ())
    (1 . 3)
*  (EVAL* (IF X Y Z) ((W T)(X T)(Y 34)(Z Z)))
    34
*  (EVAL* ((LAMBDA* (N) (+ N N)) 21) ())
    42
*  (EVAL* (COND* (X Y) (Z T)) ((X NIL)(Y 55)(Z T)))
    T
```

Our universal example, the factorial function, is defined in the following experiment. Notice that the environment is initially empty and that LABEL* is used to preserve the definition of FACT* in the environment. FACT* had no bindings accessible to GCLISP.

```
*  (EVAL* ((LABEL* FACT* (LAMBDA* (N)
            (IF (= N 0) 1 (* N (FACT* (- N 1)))))) 4) ())
    24
```

The following test shows that EVAL* can evaluate itself if the definition of EVAL* is in the environment.

```
*  (EVAL* (EVAL* 999 ()) ENV0)
    999
```

Rather than return an error when an unbound constant or function-name is encountered, toyLISP returns NIL.

```
*  (EVAL* (EVAL* 999 ()) ())
    NIL
```

Finally, a closure is used.

```
*  (EVAL*
   ((FUNCTION* (LAMBDA* (N) (+ M N)) ((M 987))) 13)
   ((M 0)) )
  1000
```

Notice that the closure's private environment – rather than the public environment given to EVAL* – was used in computing the value of the closure's term.

6.2.2   A call-by-name interpreter for LISP

The following LISP interpreter, for generating call-by-name computations, is based on the interpreter given in chapter 10 of McCarthy&Talcott[1980]. In this interpreter the evaluation of expressions defining the arguments for a function call may be delayed or never performed. This delay requires that a function's variables be bound to expressions (rather than values of expressions). Later, when the variables are used, the expressions are evaluated. This delayed evaluation takes place in the environment of the original function call (i.e., the environment in which the variable-to-expression bindings were created). We have expressed the interpreter in LISP code.

C(*all*)B(*y*)N(*ame*)-EVAL does not use APPLY.

```
*   (DEFUN CBN-EVAL (FORM ENV)
    (COND

     ((ATOM FORM)
      (COND
       ((EQ FORM 'T)   FORM)
       ((EQ FORM 'NIL)  FORM)
       ((NUMBERP FORM)  FORM)
       (T                              ;Arg is a variable.
        (CBN-EVAL
    ;The evaluation of ARG's unevaluated expression in
                             ;the original environment.
         (CADR (ASSOC FORM ENV))
         (CDDR (ASSOC FORM ENV))
    ))))

     ((ATOM (CAR FORM))
      (COND
       ((EQ (CAR FORM) 'ATOM)
        (ATOM (CBN-EVAL (CADR FORM) ENV)))
       ((EQ (CAR FORM) 'CAR)
```

```
      (CAR (CBN-EVAL (CADR FORM) ENV)))
     ((EQ (CAR FORM) 'CDR)
      (CDR (CBN-EVAL (CADR FORM) ENV)))
     ((EQ (CAR FORM) 'CONS)
      (CONS
       (CBN-EVAL (CADR FORM) ENV)
       (CBN-EVAL (CADDR FORM) ENV) ))
     ((EQ (CAR FORM) 'COND)
      (CBN-EVCOND (CDR FORM) ENV))
     ((EQ (CAR FORM) 'EQ)
      (EQ
       (CBN-EVAL (CADR FORM) ENV)
       (CBN-EVAL (CADDR FORM) ENV) ))
     ((EQ (CAR FORM) 'NULL)
      (NULL (CBN-EVAL (CADR FORM) ENV)))
     ((EQ (CAR FORM) 'NUMBERP)
      (NUMBERP (CBN-EVAL (CADR FORM) ENV)))
     ((EQ (CAR FORM) 'QUOTE)   (CADR FORM))
     ((EQ (CAR FORM) 'BREAK)   (BREAK))
     (T        ;A LABELed function name is bound in E.
      (CBN-EVAL
  ;Function's name in FORM replaced by the associated
                                  ;lambda expression.
       (CONS (CDR (ASSOC (CAR FORM) ENV))
        (CDR FORM) )
       E ))))

    ((EQ (CAAR FORM) 'LAMBDA)          ;LAMBDA function.
     (CBN-EVAL                   ;Evaluation of the body of
      (CADDAR FORM)     ;lambda expression in new env.
      (CBN-PAIRLIS (CADAR FORM) (CDR FORM) ENV)
     ))

    ((EQ (CAAR FORM) 'LABEL)           ;LABELed function.
     (CBN-EVAL
      (CONS                            ;new argument
       (CADDAR FORM)   ;LABELed function's lambda expr
       (CDR FORM))             ;the original argument list
      (CONS                            ;new environment
       (CONS (CADAR FORM) (CAR FORM))
       E )))))  ;(fun-name.(LABEL...)) is added to the
                                       ;environment.

(DEFUN CBN-EVCOND (FORM-PAIRS ENV)         ;Subroutine
  (COND                                    ;for COND.
```

```
((NULL FORM-PAIRS)   NIL)
((CBN-EVAL (CAAR FORM-PAIRS) ENV)
 (CBN-EVAL (CADAR FORM-PAIRS) ENV))
(T   (CBN-EVCOND (CDR FORM-PAIRS) ENV)) ))

(DEFUN CBN-PAIRLIS (SYMBOLS VALUES ALIST)
                                  ;PAIRLIS version.
 (COND
  ((NULL SYMBOLS)   ALIST)
  (T
   (CONS
    (CONS              ;Add first new association.
     (CAR SYMBOLS)              ;New symbol with its
     (CONS (CAR VALUES)    ;unevaluated argument and
     ALIST ))                          ;environment,
    (CBN-PAIRLIS           ;to remaining new alist.
     (CDR SYMBOLS) (CDR VALUES) ALIST) ))))
```

The CADDAR used above may have to be defined.

CBN-EVAL differs from EVAL in the way that arguments for function calls are evaluated. When CBN-EVAL encounters a term of the form

$$((\text{LAMBDA } (var_1...) \; body) \; expression1...)$$

in the environment $\text{ENV}=(e_1 \; ...)$, it returns on the function's body with the extended environment

$$\text{ENV2} = ((var_1 \; expression_1 \; . \; \text{ENV})...e_1...),$$

where *expression*1 is not yet evaluated. If the value of *var*1 is needed later, then ASSOC retrieves (*var*1 *expression*1 ENV) and evaluates *expression*1 in the original environment ENV. Notice that CBN-PAIRLIS adds associations of the form

$$(variable \; expression \; . \; environment)$$

and

$$(function\text{-}name \; \text{LABEL} \; function\text{-}name \; (\text{LAMBDA}...))$$

to the environment.

Example 9:   BREAK can be used to examine the environment.

```
*   (CBN-EVAL '((LABEL LOOK (LAMBDA (X) (BREAK)))
              (CONS 1 2))   ())
   BREAK, (CONTINUE) TO CONTINUE.

1> ENV
```

```
==> ((X (CONS 1 2) (LOOK LABEL LOOK (LAMBDA ...)))
     (LOOK LABEL LOOK (LAMBDA (V) (BREAK))) )
```

```
1> (CONTINUE)
   ==> NIL
```

Example 10: It is a well-known consequence of the Church-Rosser theorem that the values returned by call-by-value computations are the same as those of call-by-name computations. However, a call-by-name computation may return a value when the corresponding call-by-value computation does not. First, establish the preceding definitions in our usual LISP.

```
*   (DEFUN CBN-EVAL ...)
    ==> CBN-EVAL
*   (DEFUN CBN-COND ...)
    ==> CBN-COND
*   (DEFUN CBN-PAIRLIS ...)
    ==> CBN-PAIRLIS
```

Run it as a front-end to the existing listener.

```
*   (DEFUN CBN-FRONTEND ()
     (TERPRI) (TERPRI) (PRINC "? ")
     (PRINT (CBN-EVAL (READ) (TERPRI)))
     (CBN-FRONTEND) )
    ==> CBN-FRONTEND
*   (CBN-FRONTEND)
```

Then, submit an expression to CBN-EVAL which has a value (8 in this case) but which would lead to an infinite computation in EVAL.

```
?   ((LABEL CBN-TEST (LAMBDA (X) 8))
     ((LABEL O (LAMBDA () (O)))) )
8
```

The function (LABEL CBN-TEST (LAMBDA (X) 8)) has a value for every argument value returned. However, the argument ((LABEL O (LAMBDA () (O)))) has no value. Return to the regular EVAL and evaluate the equivalent form, and no value is returned.

```
*   (LABELS ((CBN-TEST (X) 8) (O () (O)))
     (CBN-TEST (O)) )
    ERROR: STACK OVERFLOW.
```

Which LISP was correct?

For additional reading, *The Art of the Interpreter*, Steele and Sussam[1978], is outstanding.

6.2.3   Put the Interpreter Inside, Keep the User Out (optional)

Inside the machine, the data objects are addresses of implemented s-expressions. Outside, the data objects are s-expressions. Thus, the word "s-expression" is being used for external objects only. We've defined these interpreters from the point of view of the user – outside of the machine. In truth, the interpreter belongs inside, the user belongs outside.

Let *iNSIDE* be the set of all addresses for registers available to represent s-expressions, and *Outside* be the set of all s-expressions.

Let $atom\langle\,\rangle$, $car\langle\,\rangle$, $cdr\langle\,\rangle$, $cons\langle\,\rangle$, ..., $prim\text{-}funs\langle\,\rangle$, ..., be internal versions of the primitive functions from which the interpreter was constructed. Specifically,

$$atom : iNSIDE \rightarrow iNSIDE, \quad ..., \quad cons : iNSIDE^2 \rightarrow iNSIDE, ... $$

For example, if 19AA6 and 08B33 are the addresses of internal objects and

$$A0091 = cons\langle 19AA6, 08B33\rangle,$$

then A0091 is the address of a register containing the pointers 19AA6 and 08B33. Nonnumerical constants and symbols are represented in iNSIDE by their addresses. For example, A0000 might represent NIL and A0001 might represent T. In this case, we would have

$$atom\langle A0091\rangle = A0000 \text{ and } atom\langle A0000\rangle = A0001.$$

An internal representation of the interpreter's primitives can be extended (just as in the external case) to an internal representation

$$eval\langle form\text{-}address, env\text{-}address\rangle$$

and

$$apply\langle fun\text{-}address, \ arg\text{-}list\text{-}address, \ env\text{-}address\rangle$$

of EVAL$\langle\,\rangle$ and APPLY$\langle\,\rangle$. The internal definitions are essentially the same as the external definitions.

Let r: Outside $\longrightarrow$ iNSIDE be an operation which, given an s-expression, creates an internal implementation of the s-expression and then returns its address as the value. Let P: iNSIDE $\longrightarrow$ Outside be an operation which given the address of an internal object returns the corresponding s-expression. A real LISP may be constructed as a loop program similar to

1   P$\langle$ $eval\langle$ r$\langle input\rangle$, A0000 $\rangle\rangle$ (o)

go to 1 ,

where the initial environment is r⟨NIL⟩—represented here by A0000. Notice that r⟨ ⟩ and P⟨ ⟩ are similar to READ and PRINT, and that they satisfy

$$P\langle\ r\langle s\text{-}expression\rangle\ \rangle = s\text{-}expression \tag{i}$$

for every external dotted-list, list, constant, or symbol.

Strictly speaking, r and P are not functions because they are not single-valued. Two successive evaluations

r⟨*s-expression*⟩

r⟨*s-expression*⟩

will usually return two different addresses, even if the s-expression does not change. Evaluations

P⟨*address*⟩

. . .

P⟨*address*⟩

for the same address will return different s-expressions if there has been a garbage-collection and reallocation of the address in between. All of the other internal representations of primitive functions have this problem. Does this undermine the validity of our interpreter?

We must be able to say—even in the face of the last paragraph—that the program above appears to the user to be the same LISP as the one defined by EVAL⟨ ⟩. In other words,

$$\text{EVAL}\langle form, \text{NIL}\rangle = P\langle eval\langle r\langle form\rangle, r\langle \text{NIL}\rangle\rangle \tag{ii}$$

for every valid LISP form.

First, change r⟨ ⟩ and P⟨ ⟩ into functions by (1) selecting a particular LISP form (thereby fixing the computation both iNSIDE and Outside), and (2) replacing iNSIDE by

$$(iNSIDE \times \{0, 1, 2, ...K\}),$$

where K is the number of steps in the computation of eval⟨r⟨form⟩, r⟨NIL⟩⟩ for the given form. Partition (iNSIDE ×{0,1,2,...K}) into sets:

$$[x] = \{(address, i)|\ x = P\langle address\rangle \text{ between the } i\text{th and } i + 1\text{th step}\}$$

for each s-expression x, and

$$[\#] = \{(address, i)|P\langle address\rangle \text{ is undefined}\}.$$

Let iNSIDE! be this partition. Each [x] in iNSIDE! is the set of all possible internal representations, $(address, i)$, for the s-expression x.

Now, define the new functions

$$r! : Outside \longrightarrow iNSIDE! \quad \text{and} \quad P! : iNSIDE! \longrightarrow Outside$$

for each s-expression x by

$$r!\langle x \rangle = [x] \quad \text{and} \quad P!\langle [x] \rangle = x. \tag{i!}$$

(Notice that (i!) is the new version of (i).) Replace primitive internal constants by the set which contains their address. In particular, replace

$$nil \text{ by } [NIL], \ t \text{ by } [T], \text{ etc.}$$

Replace primitive functions by their !-analogs. In particular, replace

$$atom\langle \rangle \text{ by } atom!\langle [x] \rangle = [ATOM\langle x \rangle],$$

$$car\langle \rangle \text{ by } car!\langle [x] \rangle = [CAR\langle x \rangle],$$

etc.

EMBEDDINGS PRESERVE STRUCTURE:

A function between algebras
H: (DOMAIN,C1,...,F1,F2,...) $\longrightarrow$ (domain,c1,...,f1,f2,...)
is an embedding if it preserves structure. Specifically,
(1) H is one-one, (2) $H\langle Cj \rangle$ = cj for all Cj, and
(3) $H\langle Fj\langle x1,... \rangle \rangle = fj\langle H\langle x1 \rangle,... \rangle$ for all Fj.

The range algebra, (domain,c1,...,f1,f2,...), may have elements, constants, and functions which do not correspond to anything in the domain. The important thing is that the range algebra contain an exact image of the domain algebra. For this reason, H is said to be an embedding of (DOMAIN,...) into (domain,...).

If $G\langle x1,... \rangle$ is a function defined in (DOMAIN,C1,...,F1,F2,...) and $g\langle w1,... \rangle$ has the corresponding definition in (domain,c1,...,f1,f2,...), then a simple induction argument generalizes property (3) to (3+) $H\langle G\langle w1,... \rangle \rangle = g\langle H\langle w1 \rangle,... \rangle$.

Embedding Theorem. Outside, the primitive constants and the primitive functions define an algebra (Outside; ..., NIL, ...; ATOM, ...). The previous paragraph defines a corresponding internal algebra (iNSIDE!; ..., [NIL], ...; atom!, ...). Between these algebras, the function

$$r! : (Outside; \text{NIL}, ...; \text{ATOM}, ..) \longrightarrow (iNSIDE!; [\text{NIL}], ..; atom!, ..)$$

is an embedding.

Proof.

1. $r!\langle x \rangle = r!\langle y \rangle$ implies

$$x = P!\langle [x] \rangle = P!\langle r!\langle x \rangle \rangle = P!\langle r!\langle y \rangle \rangle = P!\langle [y] \rangle = y.$$

Thus, $r!$ is one-one.

2. Constants are preserved: $r!\langle \text{NIL} \rangle = [\text{NIL}]$, $r!\langle \text{T} \rangle = [\text{T}]$, etc.

3. Functions are preserved:

$$r!\langle \text{ATOM}\langle x \rangle \rangle = [\text{ATOM}\langle x \rangle] = atom!\langle [x] \rangle = atom!\langle r!\langle x \rangle \rangle,$$
$$r!\langle \text{CONS}\langle x,y \rangle \rangle = [\text{CONS}\langle x,y \rangle] = cons!\langle [x],[y] \rangle$$
$$= cons!\langle r!\langle x \rangle, r!\langle y \rangle \rangle,$$

etc.

In each case, the first and third equality are justified by the definition of r!, while the second equality is justified by the definition of the function involved (i.e., that of atom!, cons!, etc.).

By the embedding theorem, (3+), and (i!)

$$r!\langle \text{EVAL}\langle form, \text{NIL} \rangle \rangle = eval!\langle r!\langle form \rangle, r!\langle \text{NIL} \rangle \rangle.$$

Apply P! to each side of the equation to get

$$P!\langle r!\langle \text{EVAL}\langle form, \text{NIL} \rangle \rangle \rangle = P!\langle eval!\langle r!\langle form \rangle, r!\langle \text{NIL} \rangle \rangle \rangle$$
$$= P!\langle eval!\langle [form], [\text{NIL}] \rangle \rangle,$$

then use (1!) to cancel $P!\langle r!\langle ... \rangle \rangle$ on the left-hand side:

$$\text{EVAL}\langle form, \text{NIL} \rangle = P!\langle eval!\langle [form], [\text{NIL}] \rangle \rangle. \qquad (ii!)$$

This completes the proof that the program (o) above (or at least the (o!) version of it) is identical with $\text{EVAL}\langle \rangle$ in the Outside algebra.

Exercises

1. Which functions do not have to use the APPLY$\langle \rangle$?

2. Why is the EVAL defined by these rules a nonmonotonic recursion?

3. An implementation of V(ery)T(iny)LISP (a variant of Lispkit LISP, Peter Henderson, 1980) is described in *Using Pascal to Implement Functional LISP*, Thompson[1987].

4. Define the CBN-functions in LISP, then use CBN-EVAL to compute the factorial of 3. The function's definition must be bound by LABEL.

5. What sort of exceptional problems would be encountered in computing with a call-by-name implementation of READ?

6. An interesting interpreter, in which all functions (except ATOM, CAR, CDR, CONS, COND, EQ, NULL, and QUOTE) are locally bound by LABEL, is defined in McCarthy[1978]. DEFUN this version of EVAL and experiment with it. In particular, use the substitute operation in your editor to change the names of the interpreter's functions (say, from EVAL to EVAL*, CAR to CAR*, etc.) so that there is no chance of the functions of the underlying LISP covering for those of the interpreter. Now, experiment to find out just which functions from the underlying LISP must be used.

7. Trace the computation of (FACT* 3) through the interpreter of section 6.2.1.

8. Show that r! is not onto (iNSIDE!;[NIL],...;atom!) – in other words, there is at least one [x] in iNSIDE! which is not a value of r!.

9. Describe an algebraic approach to pattern processing.

6.3 Compiled LISP

HISTORY:

"The implementation of LISP began in Fall 1958. The original idea was to produce a compiler, but ... we needed some experimenting to get good conventions ... . Therefore, we started by hand-compiling various functions into assembly language and writing subroutines ... . The first attempt at a compiler was made by Robert Brayton, but was unsuccessful. The first successful LISP compiler was programmed by Timothy Hart and Michael Levin. It was written in LISP."

McCarthy[1981]

If COMPILE is originally written in LISP, then its efficiency can be increased by using COMPILE to compile COMPILE.

A LISP compiler is a program which translates functions written in LISP as s-expressions into compiled object code (i.e., machine-language subroutines). COMPILE is a function,

(COMPILE *function-name*)

or

(COMPILE *function-name lambda-expression*),

which has the effect of converting a function-name defined as an s-expression (i.e., (LAMBDA ...), (LABELS ....), or (FUNCTION ...)) into equivalent compiled object code. Compiled functions can run tens of times faster than they would have run as an interpreted s-expressions. If function-name is a non-NIL symbol, then the subroutine is assigned (as if by DEFUN) to the name and the name is returned as the value. If NIL is used for the function-name, then no assignment is made but the subroutine is returned as the value. Compiling a function obviously changes the way in which the interpreter responds to it. Basically, the interpreter handles compiled functions as it would handle primitive functions. However, compiling is done in such a way that if a compiled function calls on a function which is not compiled then the computation returns to the control of the interpreter. The successful evaluation of

(MEMBER *element list* : TEST '(LAMBDA (X Y)...))

is an example of this. Thus, not every function downstream from a compiled function needs to be compiled.

Example 11: The following session is an extension of the FIBONACCI example given in 5.1.3 carried out on the TI Explorer. The first definition of FIBONACCI (in 5.1.3) is, in the first case below, interpreted.

```
*   (TIME (FIBONACCI 20))
    88,400,173 microseconds
    ==> 10,946
*   (COMPILE 'FIBONACCI)
    ==> FIBONACCI
*   (TIME (FIBONACCI 20))
    699,282 microseconds
    ==> 10,946
```

The first version of FIBONACCI is a LAMBDA expression, the second is a compiled version of the first.

For additional reading try Steele[1984], your system's manual, and Pumplin[1987].

7

Mathematical Foundations for LISP

This chapter presents a highly simplified look at the lambda calculus—an algebraic formalization of computation. As our presentation proceeds, we will compare it to LISP. Now, LISP is not really an implementation of the lambda calculus, but it has inherited (deliberately and otherwise) some of its most important features. The comparison will throw some light on the issue of LISP's relation to the lambda calculus.

Like Boolean algebra, logic, automata theory, etc., the lambda calculus is a bit too abstract to impress every programmer. The value of these areas of discrete mathematics to computer science is as a source of new ideas and techniques at a high level.

7.1 The lambda calculus defined

The *lambda calculus* is a computational system composed of (1) a term algebra,

$$(\lambda-terms; \quad apply, \lambda-abstraction);$$

(2) a description of the (reduction) steps making up computations; and (3) a description of the meaning of terms. The last two items are usually presented as axioms for a formal logic—see Revesz[1988]. But, we will handle them informally.

The *terms* of the lambda calculus consist of (1) variables u,v,w,. . . , and (2) composite terms $(t_1 \ t_2)$ and $(\lambda \ v \ t_1)$, for simpler terms t_1, t_2, and variables v. There are no constants. The term $(t_1 \ t_2)$, called "t_1 applied to t_2", is the value returned by "apply". The term $(\lambda \ v \ t_1)$ is the value returned by lambda-abstraction. In writing terms, we will follow the convention that left-most pairs of parentheses are omitted. Thus, the abbreviation $t_1 t_2...$ represents $((t_1 \ t_2) ...)$. Terms of the form

Figure 7.1. Alonzo Church, (about 1970) father of the lambda calculus.

$$(\lambda v_1 \ (\lambda v_2 \ (\ldots \text{ term})))$$

will be abbreviated $(\lambda \ (v_1 \ v_2 \ \ldots) \text{ term})$.

The term algebra begins with two real functions on terms —"apply" and "lambda abstraction". However, we've just seen that new function-like objects (e.g., $(\lambda \ v \ t_1)$) are created as terms. Although "apply" gives us the illusion that such terms are functions, they are not true functions in our algebra. They don't, by themselves, operate on elements of the domain to produce other elements. When it is necessary to preserve the distinction, terms which are acting as functions will be called *object functions*, "apply" and "lambda-abstraction" will be the only *true functions*.

The definitions of "computation" and "meaning" are given in terms of formulas. *Formulas* are constructed from terms t_1 and t_2 as

$$t_1 \rightarrow t_2 \text{ and } t_1 = t_2.$$

The formula $t_1 \rightarrow t_2$ is read as "t_1 reduces to t_2", $t_1 = t_2$ is read as "t_1 is semantically equal to t_2".

Example 1: The expressions

> v,   (λ u (u v)),   (v (λ u (u v))),   ((λ u (u v)) v),
> (v v),   and   ((λ u (u v))(λ u (u v)))

are lambda terms. Examples of formulas are

> ((λ u (u v))(λ u (u v))) → ((λ u (u v)) v),
> ((λ u (u v)) v) → (v v),
> (λ u uv)(λ u uv) → vv,   and
> (λ u uv)(λ u uv) = vv .

The convention of omitting left-most parentheses was followed in the last two formulas, as was writing uv for (u v).

Already, we can see important similarities and differences between the lambda calculus and LISP. The two are similar in that (1+) in both systems "apply" plays the central role of allowing objects to act as functions; (2+) lambda-abstraction converts a variable/variable-list and a term into an object function; and (3+) lists of the form *(function argument)* are terms representing the application of a function to an argument. The lambda calculus differs from LISP in that (1-) it (the lambda calculus) has only two primitive functions— "apply" and "lambda-abstraction"; (2-) every object-level function is ultimately unary; and (3-) absolutely every term can play three roles—function, argument, or value.

The notion of free and bound variables is almost the same as in LISP. In particular, v occurs *free* in a term t if it is not within the scope of a (λ v...,) otherwise it occurs *bound*. A term is a *form* if it has no free variables. The notation $t[x/s]$ is used to represent the result of substituting s for the free occurrences of x in t. (We assume that no free variable in s becomes bound in t[x/s]. If necessary for this, bound variables of t may be renamed.)

A *computation* is a series of terms

$$t_0 \rightarrow t_1 \rightarrow \ldots \rightarrow t_j \rightarrow t_{j+1}, \ldots$$

such that each t_i reduces to t_{i+1}. (There are no environments outside of the functions.) The permissible reductions are defined by the following axioms.

First, the axiom known as *β-reduction* says that lambda-variables may be replaced by their arguments:

> (br)   ((λ v t) s) → t[v/s].

Second, reduction is a partial ordering of the terms:

(po1) $t_1 \rightarrow t_1$,
(po2)   if $t_1 \rightarrow t_2$ and $t_2 \rightarrow t_3$ then $t_1 \rightarrow t_3$.

Finally, the reduction relation is preserved under application and lambda-abstraction:

(a1)   if $t_1 \rightarrow t_2$ then $(s\ t_1) \rightarrow (s\ t_2)$,
(a2)   if $t_1 \rightarrow t_2$ then $(t_1\ s) \rightarrow (t_2\ s)$,
(la)   if $t_1 \rightarrow t_2$ then $(\lambda\ v\ t_1) \rightarrow (\lambda\ v\ t_2)$.

These rules hold for every choice of terms s, t_1, t_2, and variable v.

The description of the meaning of terms is given by the following rules for semantic equality. First, reduction preserves semantics:

(rps)   if $t_1 \rightarrow t_2$ then $t_1 = t_2$.

Second, equality is an equivalence relation:

(eq1)   if $t_1 = t_2$ then $t_2 = t_1$,
(eq2)   if $t_1 = t_2$ and $t_2 = t_3$ then $t_1 = t_3$.

It follows from the reduction axioms (a1), (a2), and (la), together with (rps), that equality is preserved under apply and lambda-conversion. Finally, there is *η-reduction*:

(er) $(\lambda\ x\ tx) \rightarrow t$

for x a variable not free in t. (Strictly speaking, when (er) is present, we have an extension of the lambda calculus known as the lambda,eta calculus.)

Example 2:   The computation determined from a given starting term by the preceding rules is not unique. The first computation performs the left-most reduction first.

$(\lambda\ w\ ww)\ ((\lambda\ v\ vv)\ u)$
$\rightarrow (\lambda\ v\ vv)\ u\ ((\lambda\ v\ vv)\ u)$ by (br)
$\rightarrow u\ u\ ((\lambda\ v\ vv)\ u)$ by (br) and (a2)
$\rightarrow u\ u\ (u\ u)$ by (a1) and (br).

Another approach is to perform the innermost reduction first.

$(\lambda\ w\ ww)\ ((\lambda\ v\ vv)\ u)$
$\rightarrow (\lambda\ w\ ww)\ (u\ u)$ by (br) and (a1)
$\rightarrow u\ u\ (u\ u)$ by (br).

In these computations, the final values are syntactically equal, so we know that they are semantically equal. This is interesting in light of the fact that in the first computation the top-level function was applied to the value of its arguments, while in the second computation, it was applied to the syntactic expressions defining its arguments! Is there some intelligence hidden here?

Continuing our comparison of the lambda calculus with LISP, β-reduction gives us a similarity and a difference. The similarity is (4+) if we choose to evaluate arguments first, then β-reduction corresponds to the kind of call-by-value computation step we have in the usual LISP. The difference is that (4-) β-reduction does not require us to evaluate a function's arguments before applying the function—thus computation in the lambda calculus is not necessarily call-by-value.

In the previous example, our computation stopped when a normal form was reached. A term t_1 is in *normal form* if it has no subterms of the form

$$(\lambda\, v\, t_2)t_3 \quad\text{or}\quad (\lambda\, v\, t_4 v)$$

with v not in t_4. A computation which ends in a normal form term is said to terminate. A term which can be reduced to a normal form is said to have a normal form. Obviously, the terms in the previous example all have normal forms.

The previous example illustrates that there may be more than one way to compute the value of a term. Are all such computations equivalent? Axioms (rps), (eq1), and (eq2) tell us that

$$t_0 \to \ldots \to t_1 \quad\text{and}\quad t_0 \to \ldots \to t_2 \quad\text{imply}\quad t_1 = t_2.$$

The picture is completed by the following fundamental theorem.

The Church-Rosser Theorem. If $t_1 = t_2$ (is provable from the nine reduction and equality axioms given above), then for some t_3 we have

$$t_1 \to \ldots \to t_3 \quad\text{and}\quad t_2 \to \ldots \to t_3.$$

This theorem does not assume that t_1 and t_2 are reductions of a common t_0 (as is suggested in the previous paragraph). However, in case they do have a common ancestor, the C-R theorem has the following corollary. (A proof by Tait & Martin-Löf of this theorem is given in Barendregt[1977].)

Corollary. If t_0 has a normal form, then it has a unique normal form.

Together, these results tell us that, if t_0 has terminating computations $t_0 \longrightarrow \ldots\longrightarrow t_1$ and $t_0 \longrightarrow \ldots\longrightarrow t_2$, then since t_1 and t_2 are normal forms, they are the same term. Thus, the preceding example is representative of terminating computations in general.

A computation *halts* when it reaches a normal form term.

Exercises

1. Show that t $\longrightarrow$ ... $\longrightarrow$ t' is equivalent to t $\longrightarrow$ t'.

2. Justify the assertion that "a term's normal form may be considered to be its value".

3. In light of the preceding assertion, we would like to know that if a term has a "value" then it can be found by a computation. In other words, if t = t' and t' is in normal form, then t$\longrightarrow$ t' Prove this statement.

4. Some terms, such as

   $(\lambda$ v vv$)(\lambda$ v vv$)$,

   do not have normal forms. Terms without normal forms do not have terminating computations. Why is the problem "t has a normal form?" like the halting problem? Would you expect it to be decidable?

5. *Extensionality* is an axiom of semantic equality for functions:
   if fx = gx for all x then f = g ,
   which can be proved using η-reduction. Prove it.

6. Can the lambda calculus be accurately implemented within LISP?

7. Does the Church-Rosser theorem hold in LISP? How is LISP's call-by-value style of evaluation related to the question?

8. Does extensionality hold in LISP? Is there a problem with it?

9. Let L be a computationally complete (i.e., every algorithm which is Turing machine programmable, or expressible as a function in the lambda calculus, is programmable in L) language for programming algorithms. Must L contain variables and allow substitution? Must L contain constants? Explain.

7.2 Straightforward computation in the lambda calculus

In this section, we represent truth values, T and F, and natural numbers, 0 , 1 , 2 , ..., as lambda terms. Nonrecursively defined functions, such as I(dentity), AND, OR, NOT, IF_THEN_ELSE_, CAR, CDR, and CONS, are also programmed as lambda terms.

Define the identity function I and the truth values T and F as follows:

$$I = (\lambda u \; u)$$
$$T = (\lambda u \; (\lambda v \; u))$$
$$F = TI.$$

With these definitions, the conditional can be defined by

$$(\text{IF } t_1 \text{ THEN } t_2 \text{ ELSE } t_3 \;) = t_1 t_2 t_3 \; .$$

Example 3: The following computations show that these definitions really work.

$$I \; t_1 \longrightarrow (\lambda u \; u) \; t_1 \longrightarrow t_1$$

$(\text{IF } \; T \; \text{ THEN } \;\; t_1 \text{ ELSE } t_2) \longrightarrow T \; t_1 \; t_2$
$\longrightarrow (\lambda u \; (\lambda v \; u)) \; t_1 \; t_2$
$\longrightarrow (\lambda v \; t_1) \; t_2$
$\longrightarrow t_1$

$(\text{IF } \; F \; \text{ THEN } t_1 \text{ ELSE } t_2) \longrightarrow F \; t_1 \; t_2 \longrightarrow T \; I \; t_1 \; t_2$
$\longrightarrow (\lambda u \; (\lambda v \; u)) \; I \; t_1 \; t_2$
$\longrightarrow (\lambda v \; I) \; t_1 \; t_2$
$\longrightarrow I \; t_2$
$\longrightarrow t_2$

The second and third arguments of IF_THEN_ELSE_ need not be Boolean valued.

Boolean functions can be defined from the conditional and the truth values. We assume that t_1 and t_2 return either T or F or are undefined (i.e., have no normal form). First, let's consider the structure of the values to be returned (AND $t_1 \; t_2$) may be defined as (IF t_1 THEN (IF t_2 THEN T ELSE F) ELSE F) which is (t_1 (t_2 T F) F). So, as a function

$$\text{AND} = (\lambda \; (u \; v) \; u(v\text{TF}) \; \text{F})$$

Similarly,

$$\text{OR} = (\lambda \; (u \; v) \; u\text{T}(v\text{TF})),$$

and

$$\text{NOT} = (\lambda u \; u\text{FT}).$$

These Boolean functions behave correctly when their arguments have values of either T or F, or are undefined. For such arguments, AND, OR, and NOT return similar values.

Ordered pairs, CAR, CDR, and then CONS, can be defined using the conditional and truth values. The ordered pair consisting of t_1 and t_2 is

$$[t_1 t_2] = (\lambda w \; w t_1 t_2).$$

Given an ordered pair, CAR and CDR must return the first and second elements (respectively):

CAR = (λ v vT)
CDR = (λ v vF) .

CONS returns an ordered pair whose first and second elements are its first and second arguments:

CONS = (λ (u v w) wuv) .

Example 4: The following computations demonstrate the operation of these functions. For an argument, we'll use

$$[t_1 t_2] = (\lambda w \ (wt_1 t_2)).$$

Now, CAR should return the first element of the pair while CDR returns the second.

CAR $[t_1 \ t_2] = (\lambda$ v vT) (λ w (w $t_1 \ t_2$))
$\longrightarrow$ (λ w (w $t_1 \ t_2$)) T
$\longrightarrow$ T $t_1 \ t_2$
$\longrightarrow t_1$

CDR $[t_1 \ t_2] = (\lambda$ v vF) (λ w (w $t_1 \ t_2$))
$\longrightarrow$ (λ w (w $t_1 \ t_2$)) F
$\longrightarrow$ F $t_1 \ t_2$
$\longrightarrow t_2$

The original argument should be returned by CONS given t_1 and t_2.

CONS $t_1 \ t_2 = (\lambda$ u (λ v (λ w wuv))) $t_1 \ t_2$
$\longrightarrow$ (λ v (λ w (w t_1 v))) t_2
$\longrightarrow$ (λ w (w $t_1 \ t_2$)) = $[t_1 \ t_2]$

The natural numbers, $0, 1, 2, \ldots$, are coded as follows:

0 = I;

and given a natural number code n, its successor is coded

n+1 = (CONS n T) = (λ w wnT).

With these definitions, the functions 1+, 1−, and the predicate ZEROP can be defined.

1+ = (λ v (CONS v T))
1− = (λ v (CAR v)) = CAR   by η-reduction,
ZEROP = (λ v (CDR v)FT)

Example 5: In the following computation from (ZEROP m+1), notice that m does not have a specific value.

$(ZEROP\ 0) = (\lambda\ v\ (CDR\ v)FT)\ I$
$\longrightarrow (CDR\ I)FT = ((\lambda\ v\ vF)\ I)FT$
$\longrightarrow (IF)IT$
$\longrightarrow FIT$
$\longrightarrow T$

$(ZEROP\ m+1) = (\lambda\ v\ (CDR\ v)FT)\ (CONS\ m\ T)$
$\longrightarrow (CDR\ (CONS\ m\ T))FT$
$\longrightarrow TFT$
$\longrightarrow F$

Another difference between LISP and the lambda calculus: (5-) the strange
implementations of data objects, such as the integers and the Boolean values,
seen in the lambda calculus are not necessary in LISP.

Exercises

1. Prove that
   $$(CAR\ (CONS\ t_1\ t_2)) \longrightarrow t_1 \text{ and } (CDR\ (CONS\ t_1\ t_2)) \longrightarrow t_2.$$

2. Are truth values in normal form? Does each natural number have a normal
   form?

3. What basic function is the value of $(NOT\ NOT)$? What can happen if AND
   and OR are given values other than T and F?

4. If $t \longrightarrow n$, where n is a natural number, then is n the value of (i.e., final
   term in a computation from) t?

7.3   Fixed-points for object functions

The fixed-point theorem for object-level functions is interesting for its elegance
and as a truly bizarre way of constructing recursive functions.

The fixed-point theorem. For every F there is an O such that

$$FO = O.$$

(O is called a fixed-point of F.)

Proof. For O equal to $(\lambda\ v\ F(vv))(\lambda\ v\ F(vv))$, we have

$$O = (\lambda\ v\ F(vv))(\lambda\ v\ F(vv)) \longrightarrow F((\lambda\ v\ F(vv))(\lambda\ v\ F(vv))) = FO.$$

The preceding computation involved a substitution, a β-reduction, and a substitution. By (rps) and (eq1) of 7.1, FO=O.

Notice that the theorem assumes that F is unary. But, since the first occurrence of the free variable v in (vv) must be a unary function, the proof assumes that every function is unary. Thus, (6-) this theorem does not hold in LISP or in most of the other algebraic systems of mathematics. On the other hand, (5+) it might be made to hold if we used closures to Curry LISP's nonunary functions.

Example 6: The following examples of the fixed-point theorem certainly do not hold in LISP—at least not if the fixed-point must be an s-expression. For the CAR of the lambda calculus, the first half of the fixed-point is

$$O_{/2} = (\lambda\ u\ CAR(uu)) = (\lambda\ u\ (\lambda\ v\ vT)(uu))$$
$$\longrightarrow (\lambda\ u\ uuT) \qquad\qquad\qquad\qquad\qquad \text{by (la).}$$

Thus, the whole fixed-point is

$$O = O_{/2}\ O_{/2} = (\lambda\ u\ uuT)(\lambda\ u\ uuT).$$

The proof of (CAR O)=O is in the following computations.

$$O = (\lambda\ u\ uuT)(\lambda\ u\ uuT)$$
$$\longrightarrow (\lambda\ u\ uuT)(\lambda\ u\ uuT)T$$
$$CAR\ O = (\lambda\ v\ vT)((\lambda\ u\ uuT)(\lambda\ u\ uuT))$$
$$\longrightarrow (\lambda\ u\ uuT)(\lambda\ u\ uuT)T = O$$

Notice that this fixed-point for CAR does not have a normal form.

Example 7: For the function 1+, the first half of the fixed-point is

$$INFINITY_{/2} = (\lambda\ u\ \ 1+(uu))$$
$$= (\lambda\ u\ (\lambda\ v\ (CONS\ v\ T))(uu))$$
$$= (\lambda\ u\ (CONS\ (uu)\ T)) = (\lambda\ u\ (\lambda\ w\ w(uu)T)),$$

so the whole fixed-point INFINITY is

$$(\lambda\ u\ (\lambda\ w\ w(uu)T))(\lambda\ u\ (\lambda\ w\ w(uu)T)).$$

Again, the computation has two halves

$$INFINITY \longrightarrow (\lambda\ w\ (w\ INFINITY\ T))$$

and

$$1+INFINITY = (\lambda\ v\ (CONS\ v\ T))\ INFINITY$$
$$\longrightarrow (CONS\ INFINITY\ T) = (\lambda\ w\ (w\ INFINITY\ T))$$
$$= INFINITY\ .$$

Exercises

1. If we allow arguments other than s-expressions, then can CDR and CAR have fixed points in the usual LISP?

2. What elementary function is returned as the value of (CAR CAR)?

3. Is there a function f, other than I, which is its own fixed point. In other words, ff = f.

4. Is there a function other than I such that fx = x for all x?

5. Define a fixed-point operator FIXEDPOINT such that: for any λ function f, (FIXEDPOINT f) is a fixed-point of f.

6. The unsolvability of semantic equality in the lambda calculus is equivalent to the nonexistence of a lambda term E satisfying
$$(E\ t_1\ t_2) \longrightarrow T \text{ if } t_1 = t_2, \text{ otherwise } (E\ t_1\ t_2) \longrightarrow F.$$
Prove that semantic equality cannot be computed by a term in the lambda calculus.

7. What changes in LISP would be required to make the fixed-point theorem hold?

7.4   Recursive functions in the lambda calculus

A recursive definition of an object R is a formula of the form R=...R..., where the right-hand side is an expression involving R. This notion of "recursive definition" is motivated by the following definition of "+".

```
+ m n = IF (ZEROP m) THEN n ELSE (+ (1- m) (1+ n))
```

However, once the notion is established, its reasonable to ask if

$$x = x^3 + x^2 + 15$$

and

$$f(t) = \tfrac{d}{dt} f(t) \text{ and } f(0) = 1$$

are recursive definitions. The fact that they can be algebraically transformed into explicit solutions,

$$x = -3 \text{ and } f(t) = e^t,$$

might lead one to conclude that they aren't. On the other hand, the thought of solving these equations iteratively leads to the correct conclusion—that they are recursive equations. In this section, we will use the fixed-point theorem to solve recursive definitions of programs algebraically.

The preceding equation defining + can be abstracted with respect to m and n to give the recursive equation

```
+ = (λ (m n)
     IF (ZEROP m) THEN n ELSE (+ (1- m) (1+ n)) ) ),
```

or further abstracted to get

```
+ = A + ,
```

where

```
A = (λ (f m n)
     IF (ZEROP m) THEN n ELSE (f (1- m) (1+ n)) ) .
```

Since + is a fixed point of A, it seems reasonable to use the construction given in the fixed-point theorem to create its program.

The construction of + proceeds as usual.

$$+_{/2} = (λ k A(kk))$$
```
     = (λ k (λ (l m n
       IF (ZEROP m) THEN n ELSE (l (1- m) (1+ n)) ) ) (kk))
     = (λ k (λ (m n)
       IF (ZEROP m) THEN n ELSE (kk (1- m) (1+ n)) )))
     = (λ (k m n)
       IF (ZEROP m) THEN n ELSE (kk (1- m) (1+ n)) )
     = (λ (k m n) (ZEROP m) n (kk (1- m) (1+ n)))
```
$$+ = +_{/2} +_{/2}$$
```
     = (λ (k m n) (ZEROP m) n (kk (1- m) (1+ n)))
       (λ (k m n) (ZEROP m) n (kk (1- m) (1+ n)))
```

Example 8: Now, assuming that 1+, 1−, and ZEROP work as planned, we can add 4 to 2.

```
+ 2 4

   ⟶ (λ (k m n) (ZEROP m) n (kk (1- m) (1+ n))) +_{/2} 2 4
   ⟶ (ZEROP 2) 4 (+_{/2} +_{/2} (1- 2) (1+ 4))
   ⟶ (+_{/2} +_{/2} (1- 2) (1+ 4))
   ⟶ + 1 5
   ⟶ (λ (k m n) (ZEROP m) n (kk (1- m) (1+ n))) +_{/2} 1 5
   ⟶ (ZEROP 1) 5 (+_{/2}+_{/2} (1- 1) (1+ 5))
   ⟶ (+_{/2}+_{/2} (1- 1) (1+ 5))
   ⟶ + 0 6
```

$\longrightarrow (\lambda (k\ m\ n)\ (ZEROP\ m)\ n\ (kk(1-\ m)\ (1+\ n)))\ +_{/2}\ 0\ 6$
$\longrightarrow (ZEROP\ 0)\ 6\ (+_{/2}\ +_{/2}\ (1-\ 0)\ (1+\ 6))$
$\longrightarrow 6$

TIMES for natural numbers is defined implicitly as the solution to

TIMES = P TIMES,

where

```
P = (λ (f m n) IF (ZEROP m) THEN   0
    ELSE   (+(f(1-   m)n)n) ).
```

Thus, the explicit definition is

TIMES = FIXEDPOINT P,

where FIXEDPOINT is from problem 5 of 7.3.

EQ(uality)N for the natural numbers can be constructed as follows:

EQN = FIXEDPOINT E,

where

```
E = (λ (e m n)
    IF (ZEROP m) THEN (ZEROP n)
    ELSE (e(1- m)(1- n)) ).
```

Minimization and search functions are also constructed as fixed-points. For example, suppose that for each m we need to find the least natural number n for which $0 = Xmn$—where X is a term of the lambda calculus. We begin with an implicit definition of SEARCH in terms of its values

```
SEARCH m =
IF (ZEROP Xmn) THEN n ELSE SEARCH(1+m)
```

of SEARCH. Then, abstract the idea from m,

```
SEARCH  =
(λ m (IF (ZEROP Xmn) THEN n ELSE   SEARCH(1+m))),
```

and from SEARCH to get

```
DEF = (λ (s m) (IF (ZEROP Xmn) THEN n ELSE s(1+m))).
```

SEARCH is the fixed point of DEF, and so we have

```
SEARCH = (λ  v DEF(vv)) (λ v DEF(vv))
```

as an explicit definition of SEARCH.

Exercises

1. Let ADD_0 be any function and define $ADD_{k+1} = A\ ADD_k$, where A is as defined in this section. Show that the ADD constructed as the fixed point of A satisfies

$$ADD = \lim_{k \to \infty} ADD_k$$

Hint: For $m < k$, $ADD_k\ m\ n = m+n$.

2. Assuming that + works properly, show that $(TIMES\ 2\ 4) \longrightarrow 8$.

3. Construct the predicate < for the natural numbers.

4. The finite-state automaton (illustrated by the transition diagram in exercise 5 of Section 5.5) can be represented in the lambda calculus as a solution to the equations $AT = A$, $AF = B$, $BT = C$, $BF = A$, $CT = A$, $CF = C$. Find this solution.

7.5   Pure LISP in the lambda calculus

The s-expressions consist of the "atoms"

$$NIL = (\lambda\ w\ wTF).$$

T, and F, the natural numbers; and the "nonatomic" values produced by CONS. Of course, our notion of "atomic" is meaningful only from the point of view of LISP.

The remaining basic predicates are defined as follows:

$$NULL = (\lambda x\ \ AND(CAR\ x)(NOT(CDR\ x)))$$

and

$$ATOM = (\lambda x\ \ OR(OR(NULL\ x)(NUMBERP\ x))(OR\ x\ (NOT\ x))),$$

where NUMBERP is implicitly defined by

$$NUMBERP\ m\ =\ IF(ZEROP\ m)THEN\ T\ ELSE(NUMBERP(1-\ m))$$

and explicitly as the fixed point of

$$(\lambda\ n\ (\lambda\ x\ \ IF(ZEROP\ x)THEN\ T\ ELSE\ (n\ (1-\ x)))).$$

EQ is extended to all atoms by

$$EQ = (\lambda\ (x\ y)$$
$$OR(OR(AND\ x\ y)(AND(NOT\ x)(NOT\ y)))$$
$$(OR(AND(NULL\ x)(NULL\ y))(EQN\ x\ y))).$$

Then, EQUAL is defined by

```
EQUAL   =   (FIXEDPOINT
  (λ (e   x   y)
     IF(OR(ATOM   x)(ATOM   y))
     THEN(EQ   x   y)
     ELSE(AND(e(CAR x)(CAR y))(e(CDR x)(CDR y)))))) .
```

HISTORY:

> With respect to the need to be able to treat functions as data, we
> have... "And so the way to do that was to borrow from Church's
> Lambda Calculus, to borrow the lambda notation. Now, having
> borrowed this notation, one of the myths concerning LISP ... is that
> LISP is somehow a realization of the lambda calculus, or [that] that
> was the intention. The truth is that I didn't understand the lambda
> calculus, really. In particular, I didn't understand that you really
> could do conditional expressions ... in the pure lambda calculus. So
> it wasn't an attempt to make the lambda calculus practical, although
> if someone had started out with that intention, he might have ended
> up with something like LISP." McCarthy[1981]

Exercises

1. Paternity. What are the two or three most important similarities between
   the lambda calculus and LISP? ... the most important differences?

2. Library exercise. Find and read J. Barkley Rosser's article *Highlights in
   the History of the Lambda-Calculus*, in the Proceedings of the ACM's
   1982 Symposium on LISP and Functional Computing.

3. Combinatory algebra. Define a CA-REDUCE in LISP such that terms in
   the combinatory algebra built up from S and K are evaluated as their
   rewrite rules [defined in exercise 5 of 6.1] dictate.

4. Combinatory algebra. Define S and K as lambda terms so that the APPLY
   of the lambda calculus makes them behave as dictated by their rewrite
   rules. Deduce that combinatory algebra is no stronger than the lambda
   calculus.

5. Combinatory algebra. Define lambda-abstraction

   $$v, term \longrightarrow (\lambda \quad v \quad term)$$

   in terms of S and K so that CA-REDUCE can be used to evaluate terms of
   the lambda calculus. Deduce that the lambda calculus is no stronger than
   combinatory algebra.

7.6 Additional reading

For ideas on the significance of the lambda calculus to computing, see Landin [1965] and Evans[1972]. An original presentation of these ideas is present in Church [1941]. For a less superficial treatment of the lambda calculus—Revesz [1988]. Church's thesis is justified in great detail in Davis [1958]. SCHEME—an interpreter for the lambda calculus is described in Sussman&Steele [1975]. An interesting philosophical discussion of combinatory algebra is given in Curry [1978]. Clarke[1980] describes a simple reduction machine for combinatory algebra. For fun with combinatory algebra, try Smullyan[1985].

8

Automatic Reasoning, Algebraic Intelligence

What is really happening when a machine does something that seems to be intelligent? If it recognizes a spoken word, proves a theorem, plays a good chess game, or solves a problem in calculus, then does it have some idea of what is going on? Of course not. Machine intelligence is fundamentally different from human intelligence. It is an illusion based on algebraic links between syntax and semantics. The semantics of a language represents meaning in terms of an object world. When a machine's behavior seems intelligent, it is because it is semantically appropriate. However, the machine is simply a symbol shuffler—its abilities are limited to syntactic processing. Algebraic systems which provide strong formal connections between their semantics and their syntax make it possible for a symbol shuffling machine to appear to understand what it is doing.

This chapter covers logic, PROLOG, and a view of intelligence. Propositional logic and its role in automatic reasoning are used to (1) demonstrate algebraic connections between syntax and semantics which make algebraic languages important in computing, (2) return to one of the original applications of LISP, and (3) look into the classical algebraic approach to artificial intelligence. A glimpse of predicate logic sets the stage for PROLOG. PROLOG is important as an algebraic language whose relation to predicate logic is approximately the same as LISP's to the lambda calculus. Finally, we close with speculation on the strengths and limitations of algebraic intelligence—intelligence based on the links between syntax and semantics provided by algebraic languages.

8.1 Logics

HISTORY:

"IBM 704: 220 theorems (in the propositional calculus) in three
minutes.

...

Results are reported here of a rather successful attempt at proving
all theorems, totalling nearly 400, of [Bertrand Russell's] *Principia
Mathematica* which are strictly in the realm of logic, viz., the
restricted predicate calculus with equality. ... It is suggested that the
time is ripe for a new branch of applied logic which may be called
'inferential' analysis, which treats proofs as analysis does
calculations. This discipline seems capable, in the not too remote
future, of leading to machine proofs of difficult new [mathematical]
theorems. ... "

Hao Wang, Toward mechanical mathematics, the IBM Journal,
1960. ©1960 International Business Machines Corporation.
Reprinted with permission.

Many logics and algebras are the mathematical formalizations of natural reasoning mechanisms whose fossilized remains can be seen in natural language.
Propositional logic is the formalization of mechanisms involved in the construction, interpretation, and processing of simple statements. Statements are
variable-free sentences having a truth value and are built up using logical operators such as ¬ (not), ∧ (and), ∨ (or), ⟶ (implies), etc. For example,

> If it is raining or snowing,
> then the game will not be played.

can be formalized in propositional logic as

$$(R \vee S) \rightarrow \neg G$$

where R, S, and G are variables bound to "it is raining," "it is snowing," and
"the game is played." This abstraction captures everything except the notion of
future time—we would have to go to temporal logic for that.

Predicate logic is an extension of propositional logic designed to formalize
more complex statements involving functions on objects and properties of, or
relations between, objects. This domain is an algebra providing constants, variables, functions, and formulas. The formulas are treated as atomic statements in
building up more complicated expressions. For example,

> Every child's mother loves it.

is formalized in the predicate calculus as

∀x (CHILD⟨x⟩ → LOVES⟨MOTHER-OF⟨x⟩, x⟩),

where MOTHER-OF⟨⟩ is a function whose value represents the mother of its argument, and CHILD⟨⟩ and LOVES⟨⟩ are truth-valued relations.

Other logics include modal logic, logic of knowledge, second-order logic, process logic, temporal logic, program logic, etc. All of these formalize an aspect of human reasoning that originated in a more or less natural context. They are all essentially term algebras, and as such they put an aspect of natural reasoning within reach of a machine.

8.1.1 Propositional logic

The *formulas* of propositional logic consist of: (1) propositional constants T and F, (2) propositional variables A,B,... from some finite set VARIABLES of symbols, and (3) composites

$$(\neg\alpha), (\alpha \vee \beta), (\alpha \wedge \beta), \text{ and } (\alpha \to \beta),$$

where the Greek letters stand for simpler propositional formulas. A logical constant, variable, or the negation of a constant or variable is a *literal*. An ∨-*clause*(∧-*clause*) is the disjunction (resp. conjunction) of literals.

The semantics of a logical language is defined in terms of truth-valued interpretations. In the case of propositional logic, an environment

$$m : \text{VARIABLES } (\alpha) \to \{T, F\},$$

assigning truth values to the variables of a formula α can be extended to α by the following:

$$
\begin{aligned}
m\langle T\rangle &= T \text{ and } m\langle F\rangle = F,\\
m\langle\neg\beta\rangle &= T \text{ if } m\langle\beta\rangle = F,\\
&= F \text{ otherwise},\\
m\langle(\beta \vee \gamma)\rangle &= F \text{ if } m\langle\beta\rangle = m\langle\gamma\rangle = F,\\
&= T \text{ otherwise},\\
m\langle(\beta \wedge \gamma)\rangle &= T \text{ if } m\langle\beta\rangle = m\langle\gamma\rangle = T,\\
&= F \text{ otherwise}.
\end{aligned}
$$

$\alpha \leftrightarrow \beta$ is an abbreviation for $(\alpha \to \beta)\wedge(\beta \to \alpha)$, and $\alpha \to \beta$ is an abbreviation for $(\neg\alpha)\vee\beta$. An interpretation is also known as a *model*. α is *satisfied* in m if m⟨α⟩=T. It is *valid* if it is satisfied in every possible model of the language. Given formulas $\alpha_1, ..., \alpha_k$ and β, β is a *consequence* of $\alpha_1, ..., \alpha_k$, if for every m,

$$m\langle\alpha_1\rangle = ... = m\langle\alpha_k\rangle = T \text{ implies } m\langle\beta\rangle = T.$$

To the extent that artificial intelligence involves programming a machine to reason about a real world, questions of the form

Is β true in the world when $\alpha_1, ..., \alpha_k$ are true?

are fundamental. If the issues can be represented in propositional logic, then we are asking

Is β is a consequence of $\alpha_1, ..., \alpha_k$?

because propositional models are our formalizations of the real world. These issues will be referred to as "automatic reasoning".

Algorithm 1. The simplest approach to determining validity is to use a truth table. A truth table for α is a table listing all models for α's variables, together with computations of the truth values of α. Models and their computations are lines in the table. Thus,

α *is valid if it is true* in *every line of the table.*

Since there are only finitely many models and lines, the computation will eventually halt. However, the number of lines (i.e., models) is 2^j, where j is the number of variables, so the computation time will generally grow exponentially in j.

Example 1: Is $(\alpha \to (\beta \to \gamma))$ a consequence of $((\alpha \to \beta) \to (\alpha \to \gamma))$? The following truth table shows us that it is.

α	β	γ	α	$\to$	$(\beta \to \gamma)$	$(\alpha \to \beta)$	$\to$	$(\alpha \to \gamma)$
T	T	T		T	(T)		T	(T)
T	T	F	(T)	F	(F)	(T)	F	(F)
T	F	T		T	(T)		T	(T)
T	F	F		T	(T)	(F)	T	(F)
F	T	T		T	(T)		T	(T)
F	T	F	(F)	T	(F)		T	(T)
F	F	T		T	(T)		T	(T)
F	F	F		T	(T)		T	(T)

There is an inadequacy to this model-listing approach. If the number of models is infinite (or just grows exponentially with the size of the input), then model-listing algorithms may not produce a value (within a reasonable time). This suggests that we should work with descriptions of large families of models rather than with the models themselves. Such a syntactic approach is seen in proving theorems from axioms.

Syntactic computing in the propositional calculus is based on using axioms and deduction rules to produce theorems. Kleene[1967] gives the following axiom schemas:

(1a) $\alpha \to (\beta \to \alpha)$,
(1b) $(\alpha \to \beta) \to ((\alpha \to (\beta \to \gamma)) \to (\alpha \to \gamma))$,
(2a) $\alpha \to (\beta \to (\alpha \wedge \beta))$,
(2b) $(\alpha \wedge \beta) \to \alpha$,
(2c) $(\alpha \wedge \beta) \to \beta$,
(3a) $\alpha \to (\alpha \vee \beta)$,
(3b) $\beta \to (\alpha \vee \beta)$,
(3c) $(\alpha \to \gamma) \to ((\beta \to \gamma) \to ((\alpha \vee \beta) \to \gamma))$,
(4a) $(\alpha \to \beta) \to ((\alpha \to \neg\beta) \to \neg\alpha)$,
(4b) $(\neg\neg\alpha) \to \alpha$.

An *axiom* is an expression produced by replacing the Greek variables of an axiom schema by propositional formulas. The *deduction rule* is modus ponens:

$$\frac{\alpha, \ (\alpha \to \beta)}{\beta}$$

which is read as "β is a consequence of α and $(\alpha \longrightarrow \beta)$".

A *proof* is a list of formulas

$$\gamma_1, \gamma_2, ..., \gamma_k$$

such that each γ_j is either an axiom or the result of applying a deduction rule to some previously occurring γ_i and $(\gamma_i \to \gamma_j)$. A formula is a *theorem* if it is the last formula in a proof. This notion can be relativised. Given hypotheses $\alpha_1, ..., \alpha_j$ and β, β is *provable from* $\alpha_1, ..., \alpha_j$ if there is a sequence of formulas

$$\gamma_1, \gamma_2, ..., \gamma_k$$

such that each γ_i is an axiom, one of the hypotheses $\alpha_1, ..., \alpha_j$, or a deduction from preceding formulas and $\gamma_k = \beta$. The existence of a proof of β from $\alpha_1, ..., \alpha_j$ is denoted

$$\alpha_1, ..., \alpha_j \vdash \beta.$$

Thus, $\vdash \beta$ denotes "β is a theorem."

Example 2: A proof of $(A \to B) \to (A \to C)$ from $A \to (B \to C)$ using Kleene's axions as follows.

1. $A \to (B \to C)$ given
2. $(A \to (B \to C)) \to ((A \to B) \to (A \to (B \to C)))$ axiom of schema 1a
3. $((A \to B) \to (A \to (B \to C)))$ modus ponens on lines 1 and 2
4. $((A \to B) \to (A \to (B \to C))) \to (((A \to B) \to ((A \to (B \to C)) \to (A \to C)))$
   $\to ((A \to B) \to (A \to C))$) an axiom of schema 1b
5. $((A \to B) \to ((A \to (B \to C)) \to (A \to C))) \to ((A \to B) \to (A \to C))$
   modus ponens on lines 3 and 4

    6. $(A{\rightarrow}B){\rightarrow}((A{\rightarrow}(B{\rightarrow}C)){\rightarrow}(A{\rightarrow}C))$ an axiom of schema 1b

    7. $(A{\rightarrow}B){\rightarrow}(A{\rightarrow}C)$ modus ponens on lines 5 and 6.

Thus, we have $A{\longrightarrow}(B{\longrightarrow}C){\vdash}(A{\longrightarrow}B){\longrightarrow}(A{\longrightarrow}C)$. This demonstration should convince the reader that formal theorem proving is an excruciatingly tedious process, best left to a machine.

Automatic theorem proving deals with deciding whether or not formulas are theorems, whether or not they are provable from other given formulas, whether or not lists of formulas are proofs (i.e., proof checking), and constructing or finding proofs. We will consider decision procedures for these questions.

Algorithm 2. Theorem proving by the British Museum algorithm: How can we determine whether or not there is a proof of a given formula α? One approach is to use a search through all proofs. Every formula is a finite string of basic symbols from VARIABLES together with $\longrightarrow, \wedge, \vee, \neg$, (, and). An ordering of these basic symbols can be extended to a lexicographic ordering of formulas just as an ordering of the letters a,b,c,...,z determines an ordering of words in the dictionary. Extend this ordering of the formulas to an ordering of finite lists of formulas. Remove all lists of formulas which are not proofs (exercise 3 describes a proof checker). We now have (in principle at least) a computable listing

$$\pi_1 \ \pi_2 \ \pi_3 ... \pi_k ...$$

of all proofs. As the proofs, π_i, are generated, perform the tests (MEMBER $\beta \ \pi_i$) and (MEMBER $\neg\beta \ \pi_i$). If a proof passes one of the tests, then halt and return the value T (in case the first test was passed) or F (if the second test was passed). If the answer to our question is "yes", then this algorithm will always eventually halt and return "T". However, if the answer is "no", then the algorithm may halt and return "F", or it may compute for ever. Thus, we are not guaranteed a complete answer.

This algorithm is far too dumb to ever be used to make the decision. However, it does serve two purposes. First, it provides a quick and easy proof that deciding provability is not impossible. Second, it serves as an example of an extreme case of theorem proving by symbol shuffling.

There is a similarity between the semantic ideas of "valid" and "consequence of" and the syntactic "theorem" and "provable from". Are the theorems satisfied in every model? Is every valid formula provable? The next section explores links between syntax and semantics which hold in the propositional logic and are typical of other logics.

Example 3: This example moves the discussion from pure mathematics to LISP and sets the stage for the exercises. First, we develop a formalism in LISP for terms of the propositional calculus and then define functions on them.

Given the list VARIABLES of propositional variables, formulas will be represented in operator-prefix form as lists. The constants are T and F, respectively. If A and B are elements of VARIABLES, then (A ∧¬ A)⟶ B is represented in LISP by (--> (∧ A (¬ A)) B). Formulas are recognized by PC-FORMULA.

```
*    (DEFUN PC-FORMULA (X)
         (COND
          ((MEMBER X VARIABLES)   T)
          ((ATOM X)   (OR (EQ X T) (EQ X F)))
          ;Other atomics are either variables, T, or F.
          ((EQ (CAR X) '~)   (PC-FORMULA (CADR X)))
                         ;¬α is a formula if α is a formula.
          ((MEMBER (CAR X) '(--> ∧ V))
           (AND (PC-FORMULA (CADR X))
                (PC-FORMULA (CADDR X))) )
                      ; Others are of the form (binary α β)
                      ; where α and β are formulas.
          (T   NIL) ))
     ==> PC-FORMULA
```

Axioms of the first schema can be recognized by PC-AXIOM-1A.

```
*    (DEFUN PC-AXIOM-1A (X)
     (AND
      (= 3 (LENGTH X) (LENGTH (CADDR X)))
                                    ;X is (? ? (? ? ?))
      (EQUAL (CAR X) '-->) (EQUAL (CAADDR X) '-->)
                  ;X is of the form (--> ? (--> ? ?))
      (EQUAL (CAR X) (CADDR (CADDR X)))
                                    ; (--> Y (--> Z Y))
      (PC-FORMULA (CADR X))              ;Y is a formula
      (PC-FORMULA (CADR (CADDR X))) ))   ;Z is a formula
     ==> PC-AXIOM-1A
```

Exercises

Develop the following functions for automating the propositional calculus. Theorem proving by humans is generally considered an intelligent activity which requires an understanding of the meaning of mathematical formulas. These exercises show that it can be reduced to syntax.

1. Recognizing axioms. PC-AXIOM<α> returns an identifying schema number (i.e., 1a,...,4b) if its argument is an axiom, NIL otherwise.

2. Computing consequences by modus ponens. Given formulas α_1, α_2, and β, MODUS-PONENS$<\alpha_1, \alpha_2, \beta,>$ returns T if β is a consequence of α_1, α_2 by modus ponens, otherwise NIL. Given a formula β and a list of formulas FL, PC-DEDUCTION$<$FL$, \beta>$ returns (i j) if α_1, and α_2 are the ith and j^{th} elements of FL and MODUS-PONENS$<\alpha_1, \alpha_2, \beta>$=T, otherwise NIL is returned.

3. A proof checker for the propositional calculus. Given a list FL=$(\alpha_1...\alpha_k)$, PC-PROOF$<$FL$>$ determines whether or not FL is a proof. If FL is a proof, then the corresponding list $(E_1 ... E_k)$ of formula explanations (i.e., axiom identification numbers or hypothesis identification numbers) is returned. If it is not a proof, then NIL is returned.

4. A diagnostic function for bad proofs. Given a nonNIL list FL for which PC-PROOF$<$FL$>$=NIL, PC-PROOF-ERROR$<$FL$>$ returns the first element of FL which fails to be either an axiom or a consequence of its predecessors.

5. Theorems have models. Use a truth table to show that every axiom evaluates to T in every model. Show that the set of sentences that are T in every model is closed under modus ponens. Conclude that all theorems are valid. Show that the set of sentences satisfied by a single fixed model is closed under modus ponens.

6. Refutation. Use the axioms to show that given $\alpha_1, ..., \alpha_k$ and β,

$$\alpha_1, ..., \alpha_k \vdash \beta$$

if and only if

$$\alpha_1, ..., \alpha_k, \neg\beta \vdash \gamma \text{ for every formula } \gamma.$$

One particular value of γ is F.

8.1.2 Fundamental theorems for the propositional calculus

The main point of this section is to develop the completeness and model existence theorems. These theorems provide an important link between syntax and semantics from which a bit of algebraic intelligence can evolve.

Axioms for a logic are *consistent* if for every formula α at most one of $\vdash \alpha$ and $\vdash \neg\alpha$ holds.

Consistency Theorem. The propositional calculus is consistent.

Proof. By exercise 5, theorems are T in every model. Any variable A is not true in a model m for which $m(\neg A)=F$. Thus, $\neg A$ is not a theorem. Let α be a given formula. In light of axiom schema (4a), one of $A \rightarrow \alpha$ and $A \rightarrow \neg\alpha$ is not a theorem. Finally, by (1a), one of α and $\neg\alpha$ is not a theorem.

The most important theorems for any logic are its consistency theorem and its completeness theorem.

Completeness Theorem. (a) Given α, α is valid if and only if α is a theorem. (b) For formulas $\alpha_1, ..., \alpha_k$, and β, we have β is a consequence of $\alpha_1, ..., \alpha_k$ if and only if $\alpha_1, ..., \alpha_a k \vdash \beta$.

Proof. (a) Exercise 5 proves the "if" direction. Suppose that α is not a theorem. It is possible to construct a set of formulas M such that (1) $\neg\alpha$ is in M; (2) the axioms are in M; (3) M is closed under modus ponens; and (4) for every variable β, M contains either β or $\neg\beta$. (The details of this construction of M are left to the reader.) Define a model m for every variable by $m(\beta)=T$ if β is in M, $m(\beta)=F$ if $\neg\beta$ is in M. It follows that $m(\neg\alpha)=T$ and $m(\alpha)=F$. α is not valid. Thus, we have the "only if" case.

Algorithm 3. Theorem proving by truth table: The completeness theorem shows us that we may use truth tables to answer the question partially solved by algorithm 2. Given α, compute its truth table. There exists a proof of α just in case α is T in every line of the table. Notice that this algorithm always halts within a fixed time frame, consequently it answers the question of provability completely.

We may reduce the idea of relative provability (i.e., of proving β from $\alpha_1, ..., \alpha_k$) to a question of simple provability with the help of the following theorem.

Deduction Theorem. Given formulas $\alpha_1, ..., \alpha_k$ and β, $\alpha_1, ..., \alpha_k \vdash \beta$ if and only if $\vdash (\alpha_1 \wedge ... \wedge \alpha_k) \longrightarrow \beta$. A proof of this theorem is given in Kleene[1967, page 39].

Algorithm 4 (continuing from algorithms 3 and 1). There is a proof of β from $\alpha_1, ..., \alpha_k$ just in case the values of $\alpha_1 \wedge ... \wedge \alpha_k \rightarrow \beta$ in its truth table are all T. By the completeness theorem, β is a consequence of $\alpha_1, ..., \alpha_k$ just in case the values of $\alpha_1 \wedge ... \wedge \alpha_k \rightarrow \beta$ in its truth table are all T.

Algorithm 5. By the completeness theorem and the deduction theorem, β is a consequence of $\alpha_1, ..., \alpha_k$ just in case $\alpha_1 \wedge ... \wedge \alpha_k \rightarrow \beta$ is valid. Thus, every line of the truth table for $\alpha_1 \wedge ... \wedge \alpha_k \rightarrow \beta$ is T if and only if β is a consequence of $\alpha_1, ..., \alpha_k$.

8.1.3   Other approaches to automatic resaoning in PC

Another approach to bridging the gap between meaning and symbol shuffling is based on disjunctions of ∧-clauses. A formula is in disjunctive form if it is a disjunction

$$(\mu_1^1 \wedge \mu_1^2 \wedge ...) \vee ... \vee (\mu_j^1 \wedge \mu_j^2 \wedge ...)$$

of ∧-clauses. Recall that each μ_i^j of a clause is a literal. In this section, we will use ∨ and ∧ as operators on any number of arguments. Consequently, a clause may contain 0 literals, and a disjunctive form may contain 0 clauses. ∧-clauses which contain neither complementary literals (i.e., A and ¬A for some variable A), nor ¬T, nor F are *consistent*. Clearly, every consistent ∧-clause has at least one model which it directly describes. When a formula is converted into an equivalent disjunctive form, we have, in the disjunction, a list of the formula's models.

Example 4:   The formula $(A{\rightarrow}B){\rightarrow} \neg A$ is converted into a disjunctive form as follows:

$(A{\longrightarrow}B){\longrightarrow} \neg A$	
$(\neg(\neg A \vee B) \vee \neg A)$	replace $\longrightarrow$ by its definition
$((\neg\neg A \wedge \neg B) \vee \neg A)$	move all ¬'s in to literals
$((A \wedge \neg B) \vee \neg A)$	reduce multiple negations.

The consistent clauses $(A \vee \neg B)$ and ¬A describe the models

$m_1(A)=T$, $m_1(B)=F$ and $m_2(A)=F$, $m_2(B)=T$ or F.

Thus, by converting the formula into disjunctive form, we have (syntactically) converted the formula into a list of descriptions of its models. A formula with no models reduces to F. For example, $T{\rightarrow}(A \wedge \neg A)$ reduces to $(\neg T \vee (A \wedge \neg A))$, $(F \vee F)$, and finally F.

A standard way of expressing something is called a normal form. The following theorem proves the existence of a *disjunctive normal form (dnf)* for propositional formulas.

Disjunctive Normal Form Theorem. For every formula α, there is a disjunctive form dnf(α) such that α and dnf(α) have the same models.

Proof. For every model m, there is a corresponding ∧-clause γ_m (a conjunction of the literals satisfied in m) which is satisfied precisely by m. For every set $m_1,...,m_j$ of models, the disjunction $\gamma_1 \vee ... \vee \gamma_j$ of corresponding ∧-clauses is satisfied precisely by these models. Thus, if a given formula α has models $m_1,...,m_j$, then dnf(α)=($\gamma_1 \vee ... \vee \gamma_j$).

Stickel[1886] shows that a formula's dnf in not unique. In particular, $(\alpha \leftrightarrow \beta) \wedge (\beta \leftrightarrow \gamma) \wedge (\gamma \leftrightarrow \alpha)$ is equivalent to both $(\neg\alpha \vee \beta) \wedge (\neg\beta \vee \gamma) \wedge (\neg\gamma \vee \alpha)$ and $(\neg\beta \vee \alpha) \wedge (\neg\gamma \vee \beta) \wedge (\neg\alpha \vee \gamma)$.

A precise procedure for computing dnf(α) from α is important at this point. Notice that the procedure removes all $\wedge$-clauses which are not consistent.

DNF-algorithm. By applying the following rewrite rules to a given formula, we will eventually arrive at a dnf.

$$(\alpha \Longrightarrow \beta) \Longrightarrow (\neg\alpha) \vee \beta,$$
$$\neg\neg\alpha \Longrightarrow \alpha,$$
$$\alpha \wedge \beta \Longrightarrow \beta \wedge \alpha,$$
$$\alpha \vee \beta \Longrightarrow \beta \vee \alpha,$$
$$\alpha \wedge (\beta \wedge \gamma...) \Longrightarrow (\alpha \wedge \beta \wedge \gamma...),$$
$$\alpha \vee (\beta \vee \gamma...) \Longrightarrow (\alpha \vee \beta \vee \gamma...),$$
$$\alpha \wedge (\beta \vee \gamma...) \Longrightarrow (\alpha \wedge \beta) \vee (\alpha \wedge \gamma) \vee ...,$$
$$(...\alpha \wedge ... \wedge \neg\alpha...) \Longrightarrow F,$$
$$(...\alpha \vee ... \vee \neg\alpha...) \Longrightarrow T,$$
$$\alpha \wedge T \Longrightarrow \alpha,$$
$$\alpha \wedge F \Longrightarrow F,$$
$$\alpha \wedge \alpha \Longrightarrow \alpha,$$
$$\alpha \vee T \Longrightarrow T,$$
$$\alpha \vee F \Longrightarrow \alpha,$$
$$\alpha \vee \alpha \Longrightarrow \alpha,$$
$$\neg(\alpha \vee \beta) \Longrightarrow (\neg\alpha \wedge \neg\beta),$$
$$\neg(\alpha \wedge \beta) \Longrightarrow (\neg\alpha \vee \neg\beta).$$

The disjunctive normal forms produced by these rules (from a given formula) may differ in the order of their literals and clauses.

The question of model existence remains. This issue is settled by the following obvious theorem.

DNF Model Existence Theorem. Every nonempty disjunctive normal form has a model.

Corollary. A propositional formula α has a model if and only if dnf(α) is not F.

Algorithm 6. This algorithm is based on the equivalence of the following:

"β a consequence of $\alpha_1, ..., \alpha_k$,"
"$\alpha_1, ..., \alpha_k, \neg\beta$ has no model,"
"$\alpha_1 \wedge ... \wedge \alpha_k \wedge \neg\beta$ has no model,"
"dnf$(\alpha_1 \wedge ... \wedge \alpha_k \wedge \neg\beta) = F$."

The algorithm is: (1) given $\alpha_1, ..., \alpha_k$ and β compute $\gamma = dnf(\alpha_1 \wedge ... \wedge \alpha_k \wedge \neg\beta)$, (2) if γ=F, then return T, otherwise return F.

Resolution is a procedure that is, in a sense, complementary to the one just described. It is a generalization of modus ponens which operates on a set of disjunctions. Modus ponens can be expressed as

$$\frac{\alpha, (\neg\alpha \vee \beta)}{\beta}$$

If both of the hypotheses are viewed as disjunctions, then by allowing larger disjunctions, we have

$$\frac{(... \vee \alpha_i \vee \gamma \vee \alpha_{i+2} \vee ...), (... \vee \beta_j \vee \neg\gamma \vee \beta_{j+2} \vee ...)}{(... \vee \alpha_i \vee \alpha_{i+2} \vee ... \vee \beta_j \vee \beta_{j+2} \vee ...)}$$

while smaller disjunctions give

$$\frac{(\alpha), (\neg\alpha)}{F} \text{ and } \frac{(\alpha \vee ...), ()}{F}$$

Deduction by these rules is known as *resolution*. The conclusion is known as the *resolvent* of the hypotheses. Obviously, resolution is equivalent to modus ponens (together with the definition of $\longrightarrow$ and the associativity and commutativity of $\vee$). The difference is that resolution is expressed in a form that makes it convenient to use as an operation on a set of disjunctions. When resolution is used in predicate logic, a term operation known as unification is also required. Given a set S of disjunctions, the smallest set S' containing S and closed under resolution is the *closure of S*.

Resolution Theorem. Let S be a set of $\vee$-clauses, and S' be the closure of S under resolution. (a) S and S' have the same models. (b) F is in S' if and only if S has no models.

Proof. (a) Being equivalent to modus ponens, resolution preserves models (see exercise 5 of the first section). (b) F is not satisfied by any model. So, if F is in S', then there are no models for S' and, by exercise 5 of the first section, there are no models for S. Now, for "if": S_0=S has no models. Given S_i with no models, let M be a set of literals which contains one literal from each $\vee$-clause β in S_i. Any model m of M is a model of S_i, so M has no models. A set of literals M with no models contains complementary literals α and $\neg\alpha$. Form S_{i+1} from S_i by replacing $\vee$-clauses containing α and $\neg\alpha$ by their resolvent. Every model for S_{i+1} is a model for S_i, thus S_{i+1} has no models. By induction, we can continue until S_i contains F. Since each S_i is a subset of S', F is in S'.

Example 5: Resolution can be applied to automate reasoning about suburban fauna. We have Alice, Betty, Candy, Edward, Frank, and George. We are given the following facts.

1' Alice is married to either Edward or George.

2' One of the women is married to Frank.

3' If Candy is married to Frank, then George is not Alice's husband.

4' But, if Frank is married to Betty, then George is married to Candy.

5' No one has more than one spouse.

We wish to know if

6' Candy is married.

To answer this question, we will express the given facts in propositional logic using WM to denote "W(oman) and M(an) are married", where W is a woman's initial and M is a man's initial.

1	AE ∨ AG	
2	AF ∨ BF ∨ CF	
3	¬CF ∨ ¬AG	from (CF ⟶ ¬AG) of 3'
4	¬BF ∨ CG	from (BF ⟶ CG) of 4'
5_{WMN}	¬WM ∨ ¬WN	for V,W = A,B,C, and M,N = E,F,G
5_{VWM}	¬VM ∨ ¬WM	V,W = A,B,C, and M,N = E,F,G
6	CE ∨ CF ∨ CG	

We will now attempt to prove that 6 follows from 1,...,5 by deducing F from 1,...,5 plus the negation ¬6 of 6.

¬6	¬CE, ¬CF, ¬CG,	the negation of 6
7	AF ∨ BF	resolve 2 and ¬6
8	¬BF	resolve 4 and ¬6
9	AF	resolve 7 and 8
10	¬AE	resolve 9 and 5_{AEF}
11	¬AG	resolve 9 and 5_{AFG}
12	AG	resolve 1 and 10
13	F	resolve 11 and 12

Thus, Candy must be married to someone.

Algorithm 7. This algorithm is based on the equivalence of the following.

"β is a consequence of $\alpha_1, ..., \alpha_k$",
"$S = \alpha_1, ..., \alpha_k, \neg\beta$ has no models",

which by the resolution theorem is equivalent to

"S', the closure of S under resolution, has no models",
"F is in S' ".

Thus, we have

$\alpha_1, ..., \alpha_k \vdash \beta$ iff F is in resolution closure $\alpha_1, ..., \alpha_k, \neg\beta$.

Nonresolution theorem proving in developed in Bledsoe[1977].

Exercises

These exercises define functions which make up a resolution theorem prover for propositional logic. Program each function.

1. V-CLAUSES. Program a function V-CLAUSES which, given a formula α of propositional logic, returns a set of V-clauses whose conjunction is equivalent to α.

2. RESOLUTION*. Given a set S of V-clauses, RESOLUTION* returns S' the resolution closure of S. Hint: use a subordinate function which resolves with respect to one variable at a time.

3. CONSEQUENCE. Combine V-CLAUSES and RESOLUTION* into an implementation CONSEQUENCE$((\alpha_1, ..., \alpha_k), \beta)$ of algorithm 7.

4. Use the method of algorithm 7 to determine that

   H_2CO_3 and $Mg(OH)_2$
   can be synthesized from
   MgO, H_2, O_2, and C,
   given the reactions
   $2MgO + H_2 \rightarrow Mg + Mg(OH)_2,$
   $C + O_2 \rightarrow CO_2,$
   $CO_2 + H_2O \longrightarrow H_2CO_3,$
   $2H_2 + O_2 \longrightarrow 2H_2O.$

5. Can Candy be married to Edward? to Frank? to George?

6. Prove that out of our six suburbanites—Alice,...,George—there is a subset of three people P1, P2, P3 all of which know each other or all of which are strangers. Use kPQ as a representation for "P knows Q". An easy informal proof is given on page 1 of Grahm, Rothschild & Spencer[1980].

7. Wang devised a rewrite-rule-based approach to automatic reasoning in propositional logic—see Wang[1963] or McCarthy[1960]. Look it up, then develop a theorem prover based on this algorithm. More recently, rewrite rules have been used as the heart of a refutation theorem proving program by Hsiang[1985].

8.2   Predicate logic and unification

A treatment of the methods of predicate logic are beyond the scope of this chapter. Consequently, we will hit only a couple of the high points: first, the axiom schemas and deduction rules and second, the method of term unification.

Unification is a syntactic procedure for computing the common meaning or interpretation of two terms (as opposed to formulas). Thus, unification is a bridge between syntax and semantics. The power of unification can be seen in the fact that, with little more than resolution, it can be used to build a primitive theorem prover for predicate logic. It is also one of the mechanisms fundamental to PROLOG.

Just for the sake of completeness, we will look at the classical logic for the predicate calculus. The axiom schemas for the predicate calculus consist of (1) the axiom schemas 1a,...,4b of propositional logic, together with

$$\forall x\, \alpha(x) \rightarrow \alpha(r),$$

and (3)

$$\alpha(r) \rightarrow \exists x\, \alpha(x),$$

where r is a term whose variables are free at all occurrences of x in α. The deduction rules consist of modus ponens,

$$\frac{\beta \rightarrow \alpha(x)}{\beta \rightarrow \forall x\, \alpha(x)},$$

and

$$\frac{\alpha(x) \rightarrow \beta}{\exists x\, \alpha(x) \rightarrow \beta},$$

where x is not free in β. Equality for terms of the object algebra may be described by extra axioms. The computational inefficiency of deduction in this system can be seen in a frightening seventeen-line proof of n=n given in Kleene[1967, page 387].

The usual approach to automatic theorem proving relies on a procedure known as Skolemization to eliminate quantifiers, a conversion of quantifier-free formulas into equivalent ∨clauses, the use of unification to create resolvable literals, and resolution to reduce it all. In the following, suppose that we began with a set S_0 of predicate formulas.

Skolemization eliminates quantifiers at a cost of extra constants, free variables, and functions. For example, existential quantifiers, such as those of

$$\exists x(7 + x = 7) \qquad \exists z[0 = F(n, z)],$$

can be replaced by adding a new constant

$$(7 + 0 = 7) \qquad 0 = F(n, c_n).$$

Universal quantifiers, such as we have in

$$\forall x\, \exists y(x + y = 0),$$

can be eliminated by simply dropping them (making their variable free),

$$\exists y (x + y = 0),$$

and adopting the convention that free variables are to be treated as universally quantified. Since x is a free variable, the elimination of the existential quantifier on y may depend on x. This is done by replacing y by a (Skolem) function of x. Thus, our last formula becomes

$$(x + i(x) = 0),$$

with i(x)=−x as the new function. In general, an existentially quantified variable can only be replaced by a function of the existing free variables. Notice that, by the axiom schemas and deduction rules given above, the quantifier-free formulas produced in this way are logically equivalent to the original formulas. Thus, Skolemization is a syntactic process of simplification which—like constructing ∨-clause normal forms—preserves semantics. We leave it to the readers to convince themselves that it is always possible to use these procedures to convert S_0 into a semantically equivalent set S_1 of quantifier-free formulas in an expanded logical language.

Given a set S_1 of quantifier-free formulas of predicate logic, the methods of 8.1 can be used to convert it into a semantically equivalent set S_2 of ∨-clauses. Then, unification will be used to prepare the ∨-clauses of S_2 for resolution.

Unification is a procedure which, given distinct terms, determines a substitution which makes the terms equal—if such a substitution exists. By unifying terms appearing in complementary literals, we set the stage for resolution. For example, the second literals in the formulas

$$\neg(i(y) = x) \lor x + y = 0 \quad \text{and} \quad x = 0 \lor \neg(x + x = 0)$$

can be made complementary by the unifying substitution y=x:

$$\neg(i(x) = x) \lor x + x = 0 \quad \text{and} \quad x = 0 \lor \neg(x + x = 0).$$

Resolution can now be applied to get

$$x = 0 \lor \neg(i(x) = x).$$

Then, given

$$\neg(2 = 0),$$

the unifying substitution x=2 for the previous formula allows us to deduce

$$\neg(i(2) = 2).$$

Theorem proving for predicate logic is based on a unification algorithm which always finds the most general substitution possible (see Chang&Lee[1973]). Given such a unification algorithm, the resulting substitutions, into given ∨-clauses, make it possible for resolution to deduce any formula which is a consequence of the given ∨-clauses.

Example 6:   Given 1.0 and 2.0 below, 3.0 can be deduced by using the steps described so far.

1.0 Every child's mother loves it.	hypothesis
2.0 Jack is still a child, but he loves Jill.	hypothesis
3.0 Someone loves Jack.	conclusion

First, formalize the statements and negate the desired conclusion.

1.1 $\forall x[child(x) \rightarrow loves(mother\text{-}of<x>,x)]$
2.1 $child(Jack), loves(Jack, Jill)$
3.1 $\exists y[loves(y, Jack)]$
¬3.1 $\forall y[\neg loves(y, Jack)]$

Second, eliminate quantifiers by Skolemization.

1.2 $child(x) \rightarrow loves(mother\text{-}of <x>,x)$
¬3.2 $\neg loves(y, Jack)$

Notice that there is no substitution which unifies ¬3.2 and 2.1. Third, continue by expressing 1.2 as a logically equivalent ∨-clause.

1.3 $\neg child(x) \lor loves(mother\text{-}of <x>,x)$.

Fourth, 1.3 and the first formula in 2.1 can be unified by the substitution x=Jack,

1.4 $\neg child(Jack) \lor loves(mother\text{-}of <Jack>, Jack)$,

then 1.4 and 2.1 can be resolved.

4.0 $loves(mother\text{-}of <Jack>, Jack)$.

The substitution y=mother-of⟨Jack⟩ unifies ¬3.2 with 4.0.

¬3.3 $\neg loves(mother\text{-}of <Jack>, Jack)$.

Finally, resolution on ¬3.3 and 4.0 returns F. Thus, someone does love Jack.

There is an important computational difference between theorem proving in propositional and predicate logic. In propositional logic, it is possible to determine if a formula is a theorem or if it is not a theorem. In predicate logic, it is possible to determine that a formula is a theorem, but it is not possible to determine that it is not a theorem. In other words, the (theorem) decision problem of predicate logic is undecidable.

Figure 8.1. Claude Shannon (courtesy MIT Museum).

8.3 PROLOG

PROLOG is an acronym for PROgramming in LOGic. It is an attempt, by A. Colmerauer and his associates (circa 1970), to implement the predicate calculus as a programming language. It allows the programmer to specify a computation by the logcal properties of the desired result, rather than by a list of procedures to be used in reaching the result. In a sense, PROLOG is to logic as LISP is to recursion theory. Both illustrate the practical power that can be achieved when algebraic systems from mathematics are used (as the basis for) a computer languages.

The PROLOG interpreter is based on resolution and unification for Horn clauses. A *Horn clause* is a ∨-clause,

$$(\alpha_1 \vee \neg\alpha_2 \vee ... \vee \neg\alpha_k),$$

with at most one unnegated literal. In some Horn clauses, there may be no unnegated clauses. In PROLOG, a Horn clause with one negated literal is written as

$$\alpha_1 \; :- \; \alpha_2, ..., \alpha_k.$$

This notation and its meaning are suggestive of the logical implication

$$(\alpha_1 \leftarrow \alpha_2 \wedge ... \wedge \alpha_k),$$

Figure 8.2. Nathaniel Rochester (courtesy N. Rochester).

but it is not exactly equivalent. The prompt used by PROLOG's listener is ?.
Capital letters are used for variables. Each expression must end in a period.

Example 7:   So far, our standard example has been the factorial function. We
won't stop now. The relation   fact (X, Y) is read "the factorial of X is Y".
The first two lines define the program. In the last two entries, we are asking the
program questions.

```
fact(1,1) :- true.                      ;program, line 1
fact(M,N) :- (U is M-1),fact(U,V),
             (N is M*V).                 ;program, line 2

?    fact(2,2)
==> yes
?    fact(10,X)
==> X=3,628,800
```

In evaluating X, a computation similar to the following is generated.

```
?    fact(10,X)
     fact(10,X)        ;we want X to satisfy this relation
     => (U is 10-1),fact(U,V),(X is 10*V)
                                ;this must be satisfied
        U=9                 ;first addition to environment
```

Figure 8.3. Marvin Minsky (1965) (courtesy MIT Museum).

```
fact(9,V)              ;now, we want V to satisfy this
=> (U is 9-1),fact(U,V),(V is 9*V)
                               ;this must be satisfied
    U=8                ;second addition to environment
    fact(8,V)
    => ...
          . . .
    => (U is 2-1),fact(U,V),(V is 2*V)
       U=1                         ;ninth addition
       fact(1,V)                   ;now, we want
    => V=1                          ;by line 1
    (V is 2*V)                  ; previous environment
    => V=2                      ; previous arithmetic
          . . .
    => ...
    (V is 9*V)
 => V=362,880
 (X is 10*V)               ;in the original environment
=> X=3,628,800
```

Example 8: PROLOG can express list processing functions. In the following, the notation [H|T] is used to represent a list with first element H and tail T,

[G, H|T] for a list with first elements G and H, [a,b,c,...] for (a b c ...), and [ ] for ( ).

```
?   car([H|T],H) :- true.                    ;car is defined.
    recorded
?   car([1,2,3,4],X).
    ==> X=1.

?   cons(X,[],[X]) :- true.                  ;cons is defined.
    recorded
?   cons(X,[H|T],[X,H|T]) :- true.
    recorded
?   cons(1,[2 3 4],X).
    ==> X=[1,2,3,4].

?   append([],L,L) :- true.                  ;append is defined.
    recorded
?   append([H|L1],L2,[H|L3]) :- append(L1,L2,L3).
    recorded
?   append([1,2,3],[4,5,6,7,8,9],X).
    ==> X=[1,2,3,4,5,6,7,8,9].
```

A more thorough discussion of PROLOG can be found in Colmeraur[1972] or Clocksin & Mellish[1984]. In Chapter 10 of Clocksin & Mellish, the relation of PROLOG to predicate logic is discussed.

8.4   Speculation on algebraic intelligence

HISTORY:

"During the next year and during the Summer Research Project on Artificial Intelligence, I propose to study the relation of language to intelligence..."

From *A Proposal for the Dartmouth Summer Research Project on Artificial Intelligence* by John McCarthy, Marvin Minsky, Nathan Rochester, and Claude Shannon—31 August 1955.

By *algebraic intelligence*, we mean intelligence based on the bridges across the computational dichotomy (from syntax to semantics) which are present in a formal language. The idea of creating the illusion of intelligence (computation which is semantically appropriate) on a basis of syntactic processing is one of a handfull of truely great ideas in computer science.

Figure 8.4. John McCarty (courtesy MIT Museum).

However, it is not new: this idea has been around since long before 1955. After all, when a student solves a problem in algebra or calculus, it is primarily this form of intelligence that is used. The initial transformation, from word problem to equations to be solved, seems to require another form of intelligence, but (for the student at least) the equations are solved simply strictly by manipulating syntax. During this last step, the student needs no more of an idea of the meaning of the terms and equations than would a computer doing the same work. Of course, we've just seen variations of algebraic intelligence growing out of the structure of logic and interpreters. Although it wasn't discussed, this form of intelligence, or something similar, is also present in FORTRAN's ability to handle its algebraic terms and procedures, MACSYMA's ability to deal with equations symbolically, the ability of game-playing programs to generate strategies, and much more.

The original idea of intelligence originates in human information processing ability. The human brain evolved in an environment—the planes and woods of Africa?—which stressed a nonsyntactic kind of processing. In order to mate, to eat, but not get eaten, we needed to quickly process enormous data structures with a high, but less than perfect, degree of accuracy. The images, sounds, smells, and feelings that filled our brains were computationally very close to the semantics that we needed to process. (In reviewing this manuscript, George Stockman pointed out that this sort of evolution led to other forms of animal intelligence, and consequently, my definition of "original intelligence" is not restricted to humans.) On the other hand, digital computers evolved from office machines. They had to process strings of symbols quickly, and as trivial an error as a misplaced decimal point could have a negative impact on their survival. Consequently, its no surprise that machines succeed brilliantly in the symbol shuffling involved in algebraic intelligence, but struggle for minutes in their attempts to understand a single spoken sentence or interpret a simple picture. Maybe it is equally reasonable that we succeed in recognizing beauty and (to some extent) even in understanding our existence while struggling to multiply floating-point numbers. It seems that with respect to language, a machine's intelligence may be the dual of our human intelligence(s).

No one would believe that improved algorithms and training would allow a normal human to compete with a pocket calculator. The architecture of the carbon-based processor is simply not appropriate. The same seems to hold for attempts to make a serial VonNeumann style architecture compete with the human brain in distinguishing beautiful faces from those less fortunate. The point is that differences in architecture (serial VonNeumann digital vs. ultra-fine-grained distributed analog) could be the origin of two very distinct and powerful types of intelligence. Further, there is no reason to believe that there are not still other equally unique forms of intelligence waiting to be created or discovered.

The influence of architecture on computational style can be seen at the most basic level—that of search. The type of computations that a serial digital computer supports must (according to recursion theory, 4.1) involve serial searches through every possible data structure. This leads directly to the exponential complexity seen throughout artificial intelligence (a consequence of trying to solve NP-complete problems in a traditional way). This complexity problem has been the greatest single weakness of the algebraic approach to intelligence. The human brain processes data structures which are so large, and consequently so numerous in potential variety, that this kind of strictly serial search is out of the question. Computation in the brain seems to violate the traditions of recursion theory with respect to the need for search.

Along with the new, fine-grained distributed architectures being developed for electronic computers, there are fundamentally new types of algorithms. These algorithms are often focused on processing very large nonlinear data structures—as opposed to short strings of symbols. The emphasis on large data structures brings with it an examination of approximate algorithms and of analog algorithms—for example, the algorithms being developed to approximately solve NP-complete problems on connectionist architectures. This sort of research that may lead to notions of computability that go beyond the seemingly final word of algebra and recursion theory. If a robust new view of computability emerges from research into distributed processes, then we may expect with it totally nontraditional insights into the bridges between semantics and machine computation—insights which go beyond the brilliant classical algebraic strategies described in this text.

On the other hand, there is a great deal more to be done with the traditional ideas. If the success of LISP and PROLOG and the diversity of the hundreds of algebras known to mathematics are a valid indication, then the potential for algebraic intelligence has only just been tapped.

We will end this section as we began it, by stating that many of the preceeding ideas on algebraic intelligence—particularly its inadequacies—are the author's speculation. In spite of its inadequacies, the idea of algebraic intelligence is monumental.

8.5 Additional reading

Classical introductions to mathematical logic are found in Kleene[1950,1967] and Mendelson[1979]. The history of theorem proving is described in Bledsoe&Loveland[1984]. Also of historical interest are Newell,Shaw&Simon[1957], Robinson[1965], and Wang[1960,1963]. The standard introduction to the general theory of automatic theorem proving is Chang&Lee[1973]. Bledsoe[1977] describes a nonresolution theorem prover. For light reading on intelligence, try Kolata[1982], Kurzwell[1985], Waldrop[1984], and Wegner[1989].

9
Bibliography

THE REAL MEANING OF A BIBLIOGRAPHY:

"... most papers in computer science describe how their authors
learned what someone else already knew." P. J. Landin

Abelson, Harold and Gerald Sussman; 1985, *Structure and Interpretation of Computer Programs,* MIT Press, Cambridge, Mass.

Allen, John; 1978, *Anatomy of LISP,* McGraw-Hill, New York.

Backus, John; 1978, *Can programming be liberated from the VonNeumann style? a functional style and its algebra of programs,* Communications of the ACM, v.21, n.8, p.613-641, Association of Computing Machinery, New York.

Barendregt, Henk; 1977, *The type-free lambda calculus,* Handbook of Mathematical Logic, Jon Barwise (editor), North-Holland, Amsterdam.

Bledsoe, W.W. and D.W. Loveland; 1984, *Theorem proving: the last 25 years,* American Mathematical Society, Providence, R.I.

Borges, Jorge Luis; 1962, *Labyrinths, Selected Stories and Other Writings,* New Directions, San Francisco.

Brooks, Rodney and Richard Gabriel; 1984, *A Critique of Common LISP,* Record of the 1984 ACM Symposium on LISP and Functional Programming, Austin.

Cartwright, R. and John McCarthy; 1978, *Representations of recursive programs in first-order logic,* Proc. Int'n. Conf. on Math. Studies of Inf. Proc., Kyoto.

Chang, Chin-Liang and Richard Char-Tung Lee; 1973, *Symbolic Logic and Mechanical Theorem Proving,* Academic Press, New York.

Chatin, Gregory; 1988, *Algorithmic Information Theory,* Cambridge University Press, Cambridge.

Church, Alonzo; 1941, *The calculi of lambda-conversion,* Annals of Mathematical Studies, v.6, Princeton University, Princeton, N.J..

Clarke, T., P. Gladstone, C. MacLean, and A. Norman; 1980, *SKIM—the S, K, I, Reduction Machine,* Record of the 1980 LISP Conference, Stanford University and Santa Clara University, Palo Alto, Calif.

Clocksin, J.H. and C.S. Mellish; 1984, *Programming in PROLOG,* second edition, Springer, Berlin.

Conway, J.H.; 1972, *Unpredictable iterations,* Proc. 1972 Number Theory Conference, University of Colorado, Boulder.

Cook, Stephen; 1971, *The complexity of theorem-proving procedures,* Third ACM Symposium on the Theory of Computing, Association of Computing Machinery.

Curry, Haskel B.; 1978, *Some philosophical aspects of combinatory logic,* Proceedings of The Kleene Symposium, Barwise, Keisler and Kunen (editors), North-Holland, Amsterdam.

Davis, Martin; 1958, *Computability and Unsolvability,* McGraw-Hill, New York.

Denning, Peter J.; 1989, *The Internet worm,* American Scientist, v.77, pp.126-128, March-April.

Dijkstra, E.; 1978, *On-the-fly garbage collection,* Communications of the ACM, Association of Computing Machinery, New York.

Dyson, Freeman; 1988, *Infinite in All Directions,* Harper and Row, New York.

Evans, A.; 1972, *The lambda calculus and its relation to programming languages,* Proc. ACM Annual Conf., Association of Computing Machinery, New York.

Friedman, Daniel and Matthias Felleisen; 1987, *The Little LISPer,* trade edition, MIT Press, Cambridge, Mass.

Gabriel, Richard; 1987, *Memory management in LISP,* AI Expert (magazine), February.
1985 Performance and Evaluation of LISP Systems, MIT Press, Cambridge, Mass.

Gabriel, Richard and Gerald Sussman; 1978, *The Art of the Interpreter,* AI memo #453, AI Laboratory, MIT Press, Cambridge, Mass.

Glasner, H., C. Hankin, and D. Till; 1984, *Principles of Functional Programming,* Prentice-Hall, London.

Golden Hill Computers, Inc.; 1984, *Golden Common LISP Reference Manual,* Golden Hill Computers, Cambridge, Mass.

Harel David; 1987, *Algorithmics: The Spirit of Computing*, Addison-Wesley, Reading, Mass.

Henderson, Peter; 1980, *Functional Programming Applications and Implementation*, Prentice-Hall, Englewood Cliffs, N.J.

Hofstadter, David; 1980, *Gödel, Escher, Bach: An Eternal Golden Braid*, Vintage Books, New York.

Hopcroft, John and Jeffry Ullman; 1979, *Introduction to Automata Theory, Languages, and Computation*, Addison-Wesley, Reading, Mass.

Keene, Sonya E.; 1989, *Object-Oriented Programming in Common LISP: A Programmer's Guide to CLOS*, Addison-Wesley, Reading, Mass.

Kessler, Robert R.; 1988, *LISP: Objects, and Symbolic Programming*, Scott, Foresman and Company, Glenview, Illinois.

Kleene, Stephen Cole; 1950, *Introduction to Metamathematics*, D. VanNostrand, Princeton, N.J.
———1967, *Mathematical Logic*, John Wiley, New York.

Knuth, Donald; 1973, *The Art of Computer Programming*, volumes 1, 2, and 3, Addison-Wesley, Reading, Mass.
———1976, *Mathematics and computer science: coping with finiteness*, Science, v.194, n.4271, December.

Kolata, Gina; 1982, *How can computers get common sense?*, Science, v.217, September.
———1982, *Does Gödel's theorem really matter to mathematics?*, Science, v.218, November.

Kurzweil, Raymond; 1985, *What is artificial intelligence anyway?*, The American Scientist, v.73.

Lagarias, Jeffrey; 1985, *The 3x+1 problem and its generalizations*, American Math. Monthly, v.92, n.1.

Landin, Peter; 1965, *A correspondence between ALGOL-60 and Church's lambda calculus*, Communications of the ACM, v.8.
———1966, *The next 700 programming languages*, Communications of the ACM, v.9, n.3.

Machtey, Michael and Paul Young; 1978, *An Introduction to the General Theory of Algorithms*, North-Holland, Amsterdam.

Manna, Zohar and Jean Vuillemin; 1972, *Fixedpoint approach to the theory of computation*, Communications of the ACM, v.15, n.7.

Marshall, E; 1988, *The worm's aftermath*, Science v.242, pp.1121-1122.

McCarthy, John; 1959, *Programs with common sense,* Proc. Symp. on Mechanization of Thought Processes, Teddington, England, National Physical Laboratory.

——1960, *The LISP Programmer's Manual,* MIT Computing Center, Cambridge, Mass.

——1960, *Recursive functions of symbolic expressions and their computation by machine, part I*; Communications of the ACM; v.3, n.4.

——1962, Time sharing, Management and the Computer of the Future, MIT Press, Cambridge, Mass., pp.220-236.

——1962, *Computer programs for checking mathematical proofs,* in AMS Proc. of Symp. in Pure Mathematics, v.5, American Mathematical Society, Providence, R.I.

——1963, *A basis for the mathematical theory of computation,* Computer Programming and Formal Systems, Braffort and Hirschberg (editors), Studies in Logic Series, North-Holland, Amsterdam.

——1968, *Programs with common sense, Semantic Information Processing,* Marvin Minsky (editor).

——1978, *A micromanual for LISP—not the whole truth,* ACM SIGPLAN Notices, v.13, n.8, Association of Computing Machinery, New York.

——1981, *History of LISP,* History of Programming Languages, Richard Wexelblat (editor), Academic Press, New York.

——1987, *Generality in artificial intelligence,* 1971 Turing Award lecture, pp.257-267, in A.C.M. Turing Award Lectures, ACM Press, Addison-Wesley, Reading, Mass. CACM.

McCarthy, John and Claude Shannon; 1956, *Automata Studies,* Princeton University Press, Princeton, N.J.

McCarthy, John and Carolyn Talcott; 1980, *LISP: Programming and Proving,* Computer Science Department, Stanford University, Palo Alto, Calif.

McCarthy, John, Paul Abrahams, Daniel Edwards, Timothy Hart, and Michael Levin; 1965, *LISP 1.5 Programmer's Manual,* MIT Press, Cambridge, Mass.

Mendelson, Elliot; 1979, *Introduction to Mathematical Logic,* VanNostrand, New York.

Moon, David; 1974, *MACLISP Reference Manual,* MIT Press, Cambridge, Mass.

Moses, Joel; 1970, *The function of FUNCTION in LISP, or why the funarg problem should be called the environment problem,* ACM SIGSAM Bulletin, v.15, Association of Computing Machinery, New York.

Newell, A., J.C. Shaw, and H.A. Simon; 1957, *Empirical Explorations of the Logic Theory Machine,* Report P-951, RAND Corporation, Santa Monica, Calif.

Pavelle, Richard, Michael Rothstein, and John Fitch; 1981, *Computer algebra*, Scientific American, v.245, n.6.

Pitman, Kent; 1981, *The Revised MacLISP Manual*, TR295, Laboratory for Computer Science, MIT Press, Cambridge, Mass.

Pratt, Vaughn; 1979, *A mathematician's view of LISP*, Byte, v.4, n.8.

Pumplin, Bruce; 1987, *Compiling LISP procedures*, AI Expert (magazine), February 1987.

Revesz, G.E.; 1988, *Lambda-Calculus, Combinators, and Functional Programming*, Cambridge University Press, Cambridge, Great Britain.

Robinson, J.A., 1965, *A machine-oriented logic based on the resolution principal*, Journal of the ACM, p. 23-41, v.12, n.1, Association for Computing Machinery, New York.

Rogers, Hartley; 1967, *Theory of Recursive Functions and Effective Computability*, McGraw-Hill, New York.

Saint-James, Emmanual; 1984, *Recursion is more efficient than iteration*, Record of the 1984 ACM Symposium on LISP and Functional Computing, Austin, Association of Computing Machinery, New York.

Shannon, Claude E.; 1956, *A universal Turing machine with two internal states*, Automata Studies, Annals of Mathematical Studies XXXIV, Princeton University Press, Princeton, N.J.

Shoch, J.F. and J.A. Hupp; 1982, *The worm programs—early experiences with a distributed computation*, CACM, v.25, pp.172-180.

Stark, Richard and Leon Kotin; 1989, *The social metaphor in distributed computing*, Journal of Parallel and Distributed Computing, v.6, Academic Press.

Steele, Guy; 1980, *The dream of a lifetime: a lazy variable extent mechanism*, Record of the 1980 LISP Conference, Association of Computing Machinery, New York.
———1984, *Common LISP Reference Manual, Digital Press*, Bradford, Mass.
———1985, *Performance and Evaluation of LISP Systems*, MIT Press, Cambridge, Mass.

Steele, Guy and Gerald Sussman; 1978, *The Art of the Interpreter*, AI Memo 453, MIT AI Lab, Cambridge, Mass.

Stroyan, Herbert; 1984, *The early history of LISP (1956-59)*, Record of the 1984 ACM Symposium on LISP and Functional Programming, Association for Computing Machinery, New York.

Smullian, Raymond; 1985, *To Mock a Mockingbird*, Alfred A. Knopf, New York.

Sussman, Gerald and Guy Steele; 1975, *Scheme: an Interpreter for the Extended Lambda Calculus*, memo-349, Artificial Intelligence Laboratory, MIT Press, Cambridge, Mass.

Teitelman, Warren; 1978, *InterLISP Reference Manual*, Xerox, Palo Alto, Calif.

Thompson, Ken; 1984, *Reflections on trusting trust*, a Turing Award Lecture, Communications of the ACM, p.761-763, v.27, n.8.

Touretzky, David; 1984, *A Gentle Introduction to Symbolic Computation*, Harper and Row, New York.

VanHeijenoort, Jean (editor); 1967, *From Frege to Gödel: A Source Book in Mathematical Logic, 1879-1931*, Harvard University, Cambridge, Mass.

VonNeumann, John; 1966, *Theory of self-reproducing automata*, Collected Works of John VonNeumann, A.W. Burkes (editor), University of Illinois Press, Urbana.

Wagon, Stan; 1985, *The collatz problem*, The Mathematical Intelligencer, v.7, Springer-Verlag, New York.

Waldrop, Mitchell; 1984, *The intelligence of organizations*, Science, v.225, September.

Wand, Mitchell; 1984, *What is LISP?*, American Mathematical Monthly, v.91, n.1, January, 1984.

Wang, Hao; 1960, *Toward mechanical mathematics*, IBM Journal, January.
———1963, *Mechanical mathematics and inferential analysis*, Computer Programming and Formal Systems, Braffort and Hirschberg (editors), Studies in Logic Series, North-Holland, Amsterdam.

Weinreb, Daniel and David Moon; 1981, *LISP Machine Manual*, Artificial Intelligence Laboratory, MIT Press, Cambridge, Mass.

Weissman, Clark; 1967, *LISP 1.5 Primer*, Dickenson, Belmont, California.

Wilensky, Robert; 1986, *Common LISPcraft*, Norton, New York.

Winston, Patrick; 1984, *Artificial Intelligence*, Addison-Wesley, Reading, Mass.

Winston, Patrick and Berthold Horn; 1988, *LISP*, Addison-Wesley, Reading, Mass.

10
Answers to Selected Exercises

The LISP code given here is correct for GCLISP 1.01; minor modifications (e.g., the replacement of ' by #' before function arguments) may be necessary to adapt answers to other Common LISPs. Answers to certain theoretical exercises from chapters 6, 7, and 8 may be taken as representing the author's views. Please write to the author if you find better answers to these or any other exercises. Also, write if you have interesting exercises to contribute to a possible second edition.

1.2.7

3. Let the number be 3. In the evaluation of

```
*    ((LAMBDA (X) ((LAMBDA (Y) (CONS X Y)) (1+ X))) 3)
```

the outer LAMBDA (X) binds X=3, thus the argument to the inner (LAMBDA (Y) ...) is (1+ 3), Y is bound to 4. Finally, the value of (CONS X Y) is returned:

```
    ==> (3 . 4) .
```

4. Lambda abstraction is an operation which constructs functions from terms with free variables. It is the primary mechanism for user programming in LISP.

5. (a) LAMBDA is a linguistic operation. Functions with no free variables: (b), (c), (e), (f), (h), and (i); (d) is a function with the free variable Z; (g) is not a function in Common LISP. However, (g) will act as a function in SCHEME, LISP 360, LISP1.5, etc., when given the name of a function—such as AND, OR, READ, etc.—which can take 0 arguments.

```
*    ((LAMBDA (V) (V)) 'OR)
     ==> NIL           ;In SCHEME and certain other LISPs.
     ERROR UNDEFINED FUNCTION: V         ;In Common LISP.
```

(j) IF is a special form (forming function or operation).

1.2.8

2. Function-name binding experiment.

```
*   (SETQ MAKE-FUN '(LAMBDA (X) (1+ X)))
    ==> MAKE-FUN
*   (MAKE-FUN 2.718281828)
    ERROR UNDEFINED FUNCTION: MAKE-FUN
*   (APPLY MAKE-FUN '(2.718281828))
    ==> 3.718281828
*   (DEFUN MAKE-FUN (X) (1+ X))
    ==> MAKE-FUN
*   (MAKE-FUN 2.718281828)
    ==> 3.7182818283.
```

3. (READ) removes the next LISP data object from the input queue. The presence or absence of one (READ) effects the values of all subsequent (READ)s.

2.1

4. A polynomial approximation to the exponential function is

```
(DEFUN E (X) (+ 1 X (/ (* X X) 2) (/ (* X X X) 6)
    (/ (* X X X X) 24) )).
```

This definition could be made more efficient by algebraically restructuring the terms to reduce the number of multiplications.

2.2

1. Yes. Recursive functions, such as +, *, and factorial⟨n⟩, will be defined by similar equations in the lambda calculus (see 7.4).

2. Rules 1, 2, and 3 are violated in O.

6. A simple recursive program for FIBONACCI is

```
(DEFUN FIBONACCI (M)
  (IF (< M 3) 1 (+ (FIBONACCI (- M 1))
      (FIBONACCI (- M 2)))) ).
```

Better definitions for FIBONACCI are possible if an auxillary function and extra variables are used.

10.

```
(DEFUN REDUCE (LST)
 (COND
  ((ATOM LST) NIL)
  ((MEMBER (CAR LST) (CDR LST)) (REDUCE (CDR LST)))
  (T (CONS (CAR LST) (REDUCE (CDR LST)))) ))
```

Better definitions for REDUCE use extra variables and auxiliary functions, or DO.

11.

```
(DEFUN CONSEL (E L)
 (IF (ATOM L) NIL (CONS (CONS E (CAR L)) (CONSEL E (CDR
   L ))))))
```

A better definition uses MAPCAR.

12.

```
(DEFUN PERMUTE (L)
  (IF (ATOM L) (LIST NIL)
   (DO
    ((PERML NIL
      (APPEND PERML
       (CONSEL ELE (PERMUTE (REMOVE ELE L))) ))
     (ELE (CAR L) (CAR OBJL))
     (OBJL (CDR L) (CDR OBJL)) )
    ((ATOM OBJL)
     (APPEND PERML
       (CONSEL ELE (PERMUTE (REMOVE ELE L))) )))))
```

DELETE is a destructive version of REMOVE, it will not work in this program.

13.

```
(DEFUN WBRF (L)
 (AND L (NOT (ATOM L)) (WBRF (CDR L))) )
```

15.

```
(DEFUN POWER-SET (S)
 (POWER-SET-AUX (LIST ( )) (REDUCE S)) )
(DEFUN POWER-SET-AUX (PS S)
 (IF
  (ATOM S)
  PS
  (POWER-SET-AUX (APPEND PS (CONSEL (CAR S) PS))
   (CDR S)) ))
```

2.2.4

2. A DO-based definition for REDUCE.

```
(DEFUN REDUCE (L)
  (IF
   (ATOM L)
   NIL
   (DO
    ((LST (CDR L) (CDR LST))
     (OUT () (IF (MEMBER ELE OUT) OUT (CONS ELE OUT)))
     (ELE (CAR L) (CAR LST)) )
    ((ATOM LST)
     (REVERSE (CONS ELE OUT)) ))))
```

2.3

2. Add (LOAD *path\to\file-1*) ... (LOAD *path\to\file-k)* to the end of the current file.

2.4

4. The set of all s-expressions must be listed in an 0, 1, 2, ..., N, N + 1, ... ordering. Each s-expression x can be represented as a string $S=S\langle x\rangle$ of parenthesis, period, space, letters, and numbers. Order the string representations lexicographically and the s-expressions listed in an order

$$S_0, S_1, S_2, S_3, ..., S_N, ... ,$$

in which they may be searched.

2.5

4. A DO-based COLLECT* avoids the auxillary function used below.

```
(DEFUN COLLECT* ( )
 (SETQ MARK (READ))
 (AUX-COLLECT* (READ) NIL) )
(DEFUN AUX-COLLECT* (R L)
 (IF (EQUAL R MARK) L (AUX-COLLECT* (READ)
   (CONS R L))) )
```

2.6

1.

```
(DEFUN ASSOC (KEY ALIST)
  (CAR (MEMBER KEY ALIST :TEST '(LAMBDA (X)
    (EQ KEY (CAR X)))))) )
```

2.7

1. Given a differentiable function $F:R-->R$ and NEWTON+ as defined in 2.4.2, every root x of F satisfies $0 = F\langle x\rangle$ and consequently $x = $ NEWTON+$<x>$.

4. The stair-steps touch the y=f$\langle x\rangle$ curve at the points $(x_0, f\langle x_0\rangle)$, $(f\langle x_0\rangle, f\langle f\langle x_0\rangle\rangle)$, $(f\langle f\langle x_0\rangle\rangle, f\langle f\langle f\langle x_0\rangle\rangle\rangle)$, ..., as they converge to a fixed-point $(f^*\langle x\rangle, f^*\langle x\rangle)$. This fixed-point (in the top right corner) lies on both graphs, so f$\langle x\rangle$=y and y=x implies f$\langle x\rangle$=x . The illustration shows that a fixed point f$\langle x\rangle$=x may be computed as the fixed-point f*$\langle x\rangle$ obtained by repeatedly applying f to its own value.

2.8

1. We use two additional arguments to READ-CHAR to handle the end-of-file:

```
(READ-CHAR input-stream eof-error-p eof-value).
```

If *eof-error-p* is NIL, then an error is not signaled at the end of the file. Instead, the value *eof-value* is returned. We use *eof-value*=NIL.

```
(DEFUN FILE-COPY
  (SOURCE-PATH TARGET-PATH)
  (SETQ IN  (OPEN SOURCE-PATH :DIRECTION :INPUT))
  (SETQ OUT (OPEN TARGET-PATH :DIRECTION :OUTPUT))
  (DO
    ((CH (READ-CHAR IN NIL NIL)(READ-CHAR IN NIL NIL)))
    ((IF
      (EQ NIL CH)
      T
      (NULL (WRITE-CHAR (WRITE-CHAR CH OUT))) )
    (CLOSE IN)
    (CLOSE OUT) )))
```

For more on the eof arguments, see p.374 and p.379 of Steele[1984]

2.9

1. AND and OR are procedural in that their arguments are evaluated one after the other. Further, if there are side effects to the evaluation of arguments, then the order of the arguments may determine effect.

2. COND is procedural in the sense described above for AND and OR.

3. LET* is procedural in that its variable bindings are performed in serial environments and are therefore order dependent.

4. A user experiment involving SETQ and PRINT will determine whether or not COND's test terms are evaluated in parallel.

3.1

1. Yes, (1 . 2). Yes. No, CONS<*object,list*> = *list*. No.

2. = NIL:list.

5. The objective here is to compare the cost of using random-access memory, which is remote, to using stack memory, which is local. If $F\langle\rangle$ has a domain of size 2^K, then the times to access $F\langle x\rangle$ given x are something like

$$\text{ram-access-time}(2^K) = C + B*\log_2(2^K) = C+B*K$$

and

$$\text{alist-access-time}(2^K) = c + b*\tfrac{1}{2}*2^K = c + b*2^{K-1} ,$$

where B, b, C, and c are arbitrary constants, c<<C, and M=D=2^K (where M and D are the constants from the problem). Property lists will be more efficient when K is so large that

$$\text{ram-access-time}(2^K) < \text{alist-access-time}(2^K)$$
$$C+B*K < c + b*2^{K-1}$$
$$(2/b)*(C-c + B*K) < 2^K .$$

7. There are $2^{10}=1024=10^{3.0103}$ subsets of fingers. If we are counting only total functions, then it follows that there are $1024^{1024}=10^{3082.5472}=3.5253*10^{3082}$ functions from sets of fingers to sets of fingers. Each of these functions is definable in terms of association lists of length only 1024.

3.2

4. MAX is defined in terms of DO*. DO* is the same as DO except that the variable bindings are serial rather than parallel.

```
(DEFUN MAX (NUM-LST)
 (COND
  ((ATOM NUM-LST) NIL)
  ((ATOM (CDR NUM-LST)) (CAR NUM-LST))
  (T
   (DO*
    ((SAVE-NUM (CAR NUM-LST) BIGGEST)
     (NUM-LST (CDR NUM-LST) (CDR NUM-LST))
     (BIGGEST
       (IF (< SAVE-NUM (CAR NUM-LST))
        (CAR NUM-LST) SAVE-NUM))
       (IF (< SAVE-NUM (CAR NUM-LST))
        (CAR NUM-LST) SAVE-NUM)) )
    ((ATOM (CDR NUM-LST))
     BIGGEST )))))
```

3.3

1. All expressions except CONS, (LAMBDA...), LAMBDA, (CONS), and (CAR (1 2)) are terms.

2. Answers in order: no free variables, U and V, U, no free variables, U, U. The first, fourth, and (depending on which definition of "form" you use) possibly the sixth terms are forms.

3. (O) is a form in the sense of Church.

4. Steele's definition can never be made algorithmically computable.

3.4

2. The general idea of this problem is to program some of the syntax for LISP. The following functions are a step in that direction.

```
(DEFUN CONSTANTP (OBJ)
 (IF
  (OR (NUMBERP OBJ) (EQ OBJ T) (NULL OBJ)
   (STRINGP OBJ))   T   NIL ))
(DEFUN VARIABLEP (OBJ)   (IF (SYMBOLP OBJ) T NIL) )
```

```
(SETQ FA-LIST
 '((CAR 1)(CDR 1)(CONS 2)(LISTP 1)(NULL 1)
   (ATOMP 1)(AND T)(OR T)
   (NOT 1)(ZEROP 1)(NUMBERP 1)(* T)(+ T)(- 2)(/ 2)
   (IF 3)(QUOTE 1)
   (EQ 2)(EQUAL 2) ...))
(DEFUN ARITY (FUN)
 (COND
  ((ATOM FUN) (CADR (ASSOC FUN FA-LIST)))
  ((> (LENGTH FUN) 2) (LENGTH (CADR FUN)))
  (T NIL) ))
(DEFUN ATOM-FUN-TERMP (OBJ)
 (COND
  ((EQ (CAR OBJ) 'QUOTE) (= (LENGTH OBJ) 2))
  ((EQ (ARITY (CAR OBJ)) T) (TERM-LIST (CDR OBJ)))
  ((NULL (ARITY (CAR OBJ))) NIL)
  ((TERM-LIST (CDR OBJ))  (= (LENGTH (CDR OBJ))
    (ARITY (CAR OBJ))))
  (T  NIL)))
(DEFUN LAMBDA-FUN-TERMP (OBJ)
 (COND
  ((< (LENGTH (CAR OBJ)) 3) NIL)
  ((TERM-LIST (CDR OBJ))
   (IF
    (= (LENGTH (CADAR OBJ)) (LENGTH (CDR OBJ)))
    (TERM-LIST (CDR (CDAR OBJ)))
    NIL ))
  (T NIL) ))
(DEFUN TERMP (OBJ)
 (COND
  ((ATOM OBJ) (OR (CONSTANTP OBJ) (VARIABLEP OBJ)))
  ((ATOM (CAR OBJ)) (ATOM-FUN-TERMP OBJ))
  ((EQ (CAAR OBJ) 'LAMBDA) (LAMBDA-FUN-TERMP OBJ))
  (T NIL)))
(DEFUN TERM-LIST (OBJL)
 (COND
  ((NULL OBJL) T)
  ((ATOM OBJL) NIL)
  ((TERMP (CAR OBJL)) (TERM-LIST (CDR OBJL)))
  (T NIL) ))
```

The expressions 12, NIL, T, "string", (AND NIL V (OR T)), ((LAMBDA (X) X) (+ 2 3)), and (CONS (CAR(QUOTE (1 2 3))) (CDR V)) are recognized by TERMP as being terms, while (CONS (CAR (1 2 3)) (CDR V)), (CONS (QUOTE (1 2 3))), and ((LAMBDA (X) (CONS X X X)) (CONS 1 2)) are recognized as not being terms.

```
(DEFUN FORMP (OBJ)
  (AND (TERMP OBJ) (NULL (FREE-VARIABLES OBJ))) )
```

3.5

5. The values returned should be

```
==> 100
==> 0
==> INNER
==> 100 .
```

4.1.2

1. F⟨x⟩ = min i [i+x=0] is undefined for x>0 because the partial recursive functions are defined over the nonnegative integers.

3. Yes. Composition of F⟨⟩ with G1⟨⟩,...,Gk⟨⟩ to produce H⟨⟩ is

```
(DEFUN H (N1...Nk) (F (G1 N1...Nk)...(Gj N1...Nk))) .
```

Recursion of G⟨⟩ from F⟨⟩ to produce H⟨⟩ is

```
(DEFUN H (N0 N1...NJ)
  (IF (ZEROP N0) (F N1...NJ) (G (H (1- N0) N1...NJ)
  N1...NJ ))) .
```

Minimization of N0 in F⟨⟩=0 to produce H⟨⟩ is

```
(DEFUN H (N1...NJ) (AUX-H 0 N1...NJ))
(DEFUN AUX-H (N0 N1...NJ)
  (IF (ZEROP (F N0 N1...NJ)) N0 (AUX (1+ N0) N1...NJ))) .
```

5. Probably not. Any system whose programmable functions are always totally defined will not be able to program every computable function.

4.3

1. A tail recursive definition for FACTORIAL:

```
(DEFUN FACTORIAL (IN) (AUX-FACT IN 1))
(DEFUN AUX-FACT (IN OUT)
  (IF (< IN 2) OUT (AUX-FACT (1- IN) (* IN OUT)))) )
```

2. Structural recursion was used in SUBST.

4. If EVAL and APPLY have tail recursive definitions, then the program for A given in this section can be made tail recursive by reducing it to data in in the tail recursive APPLY.

```
(DEFUN TR-ACKERMANN (N) (APPLY A (LIST N)))
```

Since this contradicts the given, EVAL and APPLY cannot have tail recursive definitions.

7. The simulation of the solution to the Tower of Hanoi puzzle involves a beautiful form of recursion. Key idea: to move m disks from pin i to pin j do:

(1) move m-1 disks from i to k (k different from i and j),
(2) move 1 disk from i to j,
(3) move m-1 disks from k to j.

Let M[m i j] be an abbreviation for "Move m disks from pin i to pin j."

```
                        M[3 1 2]
              M[2 1 3] M[1 1 2] M[2 1 2]
M[1 1 2] M[1 1 3] M[1 2 3] M[1 1 2] M[1 1 3] M[1 1 2]...
```

This unique form of recursion creates a tree whose nodes are either moves (i.e., M[1..]) or move plans (i.e., M[m..] for m>1). It terminates when all move plans have been replaced by moves. The moves are then executed from left to right.

```
(DEFUN HANOI (DISK-STACK)
   ;This is a simulation of the Tower of Hanoi puzzle.
   ;The value (1 2 ... k) is the initial contents of s1.
   (SETQ STEP 0)
   (SETQ S1 DISK-STACK)   (SETQ S2 (SETQ S3 NIL))
   (IF
   S1
   (M (LENGTH S1) 1 2)
   NIL )
   (DISPLAY)  (TERPRI)  "End of world." )
(DEFUN M (M I J)       ;m disks are moved from si to sj.
   (IF (= M 1) (DISPLAY) NIL)    ;When a disk is actually
                                         ;moved the
;contents of the stacks are displayed. Disks are moved
;from si.
   (COND
   ((= I 1) (SETQ SI 'S1))
   ((= I 2) (SETQ SI 'S2))
   (T       (SETQ SI 'S3)) )
   (COND                          ;Disks are moved to sj.
```

```
  ((= J 1) (SETQ SJ 'S1))
  ((= J 2) (SETQ SJ 'S2))
  (T       (SETQ SJ 'S3)) )
 (COND
  ((= M 1);If one disk is to be moved, then the values
          ; (of the values)  of si and sj must change.
   (SET SJ (CONS (CAR (EVAL SI)) (EVAL SJ)))
   (SET SI (CDR (EVAL SI))) )
  ((< 1 M)
   (M (1- M) I (CO I J))
   (M 1 I J)
   (M (1- M) (CO I J) J) )
  (T (BREAK)) ))
(DEFUN CO (I J)       ;The stack number not in (i j) is
 (CAR (REMOVE I (REMOVE J '(1 2 3)))) )       ;returned.
(DEFUN DISPLAY ()       ;Step number and stack contents
 (TERPRI)                                 ;are printed.
 (TERPRI) (PRINC "STEP = ")
 (SETQ STEP (1+ (PRIN1 STEP)))
 (TERPRI) (PRINC "  S1 = ") (PRIN1 (REVERSE S1))
 (TERPRI) (PRINC "  S2 = ") (PRIN1 (REVERSE S2))
 (TERPRI) (PRINC "  S3 = ") (PRIN1 (REVERSE S3)) )
```

The astronomers predict a *much earlier* end to the world than the monks.

4.4

1.

```
(DEFUN HALT? (fun args) (IF (APPLY fun args) T T)).
```

2. If semantic equality is decidable, then there is a function or macro

```
(DEF... SEM-EQUAL? (term1 term2) ...)
```

which returns T if (EQUAL *term1 term2*), otherwise it returns NIL. Now define

```
(DEFUN HP-SOLUTION (fun args)
(SEM-EQUAL? (IF (APPLY fun args) T NIL) T) ),
```

and we have a solution to the halting problem.

3. If the existence of semantic errors is decidable, then we can define a LISP function or macro

```
(DEF... SEM-ERROR (term) ...)
```

such that (SEM-ERROR *term*) returns T or NIL depending on whether or not the given term has a semantic error. Let V be an unbound variable, then an attempt to evaluate V will be a semantic error. Then, the term (IF (IF (APPLY fun args) T T) V T) contains a semantic error just in case the function halts for the given arguments. Contrary to the undecidability of the halting problem, this decides the halting problem.

5.2

2.

```
(DEFUN EVLIS (TL) (MAPCAR 'EVAL TL))
```

3. If MEMBER is defined as simply a Boolean-valued function, then the serial environment feature is not required. Notice the (EVAL (CONS 'OR (MAP... trick in the following code.

```
(DEFUN MEMBER (E S)
 (EVAL (CONS 'OR
   (MAPCAR '(LAMBDA (O) (IF (EQUAL E O) '(T) NIL))
   S ))))
```

A second version of the MEMBER function returns the list of E and all elements of L following E. The fact that function application environments are serial in MAPCAR is used by the SETQs.

```
(DEFUN MEMBER (E S &OPTIONAL(E-IN-S NIL))
  (MAPLIST
   '(LAMBDA (ST)
     (COND (E-IN-S O)
       ((EQUAL E (CAR ST)) (SETQ E-IN-S ST)) (T O) ))
   S )
 E-IN-S )
```

4. Two approaches to SUBSET. First, use the MEMBER just defined in

```
(DEFUN SUBSET (S1 S2)
 (NOT (MEMBER NIL
   (MAPCAR '(LAMBDA (E1) (MEMBER E1 S2)) S1))) )
```

or use the (EVAL (CONS 'OR (MAP... and (EVAL (CONS 'AND (MAP... tricks

```
(DEFUN SUBSET (S1 S2)
 (EVAL (CONS 'AND
   (MAPCAR
    '(LAMBDA (E1)
      (EVAL (CONS 'OR
```

```
            (MAPCAR '(LAMBDA (E2) (EQUAL E1 E2)) S2 ))))
    S2 ))))
(DEFUN EQUAL-SETS (S1 S2) (AND (SUBSET S1 S2)
  (SUBSET S2 S1 )))
```

5.

```
(DEFUN INTERSECT (S1 S2)
 (APPLY 'APPEND
  (MAPCAR '(LAMBDA (O) (IF (MEMBER O S2) (LIST O)()))
   S1) ))
(DEFUN UNION (SET1 SET2) (REDUCE (APPEND SET1 SET2)))
```

6.

```
(DEFUN CARTESIAN-PRODUCT (S1 S2)
 (APPLY 'APPEND
  (MAPCAR '(LAMBDA (O1) (MAPCAR '(LAMBDA (O2)
 (LIST O1 O2)) S2)) S1) ))
```

7.

```
(DEFUN ROTATE (L) (IF (ATOM L) L (APPEND (CDR L)
 (LIST (CAR L)))))
(DEFUN M2 (NL)
 (LET ((NPL (MAPCAR 'CONS NL (ROTATE NL))))
  (APPLY 'APPEND
   (MAPCAR
    '(LAMBDA (NP) (IF (< (CAR NP) (CDR NP))
 (LIST (CDR NP)) NIL))
    NPL ))))
(DEFUN MAX (NL)
 (DO ((NL NL (M2 NL)))
  ((OR (ATOM NL) (ATOM (CDR NL)))
   (IF (ATOM NL) NL (CAR NL)) )))
```

5.3

1. &REST causes the variable MAC to be bound to the list of arguments.

```
(DEFMACRO CONS* (&REST MAC)
 (COND
  ((ATOM MAC) NIL)
  ((ATOM (CDR MAC)) (CAR MAC))
  (T '(CONS ,(CAR MAC) ,(CONS 'CONS* (CDR MAC)))) ))
```

3. Build the required macro using auxiliary functions from the answer given for problem 2 in 3.4.

4. The second call to FACTORIAL, the macro, is with a nonnumerical argument. The problem of recursive macros is to get the intended arguments to the macro's recursive call. When a macro recursively calls itself, the call should be during the evaluation of the expansion. This allows the arguments to be constructed during the creation of the expansion.

5.4.3

1. A structure of type O is the returned value. However, the two structures created make up a linked group.

2. If H2O really represents water, then the evaluation of (O-B1 H2O) and (O-B2 H2O) should return two different hydrogens, and the evaluation of (H-B1 (O-B1 H2O)) and (H-B1 (O-B2 H2O)) should return the same oxygen.

3.
```
(SETQ METHANE
  (BOND
   (BOND
    (BOND
     (BOND (MAKE-C) C-B1 (MAKE-H) H-B1)
     C-B2 (MAKE-H) H-B1 )
    C-B3 (MAKE-H) H-B1 )
   C-B4 (MAKE-H) H-B1 ))
```

4. DEFMETHOD is a macro which creates a function definition (if the function name is not previously used) or expands an existing function definition to cover additional cases. DEFMETHOD may be programmed using FUNCTION (to retreive existing definitions) and

```
`(EVAL (DEFUN fun-name original-var-list ,
    expanded-definition ))
```

as the expansion.

5.5

2. Well, the actual implication is that for a certain class of object there is no distinction between their roles as data and as functions. Let * be what we usually think of as a binary operator, but now it is Curried. As a unary function, *(9) returns a function/data value. However, this data value must act as a function when it is applied to the second argument—*(9)(5) = 45.

4.

```
(DEFUN RESET () (SETQ STATES '(A)))
(RESET)
(SETQ FSA1
  (CLOSURE
    '(STATES)
    '(LAMBDA (IN)
       (IF IN (TRUE) (FALSE))
       (PRINC "INPUT = ") (PRIN1 (IF IN T 'F)) (TERPRI)
       (PRINC "STATES = ") (PRIN1 STATES) (TERPRI) )))
(DEFUN FSA (&REST IN)
  (RESET)
  (TERPRI)
  (COND
   (IN  (FUNCALL FSA1 (EVAL (CAR IN)))
    (APPLY #'FSA (CDR IN)) )
   (T (TERPRI)) ))
(DEFUN TRUE ()
  (IF
   (OR (MEMBER 'A STATES) (MEMBER 'B STATES))
   (SETQ STATES (REDUCE (REMOVE 'B (CONS 'C STATES))))
   NIL ))
(DEFUN FALSE ()
  (COND
   ((MEMBER 'A STATES) (SETQ STATES (REMOVE 'A (CONS 'B
       STATES ))))
   ((MEMBER 'B STATES) (SETQ STATES (REMOVE 'B (CONS 'A
       STATES ))))
   (T NIL) )
  (SETQ STATES (REDUCE STATES)) )
(DEFUN REDUCE (S)
  (COND
   ((ATOM S) S)
   ((MEMBER (CAR S) (CDR S)) (REDUCE (CDR S)))
   (T (CONS (CAR S) (REDUCE (CDR S)))) ))
(SETQ F NIL)
```

5.6

1.

```
(DEFMACRO EXPLODE (SYMBOL)
 '(MAPCAR (QUOTE DECODE)
   (QUOTE ,(COERCE (SYMBOL-NAME SYMBOL) 'LIST)) ))
(DEFUN DECODE (NUM)   (CDR (ASSOC NUM CODE-BOOK)) )
(SETQ CODE-BOOK '((65 . A)(66 . B)(67 . C)(68 . D)
  (69 . E)(70 . F)
  (71 . G)(72 . H)(73 . I)(74 . J)(75 . K)(76 . L)
  (77 . M)(78 . N)
  (79 . O)(80 . P)(81 . Q)(82 . R)(83 . S)(84 . T)
  (85 . U)(86 . V)(87 . W)
  (88 . X)(89 . Y)(90 . Z) ))
```

2.

```
(DEFUN LEX-ORDER (SYMBOL1 SYMBOL2)
 (LET
  ((LIST1 (COERCE (SYMBOL-NAME SYMBOL1) 'LIST))
   (LIST2 (COERCE (SYMBOL-NAME SYMBOL2) 'LIST)) )
  (NUM-ORDER LIST1 LIST2) ))
(DEFUN NUM-ORDER (LS1 LS2)
 (COND
  ((AND (ATOM LS1) (ATOM LS2))   T)
  ((ATOM LS1)   T)
  ((ATOM LS2)   NIL)
  ((< (CAR LS1) (CAR LS2))   T)
  ((= (CAR LS1) (CAR LS2))
   (NUM-ORDER (CDR LS1) (CDR LS2)) )
  (( > (CAR LS1) (CAR LS2))   NIL) ))
```

5.7

1. The value of AFTER-LABOR-DAY was a part of the value of SEASONS—a *part*, not a copy of a part! Thus, when the tale of SEASONS was connected to the head of SEASONS, it was also the tail of AFTER-LABOR-DAY that was moved.

2. In applications where the total number of cells in the data being processed changes during processing.

6.1

1. The algebra's rules will use square brackets—[and]—as delimiters to indicate the beginning and end of a balanced string of parentheses. *Terms* are defined:

> the empty string $\sim$ is a term,
>) and (are terms,
> if s and t are terms, then st is a term.

Constants are $\sim$,), and (. An *expression* is the result of inserting 0-or-more pairs of square brackets into a term. Reduction rules: for terms r, s, t, and expressions u, such that the entire expression being processed is represented by the left-hand pattern

> ut → u[ ]t ,
> u([s])t → u[(s)]t ,
> u[r][s]t → u[rs]t ,
> [[s]])u → [s]u ,
> u([t] → u[t] ,
> [[s]] → s .

Keep in mind that any of r, s, t, and u may be empty. The last rule in the list above is the exit rule. This solution is a bit strange in that the entire expression must match the left-hand side. Another approach [due to J. Pedersen] uses three sets of additional brackets—{, }, [,], ⟨, ⟩—and three sets of rules. The first set of rules is used as long as one applies, then the second set, and finally the third. In this approach, the left-hand side of a rule does not have to match the whole expression but only a part of it. The idea of a three-level set of rules is the strange thing here.

2. There is no necessary relationship between $|OA|$ and $|TA|$. In the cases mentioned in the hint, we have: $2 = |OA| < |TA|$ (for the Boolean algebra) and $|OA| > |TA|$ (for the reals). For those who know set theory, TA is always a countably infinite set. In the case of the reals, OA is an uncountably infinite set.

3. The algebras discussed so far allow only the construction of data (object-valued) terms and do not allow data to play the role of functions. Thus, function construction does go beyond what these algebras can do.

7. For the most part, LISP is call-by-value. Only such things as QUOTE, IF, COND, OR, AND, ... are not call-by-value. These special functions could be thought of as call-by-need.

8. An algebra's computations are determined by its terms. If functions cannot be created, then the number of function calls in a computation is at most the number of function applications in the term's syntax. It follows that (in these algebras) the length of a computation is always less than the length of the term determining it. Thus, recursion and (unbounded) search are impossible.

9. Now,

value⟨ ⟩ : term-algebra ⟶ object-algebra

and any function of the algebra is of the type

v⟨ ⟩ : object-algebra ⟶ object-algebra .

To consider the possibility of v⟨ ⟩ representing value⟨ ⟩, we need a natural coding of syntax into objects:

code⟨ ⟩ : term-algebra ⟶ object-algebra .

Now, the question of representation becomes can an object-algebra (as we have them in this section) have a function v⟨ ⟩ which satisfies

value⟨term⟩ = v⟨code⟨term⟩⟩ ?

An environment

env : variables ⟶ object-algebra

determines value⟨ ⟩. Let U be a variable and suppose that v⟨⟩ exists. Since u=code⟨U⟩ depends only on the syntax of U, u is fixed and independent of env⟨⟩. Then, the equation

env⟨U⟩ = value⟨U⟩ = v⟨code⟨U⟩⟩ = v⟨u⟩

indicates that the environment is unique and is determined by v⟨ ⟩. Contradiction. This contradiction fails in LISP because LISP has the power to construct the representation of arbitrary finite functions evn⟨ ⟩ and then to use these representations in constructing v⟨ ⟩. In CA (defined in problem 5), there are no variables and so there is no env⟨ ⟩ tied to the definition of CAreduce⟨ ⟩ (CA's version of eval⟨ ⟩). Consequently, the preceding argument against the existence of v⟨ ⟩ fails for CA.

11. Think of K and S as being functions. The rules defining CAreduce⟨ ⟩ do not evaluate the arguments to K and S, so CAreduce⟨ ⟩ is not call-by-value.

6.2

2. Nonmonotonicity in length-of-expression is seen in rules 3a and 3b as well as in others.

5. The order of multiple (READ)s would be determined on the basis of need—need as determined by interpreter or other system evaluating expressions—rather than syntax.

7.1

1. According to (po2), the relation "$\longrightarrow$" is transitive.

2. By the corollary to the C-R theorem, (1) a term can have at most one normal form. By the C-R theorem, (2) a term having a normal form can always be reduced to its normal form. Computations are sequences of reductions by (br). Since a term in normal form cannot be further reduced by (br), (3) it represents the end of a computation.

3. By the C-R theorem, there are computations $t \longrightarrow t''$ and $t' \longrightarrow t''$. Since t' is in normal form, t'' is syntactically equal to t'. Thus, $t \longrightarrow t''$.

4. The similarity is in the fact that computations halt when they reach a normal form. Thus, it is reasonable to guess that "t has a normal form" is undecidable. Church has proved that this is true.

5. Assume that $Mx=M'x$, where x is not a free variable in either M or M'. There exists a t for which

$$Mx \longrightarrow t \text{ and } M'x \longrightarrow t;$$

by (la),

$$(\lambda \ x \ Mx) \longrightarrow (\lambda \ x \ tx)$$
$$(\lambda \ x \ M'x) \longrightarrow (\lambda \ x \ tx);$$

by (rps),

$$(\lambda \ x \ Mx)=(\lambda \ x \ tx)$$
$$(\lambda \ x \ M'x)=(\lambda \ x \ tx);$$

by (eq2) in 7.1,

$$(\lambda \ x \ Mx)=(\lambda \ x \ M'x);$$

by (er),

$$(\lambda \ x \ Mx) \longrightarrow M \text{ and } (\lambda \ x \ M'x) \longrightarrow M';$$

finally by the previous equation, (rps), and (eq 2),

$$M=M'.$$

7.2

1. Use the definitions of CAR and CONS as lambda functions from this chapter.

2. T is in normal form. However, F is not in normal form.

$$F = TI = (\lambda \ (u \ v) \ u)(\lambda \ u \ u)$$
$$\longrightarrow (\lambda \ v \ (\lambda \ u \ u)) = (\lambda \ (v \ u) \ u)$$

Thus, F's normal form differs from that of T.

2. $0 = (\lambda \ u \ u)$ is in normal form. $k+1 = (\text{CONS} \ k \ T) = (\lambda \ (u \ v \ w) \ wuv)kT \longrightarrow$ $(\lambda \ w \ wkT)$. Since w is a variable and $wkT = ((w \ k) \ T)$, $(\lambda \ w \ wkT)$ is in normal form. Thus, every natural number has a normal form. However, $k+1$ is literally an abbreviation for

$$(\lambda \ u \ (\lambda \ v \ (\lambda \ w \ wuv)))kT \ ,$$

which is not a normal form.

3.

$$\text{NOT} \ \text{NOT} = (\lambda \ u \ uFT)(\lambda \ u \ uFT) \longrightarrow (\lambda \ u \ uFT)FT \longrightarrow FTFT \longrightarrow$$
$$FT = TIT \longrightarrow I.$$

4. The normal form of n is the value of t.

7.3

1. Yes. The pointer manipulating functions can create objects which act as fixed points for some functions. For example,

```
*   (SETQ ARCTIC-EXPLORERS
        (NANSEN FRANKLIN RASMUSSEN PEARY STEFANSSON) )
    ==> (NANSEN FRANKLIN RASMUSSEN PEARY STEFANSSON)
*   (RPLACD ARCTIC-EXPLORERS ARCTIC-EXPLORERS)
    ==> (NANSEN NANSEN NANSEN NANSEN ...)
*   (EQUAL ARCTIC-EXPLORERS (CDR ARCTIC-EXPLORERS))
    ==> T
```

A fixed point for CAR may be created by using RPLACA in place of RPLACD.

2. $(\lambda v \ T)$.

3. Yes, let f be the fixed point of K. $Kf=f$, so $ff=Kff \longrightarrow f$. Let x be anything not equal to f, then $Ix=x$ and $fx=f$, and Ix is not equal to fx, so f is different from I. There is also the fixed-point of FIXED-POINT.

4. No. If $fx=x$ for all x, then $fx=Ix$ for all x. By extensionality, $f=I$.

5. FIXEDPOINT is $(\lambda \ f \ (\lambda \ v \ f(vv))(\lambda \ v \ f(vv)))$.

6. Semantic equality is solvable in the λ calculus if there is a term E such that

$$Efg \longrightarrow T \ \text{if} \ fx=gx \ \text{for all x, otherwise} \ Efg \longrightarrow F.$$

Suppose, for the sake of a contradiction that such an E exists. Define D and P by

$$D = (\lambda \text{ x IF ETx THEN F ELSE T) and DP = P.}$$

D's values are all either T or F, so by DP=P, either P=T or P=F. In either case, we can prove T=F as a consequence of the assumption. For example,

```
T = P = DP = (λ x IF ETx THEN F ELSE T) P
  = (λx IF ETx THEN F ELSE T) T = IF ETT THEN F ELSE T
  ⟶  IF T THEN F ELSE T ⟶ F.+
```

By contradiction, there does not exist a lambda term E which decides semantic equality for all terms.

7.4

4. The finite-state automaton of exercise 4, section 5.5, is defined in the lambda calculus as the solution to

```
AT = A,    AF = B,    BT = C,    BF = A,    CT = A,
and CF = C,
```

where A, B, and C represent unknown terms. The solution to these equations is constructed as follows: first, let

```
a = (λ (f g h x)  x(ffgh)(gfgh)),
b = (λ (f g h x)  x(hfgh)(ffgh)),
c = (λ (f g h x)  x(ffgh)(hfgh)),
```

then set

```
A = aabc,    B = babc, and C = cabc.
```

Each state codes the entire automaton, so the effect of inputs F and T on the starting state A can be computed by evaluating

```
AFT = aabcFT = (λ (f g h x)  x(ffgh)(gfgh))abcFT
    = F(aabc)(babc)T = babcT
    = (λ (f g h x)  x(hfgh)(ffgh))abcT
    = T(caba)(aabc) = cabc = C.
```

7.5

4. The following are, as usual, abbreviations for nested unary lambda functions:

```
S = (λ (x y z)  (x y (x z))),
```

and

K = (λ (x y) x).

Thus, CA can be embedded into the lambda calculus.

5. In combinatory algebra, the identity is I=SKK. Given a lambda function (λ term), we will define the equivalent function in CA by the following rewrite rules:

a. (CA v u) → Ku

   if the variable v does not occur in u;

b. (CA v v) → I if v is a variable;

c. (CA v (term₁ term₂)) → S(CA v term ₁)(CA v term ₂)

for composites. For example, the reversing function (λ (x y) yx) can be translated into combinatory algebra as follows:

(λ (x y) yx)
= (λ x (λ y yx))
= (λ x (λ y yx))
→ (λ x S(λ y y)(λ y x))   rule c
→ (λ x SI(Kx))   rules b and a
→ S(λ x SI)(λ x Kx)   rule c
→ S(K(SI))S(λ x K)(λ x x)   two applications c
→ S(K(SI))S(KK)I   rules a and b.

Thus, S(K(SI))S(KK)I = (λ (x y) yx).

8.1.1

5. The proof, by the truth table algorithm, that axiom 1a is true in every model follows.

α	β	α	$\longrightarrow$	(β $\longrightarrow$ α)
t	t	t	t	t
t	f	t	t	t
f	t	f	t	f
f	f	f	t	t

The truth tables for the nine other axioms are similar. The proof that modus ponens preserves the property of being true in every model: if α and (α $\longrightarrow$ β) are true in every model, then there does not exist a model α is true and β is false; in other words, β false implies α false which is impossible; thus, β is always true. By induction, theorems are true in every model—i.e., theorems are valid.

6.

$\alpha_1,...,\alpha_k \vdash \beta$ implies that there is a proof $\gamma_1, ..., \gamma_k, \beta$

of β from $\alpha_1,...,\alpha_k$ It can be extended to a proof from $\alpha_1,...,\alpha_k, \neg\beta$:

$\gamma_1, ..., \gamma_k, \beta,$	previous proof from $\alpha_1,...,\alpha_k$
$\neg\beta$	$\neg\beta$ is given
$\beta \longrightarrow (T \longrightarrow \beta)$	axiom schema 1a
$(T \longrightarrow \beta)$	modus ponens
$\neg\beta \longrightarrow (T \longrightarrow \neg\beta)$	axiom schema 1a
$(T \longrightarrow \neg\beta)$	modus ponens
$(T \longrightarrow \beta) \longrightarrow ((T \longrightarrow \neg\beta) \longrightarrow \neg T)$	axiom schema 4a
$((T \longrightarrow \neg\beta) \longrightarrow \neg T)$	modus ponens
$\neg T$	modus ponens

of $\neg T$ (=F).

8.1.3

Assume that: (COMPLEMENT α) returns $\neg\alpha$, (COMPLEMENT $\neg\alpha$) returns α, and
the value of F is F.

2.

```
(DEFUN COMPLEMENTARY-LITERALS (V-CLAUSE1 V-CLAUSE2)
 (REDUCE (APPEND
  (INTERSECT V-CLAUSE1 (MAPCAR 'COMPLEMENT V-CLAUSE2))
))))
(DEFUN RESOLVE (V-CLAUSE1 V-CLAUSE2)
 (LET*
  ((COMPLEMENT1
    (COMPLEMENTARY-LITERALS V-CLAUSE1 V-CLAUSE2) )
   (COMPLEMENT2 (MAPCAR 'COMPLEMENT COMPLEMENT1)) )
  (IF
   COMPLEMENT1
   (REDUCE (APPEND
     (SET-SUBTRACT V-CLAUSE1 COMPLEMENT1)
     (SET-SUBTRACT V-CLAUSE2 COMPLEMENT2) ))
   NIL )))
```

RESOLVE* computes a fixed point of RESOLVE.

3.

```
(DEFUN CONSEQUENCE (HYPOTHESES CONSEQUENT)
 (MEMBER F
 (RESOLUTION*
  (CONS (COMPLEMENT CONSEQUENT) HYPOTHESES) ) ))
```

Index

Abbreviations are used in this index to increase the value of references. Letters immediately following page numbers indicate the nature of the material located on that page, specifically

p = primary reference, al = algorithm, ex = example.
h = history, i = illustration, n = note, xr = exercise.

Further, functions that are an official part of Common LISP (according to Steele) have their type identified in square brackets just after the function name. For example

[CLf] = Common LISP function, [CLm] = macro,
[CLsf] = special form, [CLc] = constant, etc.

These identifications are made even when the function named is to be programmed by the user, or is an example expressed in pseudocode.

In some cases, the Commmon LISP version of these functions will not exactly match the behavior of the function described in the example or exercise.